publishing

CURIOSITY
KILLED
THE
SPAT

The Melfox Method
for Relationship Health Through
Effective Conflict Resolution

Joseph Jay Mellon

Grumpy Gills Publishing
Atlanta, Georgia USA

Grumpy Gills Publishing
Atlanta, Georgia USA
www.grumpygillspublishing.com

ISBN: 0615906141
ISBN-13: 9780615906140

To my sons Daniel, Shane, and Alexander

CONTENTS

Chapter Three - Egoity 127

Chapter Four - Interaction 195

CONTENTS

PREFACE

Welcome to the first edition of *Curiosity Killed The Spat* – a book that introduces a brand-new step-by-step system to help restore and preserve intimacy, trust, and overall health in your relationship. In fact, if you're not careful, it will totally change the way you look at relationships. Many myths and mysteries are exposed and secrets revealed.

This book will take you on an entertaining and informative journey into the very heart and soul of relationships. It answers questions I've always had regarding the restoration and preservation of intimacy. Maybe you have the same questions.

The foundation of this book came from all the painful lessons I learned from past relationships and my burning desire to understand why they failed. What I had been taught about relationships from family, friends, books, and TV was not answering my questions. I was no longer able to accept the traditional ineffective remedies for couple problems and their anemic approaches to conflict resolution as viable solutions. And I can't imagine that I am alone.

Our collective epidemic divorce rate should be testament enough that our present methods of maintaining intimacy and healthy relationships are simply not working. There is definitely something not right when one-half of lifetime ('til death do us part) commitment vows are shattered.

And what about all the unhappy couples in committed relationships that would mercifully end if not for situational circumstances? Since they haven't figured out how to fix their relationship with each other, many couples feel emotionally imprisoned. They stay in a miserable, often mostly sexless relationship just because they feel financially trapped, don't want to upset or leave their children, or simply don't want to be on their own.

Does that sound familiar? Are you just as tired as I am of trying to sweep resentment under the rug, yet still walking on eggshells? It seems to me that we could use a fresh perspective when it comes to conflict resolution and maintaining healthy relationships. So I put on my engineer's lab coat, slipped on my pocket protector, grabbed my clipboard, and waded into the murky, mysterious world of interpersonal relationships. I treated this like just another engineering project: Define the primary problem, gather the facts, ponder alternatives, and develop a viable solution.

I wasn't looking for affirmations or interesting observations, or to be told to go on date night. I needed answers. I needed to know fundamental aspects of relationships problems like:

- *Why do we lose attraction with our partner?*
- *What is the real nemesis of relationships?*
- *Why do we typically act so selfishly when we argue?*
- *Why do we feel the need to suppress our true feelings and desires?*

Questions like these had to have answers. Playtime was over. I needed to know what was really going on. And it's amazing what can be discovered when there is a relentless drive to understand and uncover answers.

Curiosity Killed The Spat introduces *The Melfox Method* - a bold, brand-new, comprehensive approach to understanding relationships and effective conflict resolution. The 5-part system is presented with the help of stories, metaphors, and real-life examples that aim to entertain and inspire. *The Melfox Method* clearly identifies the universal "enemy" of relationships, the agent of change, the regulating force, a proposed solution, and its expected results.

In researching and writing this book, I focused on stripping away any pre-conceived notions we have regarding relationships and figuring out what makes them tick at their core. Like getting rid of an unwanted bush, the focus is on exposing the root cause of relationship problems, not whacking at their branches.

I would like to express my appreciation to everyone who has leant support for this project and to me over the years. A special thank you to Helene Obst and Dianna Sinovic for their help with the manuscript, to Tom Bruton for his help with The Resentment Dumpers website, and to Don Lafferty for his help with promotion.

This book would not have been written without the amazing patience, strength, and "intelligently open-mindedness" of my partner, Meryl Fox. Thank you for your relentless encouragement and willingness to help me bring this vision to life. I love you. IBOYSA

****

"It's like, for peace or anything, it's all down to this relationship. To work on this relationship with Yoko is very hard, and we've got the gift of love. But love is like a precious plant. You can't just accept it and leave it in the cupboard, or just think it's going to get on with itself like a pet. You got to keep watering it. You've got to really look after it. And love, you have to water and be careful of it, and keep the flies off and see that it's all right, and nurture it **and to get a relationship between two people is a start....** *"*

John Lennon
"Man of the Decade" Interview
December 2, 1969

INTRODUCTION

Once upon a time, there was a normal everyday couple named Beatrice and Bruno. They had your typical court-ship, and your average run-of-the-mill relationship. And that was the problem. You see... Beatrice and Bruno were both slowly coming to the same realization that, in time, most all other couples do – their relationship was dying.

Beatrice was aware that something was wrong, yet didn't know what. She had sweet memories of when their relationship was new. They had talked on the phone for hours and hours, and were together whenever they could. Things were different now, she thought. His touch isn't as tender; his words are not as charming, his antics not as cute. She was frustrated and coming to the end of her rope.

Bruno, on the other hand, thought nothing was really wrong. In fact, he thought little of the relationship at all. Deep down Bruno knew that it wasn't the same as when it was new. He just figured that the closeness and giddiness they felt earlier could not be sustained, and that it was only natural for things to fade over time.

One evening, Beatrice made up her mind to approach Bruno. "We need to talk," she started, staring at Bruno with wet eyes. He turned off the TV and asked her to sit down. He knew when to take her seriously. "What is it?" he asked curiously, handing over his handkerchief.

Beatrice turned away, hung her head, and began to cry. "I have no idea... but I wish I did."

Just then, there was a knock at the door.

****

Welcome To *The Melfox Method!*

Have you ever felt like Beatrice? Ever have a strong feeling that something was wrong, yet you were clueless as to what it was? Ever have a passionate desire to change something, yet no idea how to do it? It's like what Morpheus said to Neo in the film *The Matrix*: "You don't know what it is, but it's there, like a splinter in your mind, driving you mad." What do you do when you feel your relationship is dying? What *can* you do? Are you desperate like Beatrice? Or are you like Bruno and feel that there is nothing you can do?

The Melfox Method addresses the very issues that sooner or later plague most relationships. In this book, we will be exploring new solutions to old problems. New solutions mean new information. To understand the solutions, you need to open your mind to new ideas that may threaten your old way of thinking.

Understand Before Proceeding

Many of us have spent our lives feeling victimized, and blaming someone or something else for all our misfortunes. We may look back and feel proud of how we were able to survive being a victim in a bad relationship and strongly identify with that pride. We may look at our current situation and marvel at our strength and fortitude for enduring, *yet again*, another verbal, emotional, or even physical abuser. We may even admit to being an abuser ourselves, yet still feel victimized for having a bad childhood and blame our caretakers for our actions.

Let's keep going. If we were to ask the caretakers, they might say they did their best yet were not raised in a healthy household either. We can go on and on. How often have you considered that those who abuse *us* may very well have been abused *themselves?* I know, I know. It's really tough sometimes to have sympathy for the devil. But to understand my point, it's not *sympathy* you need to have; it's *empathy*.

Think of the possibility that we are all just "victims" in a long line of "victims" stretching back to the beginning of humanity. And if *everyone* is or has been a "victim" of someone else, can we really place the blame on *anyone*? It reminds me of the movie *The Incredibles* in which the evil mastermind and genius inventor Syndrome explains to "super" Mr. Incredible his devious plan to disarm the "supers" of the world:

INTRODUCTION

And when I'm old and I've had my fun, I'll sell my inventions so that everyone can have powers. Everyone can be super! And when everyone's super... [chuckles evilly]...no one will be.

When we are able to see that *everyone* is or has been a "victim" of a bad childhood, abusive relationships, or other unfortunate circumstances beyond his or her control, we can begin to understand *we are all* in the same boat, and therefore *no one ever is to blame.* When we are able to take even the least bit of responsibility for the condition of our relationship, we begin to "disarm" the blaming game, break the generational cycle of victimhood and martyrdom, and open ourselves to real solutions.

If you are a proud card-carrying member of the "Victims and Martyrs Forever" honorary society, you will probably resist this book at every page. As long as you always blame someone or something else for your lot in life, you won't accept responsibility and will reject anything that requires you to do so. After all, if nothing is your fault, why should you change? If this is the case, I wish you well in your ongoing search for answers to your relationship problems. For the rest of us, let's explore what a healthy relationship looks and feels like, and how to keep it that way.

New Information and a New Way

New information is sometimes hard to accept, isn't it? There seems to be a natural skepticism and resistance to learning something that conflicts with what we think we already know. We are tempted to dismiss something that is not already known to us. When the desire is great enough, however, curiosity outweighs the skepticism and we are open to understanding new things. Yield to your curiosity and join us as we embark on this journey of discovery, a journey on which you will see a fresh way of looking at relationships and conflict resolution.

Relationships have always seemed to be one of those proverbial double-edged swords. At times of extreme closeness and trust, it would seem that the relationship itself was all that existed and that the rest of the world was irrelevant. At other times the distance, betrayal, and abuse would transform that same relationship into the least desirous thing in the world.

The Melfox Method pulls back the curtain and, in a way, demystifies relationships. Through the use of analogies, examples, experiments, charts, and diagrams, the reality of what's going on during personal conflicts will be revealed. By understanding the principles in this book, you'll see these conflicts as opportunities for relationship and personal growth, and not something to be avoided or dreaded.

Look at this book like you would a primer for learning to play the piano. Instead of banging the keys and making a bunch of noise, your conflict resolution talks (Interaction) will be purposeful, orderly, and a lot easier on the ears.

The Melfox Method Concept

The Melfox Method can be boiled down to one conceptual statement:

> The **Environment** of a relationship is cleansed
>
> when sufficient **Information** is shared,
>
> tempered by and with respect to **Egoity**,
>
> through effective **Interaction** by the partners,
>
> resulting in an **Outcome** of elevated trust and closeness.

Each line represents an individual chapter in this book. In this *Introduction* chapter, we will discuss various areas of your life that will benefit from using the concepts in this book. Here is a brief synopsis of the remaining chapters:

1. In the *Environment* chapter, we will set up the playing field and the players. The overall concept and objective will be established. The Melfox Mindset will be explained and serve as the foundation for the rest of the book.

2. The *Information* chapter delves into the process of establishing common ground and the reality of the other individual, by challenging and clarifying what each one says. This, in and of itself, serves as the cornerstone for effective conflict resolution.

3. In the *Egoity* chapter, we will discuss our natural autonomic defenses to vulnerability – potential roadblocks to healthy, effective communication. By understanding the cause and purpose of

this protective mechanism, proper respect will be granted, and proper conflict resolution can commence.

4. In the *Interaction* chapter, we will discuss combining Information and Egoity in a structured, purposeful conversation. Subjects such as disappointment, interruptions, and forgiveness will be addressed. Techniques and props will be suggested to facilitate proper and efficient exchange.

5. The *Outcome* chapter is where we list the "rewards." If the other chapters were preparations for, and the process of childbirth, this would be the child. It explains the possible results of Interaction, and lists beneficial "side effects."

The Melfox Method Model

The following diagram illustrates the basic elements of *The Melfox Method* and their interdependency:

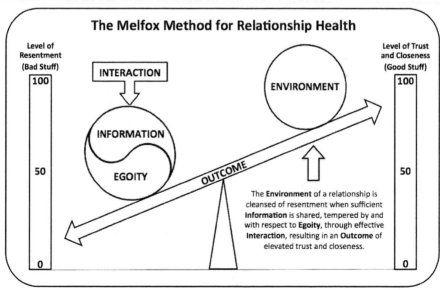

Diagram 1: *The Melfox Method* Model

Information and Egoity combined through Interaction "tips the scale" and outweighs the issues within the Environment. The *heavier* the Interaction, the more effectively it *cleanses* your relationship Environment.

Brief Overview

The Melfox Method is unique in that it does not branch off and explore the inherent differences between genders, races, nationalities, sexual orientations, ages, creeds, or even the types of relationships that two people can share. The principles contained within apply equally to all situations involving conflict with another person, whether it's your spouse, dating partner, friend, family member, life partner, coworker, or even nemesis. For the sake of simplicity, we will use the term "partner" in this book to describe the other person in the relationship with whom you are trying to resolve conflict.

This Ain't Just When Relationships Are in Trouble

How many times have you heard the expression "an ounce of prevention is worth a pound of cure"? When it comes to relationships, however, it seems many of us have yet to learn the importance of preventive maintenance. Either through pride or fear or pure ignorance, we tend to allow relationships to deteriorate until they're not worth salvaging. In this book, we will call this type of mindset *Traditional Relationship Logic*. Imagine if we had that same attitude when it came to our cars…

Automotive Event	Normal Maintenance	**Traditional Relationship Logic**
Gas tank is near empty	Stop at gas station and fill up	Let it run out and abandon car
Every 3 months / 3000 miles	Change the motor oil	Ignore it and burn up engine
Tire pressure is low	Fill tire with air	Replace tire
Engine light goes on	Have service station check the engine	Ignore it and hope for the best
A/C stops working	Have service station fix the A/C	Roll down windows and/or sweat
Muffler has a hole in it	Replace the muffler	Ride around in very noisy car
Any maintenance	Perform maintenance	Replace car

The Melfox Method is useful whether it's a last-ditch effort to save your relationship or the very first day you meet. It describes in detail, and in no uncertain terms, the proper approach to conflict resolution at any stage in your relationship. Once you learn and began using the lessons, concepts, and techniques in this book, you'll be amazed at its simplicity and effectiveness.

Success Begets Success

You will find that the more you use *The Melfox Method*, the more successes will encourage you to clean out all the issues in your relationship – some you probably didn't even know were there. You will experience a new level of closeness with your partner with each Interaction.

Think of using these lessons and concepts like the windshield wipers on your car. You don't need them when the sun is out and the vision is clear. But once the hard rain or snow comes, without functioning windshield wipers, you will not be able to see where you're going and if you blindly drive on, disaster awaits. *The Melfox Method* provides just what your relationship needs to ride through the rough times, keep you on the road, and get you home safely.

This Ain't Just for Married Folk

There are plenty of resources and counseling services that deal solely with the issue of struggling marriages or partnerships. This book does not limit itself in that respect. Think about all the other personal relationships that you have in life such as parent and child, supervisor and subordinate, neighbor and neighbor, and in-law and in-law.

At times, communication breakdowns in these types of relationships can cause just as much unhappiness or strife as the ones with an intimate partner. The techniques taught in this book can serve as a guide to keep conflict resolution sane and effective. Simply understanding the cause of relationship problems and how to avoid the typical pitfalls of conflict will make effective conversations in these areas much more of a possibility.

Two Heads Are Better Than One...

If you are reading this book to help your struggling relationship, it is highly recommended that your partner learn the lessons and techniques as well. With both people knowledgeable of what is taught, using *The Melfox Method* will be an extremely effective and even a fun experience. You will quickly develop your own style and look forward to resolving conflicts since you will know what to do, and more important, what NOT to do.

...But One Is Better Than None

Of course, using *The Melfox Method* with those unfamiliar with its techniques requires adjustments and a different mindset. Some suggested props that you will be taught to use such as the RY paddle, will need to be replaced with more conventional tools. Even if the other person is unfamiliar with the contents of this book, having a basic understanding of its concepts will enable you to drastically reduce the time and effort in understanding the other person and effectively resolving conflicts. Think of it like going on a treasure hunt. As long as one of you has a map and compass, and know how to use them, the treasure will be found.

When one partner is stuck with Traditional Relationship Logic, it is like trying to resolve conflict with one hand tied behind your back. You may see it more like fending off your partner's attacks with one hand, while resolving the conflict with the other. The thing is, you can still resolve the issue since *both* hands are not tied behind your back as in the case with Traditional Relationship Logic. In a land of blind people, it's the one-eyed man who is king.

This Even Ain't Just About Relationships!

In addition to helping you effectively resolving conflicts and restoring the health to your relationship, there are other far-reaching benefits of learning and using *The Melfox Method*.

1. **Exposing Limiting and Presuming Beliefs:** At times when two people are working through conflict resolution, the primary culprit will turn out to be a deep-seated, unknown limiting or presuming belief of one or both partners. In these cases, successful conflict resolution means the limiting or presuming belief is exposed and its effect is greatly diminished, if not totally eliminated. The effective use of the process is like turning you and your partner into virtual mirrors that can be used to look into one's own unawareness, which is where beliefs reside. We will be discussing the concept and nature of limiting and presuming beliefs in much greater detail in later chapters.

2. **Exposing Bad Habits for Better Physical Health:** Just like exposing limiting or presuming beliefs, using *The Melfox Method* exposes our bad habits as reflected back by our partner. Improving our relationship will also reduce the stress that accompanies conflict. This lessens our tendency to overeat, develop ulcers, and develop other health problems.

3. **Fostering Positive Attitude Toward Others:** Learning the concepts in this book helps us understand why people are the way they are, and why they do what they do. Understanding the root cause of relationship issues enables us to better empathize with people when they exhibit irrational behavior. It will help us maintain control and not add fuel to the conflict fire. Simply knowing what the "enemy" is (which is NOT each other) and that effective communication will enable both parties to "win," puts the whole conflict resolution subject in a new perceptive. The term "conflict" will be synonymous with "opportunity" instead of the defensive connotation it traditionally has.

4. **Enabling Us to Understand Our World Better:** The lessons in this book will also help us gain a better understanding of the world in general by demystifying the concept of conflict. You'll be better able to recognize the causes of things like prejudices and injustices, and thus possibly reduce their negative impact by exposing them.

These and more benefits are discussed in the *Outcome* chapter.

The Foreign Field of Conflict

Understanding the true nature of conflict is critical to resolving it. While there may be different ways of looking at the word "conflict" based on different assumptions, for the purpose of this book we will take away those assumptions and strip it down to its very essence:

> *Conflict: Incompatibility or interference of one idea, desire, event, or activity with another individual.*

Notice that nothing is mentioned in this definition about blame, struggle, or the belief that someone is out to get you. It simply means that something between you and your partner is not currently compatible.

Conflict Is Relative

As we will discuss later, we tend to see conflict in terms of how we experienced it as a child. If we were sufficiently taught how conflict can be effectively resolved through peaceful Interaction, the idea of conflict is not thought of as inherently bad, just a temporary inconvenience. For many of us, however, conflict in our childhood meant the suppression of feelings, the threat of punishment, and the power of authority. When there is *no chance* for resolution, conflict can *only* be seen as a struggle for survival or pride. We can only blame the other individual and defend ourselves, since we believe that other individual is out to get us.

When we take out the possibility of resolution, the definition of "conflict" becomes synonymous with this struggle:

> Wikipedia: Conflict is the process by which parties with differing wishes each believe that the other *will act or is acting against them*, and engages in behavior *seeking to damage* the other party.

This should be the definition of "irresolvable conflict" and is the sole basis for war since it *assumes* the other party is out to hurt us. Notice that there is the assumption here that the other party *will* act against you and *seeks* to damage you. Does this describe how you perceive conflict with your partner? Do you assume your partner is willfully *trying* to hurt you? Is that really necessary in conflict? It is, only when there is an absence of one thing: *trust*. If you don't "trust" someone, essentially you are saying that you feel if given the chance, he or she will hurt you.

"I Don't Trust You"

Let's say "conflict" is hitting your baseball into a neighbor's yard that has a mean dog. We have a total lack of trust that we can jump over the fence and retrieve the ball without the dog seeking to hurt us. It *just makes sense* to avoid direct contact with the dog and ask its owner to get the ball. It would be like walking into a cage with a wild lion. You *just know* that if you did that, the lion would have you for dinner. Does this really represent the degree of trust you have with your partner?

This book focuses on presenting concepts and lessons about things like conflict resolution, understanding your partner, vulnerability, defense mechanisms, and effective communication. It goes into detail describing the interworking of all these things. Understanding these concepts will expose you to valuable Information regarding relationships and arm you with the tools you need to resolve conflict. Think of it like learning the language of relationships – something most of us only partially understand.

Welcome to "Relationshipland"

When you enter into an intimate relationship, it's like being an ill-prepared tourist entering a foreign country where you don't speak the language. Since the natives don't understand your language either, you muddle through security and customs at the border by memorizing a few basic phrases and using hand gestures. As you explore this strange land, your inability to communicate effectively makes it impossible to be clearly understood.

Without the existence of a common language, misunderstandings and assumptions would be commonplace, which sets the stage for conflict. You would end up choosing between staying in Relationshipland and coping with conflict, and taking the next flight home alone. But what if you found a translator? What if you found someone who knew both languages? Think of *The Melfox Method* as a primer to understanding the language of relationships, including how to resolve conflict.

This book is not about how to cope with conflict and "soldier on" through a bad trip in Relationshipland. It is about learning concepts and methods that effectively resolve conflict and strengthen relationships. Look at these concepts like a disinfectant spray. "It doesn't mask odors, it eliminates them!"

> *A reporter asked a couple, "How did you manage to stay together for 65 years?"*
>
> *The woman replied, "We were born in a time when if something was broken we would FIX it, not throw it away..."*

The Melfox Method teaches you how to "fix" your relationship, not live with or abandon one that is seen as "broken."

Blinders and Blunders

Folks put blinders on horses so the other horses in the race won't distract them. Horses, like most animals, instinctively and constantly check around to see if there is anything coming close that they should be aware of. Without blinders, they can see all around and are fully aware of anything coming their way from just about any direction.

With blinders, their vision is limited to what is right in front of them, and the responsibility for looking around goes to the jockey. It would be irresponsible for someone to leave a horse unattended in a pasture with blinders on. The horse would be in danger of blundering into other horses or things, since it can't look around and doesn't have someone to look out and guide it.

Without understanding the language of relationships, many of us are walking around the pasture with blinders on. We are unable to see approaching danger, we blunder into problems, and we lack the ability to steer clear of them. The goal of *The Melfox Method* is to help you take off the blinders from your relationship by teaching you a way of understanding it.

Traditional Relationship Logic

Engineers know that the first step in trying to find a solution to anything is identifying the problem. In this book, the problem we're directly addressing is the disastrous level of health and failure rate of intimate relationships. How can two people who made an eternal solemn vow of trust to each other, end up not standing the sight of each other? Why are we not as close as we used to be? How and why do relationships fail?

Let's begin this exploration by looking at how we learned about relationships in the first place, and how this influences how we currently view relationships in general.

When We Were Kids

At first, we were totally dependent creatures. Everything had to be done for us by our caretakers. We were fed, bathed, and dressed with no responsibility at all but to look cute and make funny noises. In time, we were granted the privilege and responsibility of feeding, bathing and dressing ourselves. When we learned these life skills competently enough to completely care for ourselves, we became independent adults.

INTRODUCTION

During the process of learning life skills, we also learned how interpersonal relationships work. The relationships we had with our caretakers naturally had a huge influence on how we looked at relationships, and helped shape our view of how people should interact in general. The interaction we had with our caretakers taught us their style, method, and logic of interpersonal relationships, which we naturally tend to adopt in all relationships, including intimate ones.

When we see parents or guardians taking too much responsibility from their children, and not grant them the privilege of playing unattended or cutting their own food, we consider them *too responsible*. When we see children whom we consider too young to be left unattended, we label their caretakers as *not responsible*. We feel they are granting too much responsibility and privilege for the age of the children.

The proper role of caretakers is teaching and training a child to be independent, with the goal of someday releasing a self-sufficient, self-confident, and productive adult into the wild. The style, method, and logic of the interaction between caretaker and child influences the child's style, method, and logic of interpersonal relationships in the future.

The younger and less responsible children are, the less influence they have on decisions that affect their world. There is no discussion between caretaker and infant on deciding what the child will have for dinner or what clothes the child will wear. When a child's language, communication, and comprehension skills are insufficient, the caretaker is in total control and has absolute authority over those types of decisions.

Exerting Authority

As the child gets older and more responsible, opportunities will arise when the caretaker could engage the child to discuss options or the reasons behind decisions made. The earlier and more often these types of discussions, the less controlled the child feels. This depends on the time and patience of the caretaker. As an example, there may or may not be a discussion whether a toddler can play on the highway. The caretaker could try to explain why it is dangerous, yet may think it would take too much time and the child wouldn't understand it anyway. In these cases, the caretaker simply exerts *authority* over the child with no debate or discussion by making it a *rule*. But what if the caretaker does take the time, and child *could* understand the concept of the dangers of playing near speeding cars and trucks? They would understand the reasoning of not playing on the highway, agree that it is the best decision, and thus not feel manipulated and controlled.

"Just being told" what to do, without explanation, is the "traditional" way we try to keep children disciplined. To keep order, an authoritative caretaker makes a list of rules the children must follow, such as:

1. Behave yourself.
2. Play nicely with each other.
3. Care for one another.
4. Be good and don't bully!
5. Respect others. Be kind with your words and actions.
6. Share and take turns.
7. Be positive, polite, and do good.

And my personal favorite…

8. You may make decisions and choices about your behavior, as long as it doesn't *cause a problem* for authority, your peers, or yourself.

Awfully convenient for authority, isn't it? You can do what you want, as long as it doesn't cause a problem. And what's a "problem"? Anything authority doesn't like. As a child, what happened if you did anything that authority didn't like? You got punished. You were ridiculed or shunned by your peers, sent away, had privileges withheld, or worse. No negotiation, no plea-bargain, and no argument.

As a child, authority had the *power* to demand you to behave a certain way, simply because authority preferred it that way. Conflict resolution with authority was nonexistent, since authority *didn't allow you* to express the effects of conflict. You quickly learned to comply with authority, against your will and *against your nature*. You learned to suppress the effects of conflict, yet, as we all know, that does not *remove* the effects of conflict. It comes out eventually, usually with destructive consequences. This dynamic between *the oppressed* and *authority* is what we call Traditional Relationship Logic. It is the same logic many of us still use every day when faced with conflict, whether we realize it or not.

The important thing to understand is that in a healthy adult relationship, *there is no authority*. One partner does not have dominion over the other. Yet when it's the only thing we know, we have *no choice* but to assume our "childhood roles," which means one *does have* authority over the other. It's like real-life role-playing. When we take the stage and the curtain of conflict resolution goes up, Traditional Relationship Logic reverts us back to the roles of our childhood – one partner plays the role of the *oppressed*, and the other plays the role of the *authority*.

In order for someone to be *oppressive*, there has to be someone else granting control and willing to assume the "role" of the *oppressed*. The more we understand Traditional Relationship Logic, the more we see its irrationality, and the less likely we will allow anyone to ever control us again. We will be exploring this in more detail in the *Interaction* chapter.

Traditional Relationship Advice

Much of the advice out there on relationships issues regurgitates the same type of "rules" we learned as children. Instead of dealing with the conflict itself, the advice concentrates primarily on tackling the *effects* of conflict, such as anger, bitterness, contempt, distain, etc., ... Essentially anything dealing with the lack of respect and caring for (or from) your partner. Often this approach advises trying to *make* your intimate partner *feel* valued and important by doing "the little things" such as:

1. Give a card or a bouquet of flowers.
2. Be of service in a way they will appreciate.
3. Give an unexpected gentle touch on their shoulder.
4. Prepare their favorite meal.
5. Hide a love note in their lunch box.
6. Hire a babysitter and have a "date night."
7. Hold hands on a long walk.
8. Eagerly greet them after a long day apart.

These are all nice gestures, yet they do nothing themselves to directly resolve conflict. While talking during a prescribed "date night," you may stumble onto Information that instantly resolves an issue ("Oh, *that's* why you did that! I thought you were mad at me!"). You probably shouldn't count on that resolving all your conflicts. You can lead a blind horse to acorns, but that doesn't mean it'll ever find one.

Look again at that list. Aren't these exactly the type of things you *naturally* do when you're in a healthy, loving relationship? When you already feel the trust, closeness, respect, and value with an intimate partner, you don't have to be *told* to hold their hands, make them a favorite meal, or be of service to them. You naturally feel *compelled* to do those things. The less impact that conflict has on your relationship, the more you *want to* do nice things for your partner.

When things happen that naturally lower how much you honestly respect, value, or care about someone, simply *acting as if* you do does not solve anything. It's like going to a doctor after you break your arm, and instead of setting it, he tells you to flap it like a bird. Just *acting as if* something isn't broken will not magically heal it. Like Joan Cusack's character said to Tess (Melanie Griffin's character) in the film *Working Girl*: "Sometimes I sing and dance around the house in my underwear. Doesn't make me Madonna. Never will."

Of course, Tess was just "acting as if" to show Harrison Ford's character (and herself) that she had what it takes to close the merger. Traditional Relationship Logic is more like Sigourney Weaver's character. She was once the best, but now can only "act as if" she still was, and try to fool others into thinking so.

This "act as if" approach to conflict resolution tries to bring a conflict-ridden relationship back to life by making the couple do things that are *against their nature*. Yet these are the very things couples in healthy relationships *naturally do*. As if pulling a few strings on a puppet somehow brings the puppet to life. Once you let go of its strings, a puppet collapses  into a lifeless heap. Doing any of the "act as if" tasks may be inviting and bring up an opportunity, yet isn't itself conflict resolution.

Acting as if there is no resentment does not reduce resentment. A couple in a conflict-riddled relationship will not breathe new life into their relationship by simply pulling a few strings.

Burn Before Sharing

Here's another relationship-saving suggestion we sometimes see:

Start out by coming up with all the things that bother you about your partner. Sit down, by yourself, and write out all the annoying, disrespectful, crude, insensitive, and terrible things you wish you could tell your partner. Then read this letter out loud and *act as if* your partner were there to hear it. Then tear up, throw away, or burn the letter.

Oh, so close. That would feel like preparing a tempting dinner for you and your partner, pretend to eat it, and then throw it in the trash before taking one bite. As Maxwell Smart would say: "Missed it by *that* much."

Evading the Conflict Tiger

So why aren't we advised to share this annoying, disrespectful, crude, insensitive, and terrible Information with our partner? Wouldn't it make sense to let your partner know all the things that bother you? Wouldn't we want to give this Information to the *one person* who can do something about it?

For the same reasons we don't want to go inside a burning building or a cage with a man-eating tiger. It would be annoying, disrespectful, crude, insensitive, and terrible to share such Information, wouldn't it? We would unleash the wild beast, and that just wouldn't be the "nice" thing to do, would it?

Many of us were taught as children to "respect" each other by suppressing our true feelings if they are "offensive" or express conflict. When we had a beef with someone and tried to express it, authority taught us to suppress it with the threat of ridicule and punishment. "If you can't say something nice about someone, don't say anything at all."

We were taught to use Traditional Relationship Logic, which means the last thing we would want to do is share anything that expressed and exposed conflict. Or we learned that we could suppress conflict and the feelings of others by exerting our authority over them. Either way, we were taught to never voluntarily enter the cage of the conflict beast. We will be discussing more about this animal and how to train it in the *Egoity* chapter.

Those of us who are comfortable with "just tell me what to do" and suppressive type of advice are still letting Traditional Relationship Logic dictate how we deal with conflict. We are allowing the fear of conflict to suppress our true feelings by "acting as if" we didn't have any, or by imposing our authoritative will on others to suppress theirs.

With Traditional Relationship Logic, each partner is either the *oppressed* or the *authority*. You know – if you smash the words "opposed" and "authority" together and squint your eyes a bit, you may come up with a new way of looking at conflict resolution – opportunity.

Seeing Conflict as Opportunity

John F. Kennedy once said: "When written in Chinese, the word 'crisis' is composed of two characters - one represents danger, and the other represents opportunity." There's also an old proverb that goes, "In every crisis lies the seed of opportunity."

Nowhere is this truer than in the area of conflict resolution. By giving us the opportunity to look at our belief system and ourselves, conflict resolution should be thought of as more of a helpful process, rather than a painful one.

I'm not saying that you should *want* to have conflict. We all want as little of it as possible. But when conflict does arise, we could embrace it and use those opportunities to not only understand our partner better, but to understand ourselves better as well. By understanding the concepts in this book, you will greatly diminish the tendency to avoid conflict by "sweeping it under the rug."

Introducing the Belief-O-Meter®

When you use online dating services, they sometimes offer a survey to help you understand your personality and find a match. I came across one that listed 100 belief statements and asked you to rate how well it described you. One of the statements was:

> *"I feel that conflict is a negative experience."*

Why do we cringe at the thought of *conflict?* It may be because we equate conflict with *fighting.* And when there are only two of you in the room, the *fighting* must be with each other, right? When you have conflict with your partner, where do you focus your energy? Is it on fighting with your partner? Or is it on the *conflict?*

If you view conflict as *negative*, it tends to become a self-fulfilling prophecy. When you go into a conflict situation already feeling threatened, it's tough to deal with the issue in a rational way. Instead, you are more likely to eventually blow up in anger, shut down, or run away.

One of the important visual tools we will be using throughout this book is the Belief-O-Meter® shown here:

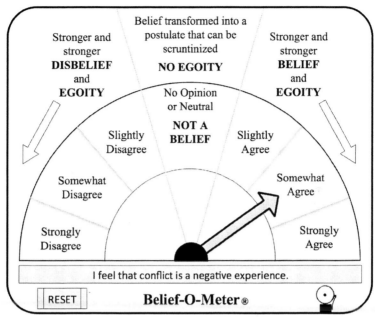

Diagram 2: Belief-O-Meter® Introduction

If you think that conflict with your partner means fighting with them, then for the "*I feel that conflict is a negative experience*" belief statement, your needle will probably point somewhere on the Agree side. After all, who would *want* to fight with the one person they have chosen to be with, forsaking all others?

If you feel that fighting with your partner is a *positive* experience, you are probably not all that interested in resolving conflict, and this book can only serve as a guide on what *not* to do.

If you do think that conflict with your partner *does* mean fighting with them, let me ask you something: Do you think someone who loves to garden feels that *weeding* is a *negative* experience?

If someone loves to garden, they understand that weeding is a normal, natural, and necessary *maintenance*. They understand that in order to have a beautiful flower garden, keeping it free of weeds is part of the deal. They *enjoy the process* of weeding since they know that without it, their garden will not be beautiful for long.

The Melfox Method teaches you how to weed your relationship garden.

So Why Don't We Know This Already?

You don't often see the host of a gourmet cooking show devote an entire segment to the joy of dishwashing or floor mopping. Why do you think the curtains or lights are lowered between the acts of a theater show? Even though cleaning up a kitchen and setting up a stage are vital elements of a production, they are hidden from the viewing public. Why? It's because they steal time away from the entertainment, glamour, and purpose of the show. You know – *the good parts*.

It's the same thing when it comes to relationships. Our attention and focus are only on *the good parts*. We would much rather experience carefree activities like skipping through a park holding hands than resolving conflicts.

And this started early on. Think about how much fun it was to play with your toys as a kid. You *wanted* to do that. You didn't have to be told seventeen times to "*Go play with your toys!*" But when it came time for clean up and putting away your toys, the fun factor suddenly dropped dramatically. You *didn't want* to do that. Think about how much more fun it is to make a mess with finger paints if you knew you didn't have to clean it up.

Clean It Up, Rosie!

Wouldn't it be cool to have a robotic maid follow you around and do all the things that you didn't want to do? For me, its duties would include picking up and washing my clothes, paying my bills, and especially vacuuming. But just because I don't have a "Rosie" to do those things doesn't mean I can just ignore them. I would soon have nothing but dirty clothes scattered on my dirty floor and bill collectors pounding on my door.

But isn't this exactly what we're doing with our relationships? During the course of getting to know someone through "fun" activities, we can't help but come across times when we disagree or have a conflict. It is as inevitable as clothes getting dirty or a bill coming due. Yet instead of making the effort to pick up our relationship and put it in the washing machine, we tend to just let it lie there, dirty, on the floor.

The fact is, for many of us, we have never really been taught how to effectively resolve conflicts nor told all the consequences if we don't. Not knowing any better, we simply let conflicts pile up on the floor, then move out when the mess gets to be too much. We sweep conflicts "under the rug," then eventually stay away from that room when the rug gets too lumpy.

We don't have a "Rosie" or little elves in our lives solving relationship issues while we sleep, nor will we ever. We have to learn how to do it for ourselves. *The Melfox Method* teaches the elements of conflict resolution and reveals the consequences when it is not effectively done.

Before Keyboarding Was Kool

I know this is going to date me, but I was in high school before the everyday presence and use of computer keyboards. When my friend signed up to take a typing class, I remember making fun of him for learning something that was only for secretaries. I was completely ignorant of the importance that proper keyboarding skills would have in the not-so-distant future.

To this day, I still "hunt-and-peck" when using a keyboard. I have improved over the years and sometimes find myself instinctively knowing what keys are where. In those brief moments, I can actually look at the screen while keying. But a lot of my energy is still spent on hunting for the right keys, and less on writing. Oh, if only I had taken that typing class in high school like my friend.

We are not born instantly knowing how to properly and effectively use a computer keyboard. The same can be said about relationships. Knowledge of effective conflict resolution, like effective keying skills, is not initially instinctive and needs to be taught. *The Melfox Method* provides you the lessons you need so you can "write" your relationship, without "hunting" for blame or "pecking" your partner with accusations.

Clean That Mouse

Speaking of computers, the first time I used a PC with a mouse for any extended period of time was at a new office job. I was working on the computer with no problems when suddenly the cursor got stuck on the screen. I moved the mouse on the pad, but the cursor stayed put. Naturally, my first move was to shake the mouse and bang it on the desk a few times. This got the cursor to jump a bit, yet it was still unresponsive to the movement of the mouse.

Bear in mind that this was a mechanical device with a ball and rollers – not one with infrared lasers or whatever folks are using now-days. Since I was ignorant about computer mice, I didn't know (or even think) to look inside, and thus considered it busted. I was looking for a replacement when a co-worker asked if I had "cleaned" it. Cleaned it? I didn't know you could clean a mouse! I was completely unaware that dust builds up on the rollers over time causing erratic cursor control. Sure enough, after I removed the cover and cleaned off the rollers, the mouse worked as good as new.

Do you know what to do when your relationship gets "stuck"? Do you just "shake and bang" it a few times, and then consider throwing it away and looking for a replacement? Isn't that the way it goes? *The Melfox Method* can show you how to open up your relationship cover, clean off its rollers, and have it working as good as new.

Understanding Relationships

Is it just my imagination, or does society as a whole look at relationships as if they have an expiration date? We have come to expect that relationships, like cut flowers, bloom fresh and sweet at the beginning, only to fade and rot until we finally decide to finally throw them out. This fading process in relationships is what we call *drifting apart*.

So why don't we ever hear or use the term *drifting together*?

> BEATRICE: You and Bob seem to be getting along better.
>
> BARBARA: I really don't know why. We just seem to have been *drifting together* lately.

Not exactly the kind of conversation you hear very often.

So why do we use terms such as *drifting apart* when we describe a failing relationship? The word "drifting" is very telling. It implies wandering around without direction. It also conjures up the idea of an external force causing the movement.

In the case of relationships, this "external force" is causing the drifting or failure. It causes a couple who at one time couldn't keep their eyes or hands off each other, to eventually walk sideways as they pass in a hallway in hopes that they don't touch. So what is this mysterious force?

To demonstrate this concept let's have fun with…

Science Experiment #1 – Magnet & Steel

Objective
To determine the effect paper has on the attraction of a magnet and steel.

Materials Needed
Magnet, steel, paper

Experimental Procedure
1. Go over to your junk drawer right now and get a horseshoe magnet or one of those magnetized hide-a-key gizmos.

2. After scraping off all the stray staples and paperclips, find a small piece of steel that is easily picked up by the magnet.

3. Remove magnet from steel, and place steel on a flat surface.

4. Drape a regular piece of paper over the steel.

5. Put the magnet on top of the paper. (Assuming it's worth the dollar you paid for it, the magnet will pick up the steel even with the paper in between. The force holding them together may not be as strong, but the attraction is still there.)

6. Separate the magnet and steel again.

7. Drape two pieces of paper over the steel. (The magnet should still pick it up, but the attraction is even weaker.)

Conclusion
With every added piece of paper between the magnet and steel, the attraction grows weaker and weaker until at some point there is no attraction at all.

In the relationship world, the paper represents the "external force" we spoke of earlier. As time goes by, these "pieces of paper" mysteriously pile up as we sense that something has "come between us."

Now granted, there are exceptions to this. There are couples out there who are just as happy together today as they were 5, 20, or 65 years ago. They've apparently figured out a way to make theirs a "paperless" relationship. This book is for the rest of us.

My Relationship, the Car

Imagine that when you begin a relationship, a magical car appears that you and your partner ride around in. When you first get into and test drive this special relationship car, you can feel the excitement. It feels like you just started a beautifully tuned engine and it's purring like a kitten. It takes you and your partner places you've never been before. Beautiful places. Then as you are traveling down life's road with your partner smiling at your side, you hear a ping. "Wow," you think. That's the first and only time that has ever happened in this car. Later on, there's another, louder ping. Then another. They get more and more frequent, and louder and louder.

Now if this engine were part of an actual car, you would probably take it in and have it looked at. But not this car. This car is special. It's going to run "happily ever after" and if it ever doesn't, well, it's a defective car and needs to be replaced. Our search then goes on for our "Mr. or Ms. Right" car, our "real soul mate" car.

Relationships are not like magical, maintenance-free cars that never require us to "take it in" and have them looked at. Your relationship needs to be regularly and properly serviced, if you want it to always purr like a kitten.

Very Attractive

Going back to our "attractive" analogy, we can see that it's not the lack of effort on the part of the magnet and steel to become closer. As much as we try to push the magnet onto the steel, the paper will always be in the way, weakening attraction.

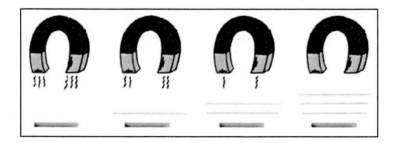

So the real trick is not *trying* to be closer. What we need to do is get rid of the obstacles between us. Obstacles that may accumulate suddenly, or slowly build up like pieces of paper. So what are these obstacles? What is it that causes us to "drift apart" and lose attraction for each other? What is the one universal enemy of relationships? Well, that's simple. The answer is...

YOUR ATTENTION PLEASE...

We Interrupt This Book for a QUICK Fairytale:

Once upon a time, there were two lonely people. Beatrice lived on one side of town and Bruno on the other. "Oh, how I wish there was someone for me so I would not have to be so lonely," Beatrice would think. Bruno would feel the same. One day, by chance, Beatrice and Bruno met. After a while they both had the same thought: Maybe this is the one who won't make me feel so lonely. They gazed into each other's eyes, held each other's hands, and took a vow to be together forever. And they lived happily ever after.

What's that you say? You want to know "how" Beatrice and Bruno did that? How did they manage to live "happily ever after" their vow? That's a very good question. Yes, I would imagine that would be valuable information to share, since so many people are not living happily after taking such a vow. But alas, I do not know. Don't shoot me, I'm only the narrator.

Fairytales Revisited

Why is there is a sense of satisfaction in a fairytale that ends with a vow or the promise of a vow? Is it just the sense of relief that "the search" is over? Many fairytales have that convenient element of ending just as a commitment begins. They make it seem that the trick is just finding that "special" someone, and having them find and accept you. Once you do that, the clouds will part, the sun will shine, the angels will sing, and the rest of both your lives will be paradise on earth.

The telling of fairytales doesn't end just because we grow up. Many books and movies have as their central theme the desire to be with that special someone. The one who will make everything all right. The one who will be the love of our life. Like fairytales, these types of stories conveniently end at the moment of commitment, leaving us to think their total happiness will effortlessly last forever.

We all love it when Richard Gere overcomes his fear of heights and rescues Julia Roberts from a life on the street. Our hearts fill with joy every time we see Dustin Hoffman win over Katharine Ross and they ride off in that bus.

Yet as satisfying as the ending to *Pretty Woman* is, how do we prevent its sequel from being *Sleeping With The Enemy*? How do we keep *The Graduate* from being *Kramer vs. Kramer* a dozen years later?

Fairytales and romantic comedies are great entertainment. They show us a magical world full of imagination and excitement. The key word there is "magical." It isn't real. Alas, there really isn't a magic slipper out there that can effortlessly make your relationship maintenance-free. It has to be done.

Relationship Maintenance

Compare the relationship you have with your partner to the relationship you have with your car. When you take possession of a car, you assume the responsibility for its care and maintenance. You fill it with gas. You check and change the oil. You check and rotate the tires. When the windshield wipers wear out, you change them. When the car gets dirty enough, you clean it. Your car's owner's manual details a lot of these things for you. It tells you what needs to be done and how often, to have a healthy relationship with your car.

So where is the "owner's manual" for the most important relationship you'll have for the rest of our life? Do you know "what to do" and "how often" to do it? Do you know *how* to do what to do?

Are we really going to accept the simple notion that "relationships go bad"? Are we really going to accept that heartbreaking feelings of despair and hopelessness are normal and natural? Assuming your answer to these questions is a resounding *"NO!"* - let's learn what to do.

CHAPTER ONE - ENVIRONMENT

"Perfect timing," Beatrice muttered to herself, getting up from the couch. She had finally gotten the nerve to talk to Bruno about their failing relationship, and boom, someone's knocking at the door. She hastily dried her eyes and opened the door.

A young man stood smiling. "Can I help you?" asked Beatrice.

"Yes, you can," a scratchy voice uttered with a cough. "May I come in?"

"Who are you? What do you want?" Beatrice asked, closing the door a bit.

"It's not really what I want. It's what YOU want."

Bruno had made his way into the hallway. "Go away," he bellowed, sweeping his arm toward the door. "We don't want anything you have."

"Oh, I think you might," the man quickly countered, with a grin and slight cough. "Once you hear what I have to say."

He had an air of confidence and warmth not common for a salesman, Beatrice thought. "Well, let me get you some water for that cough," she offered, heading toward the kitchen and nudging Bruno to let him in.

Bruno rolled his eyes and let out a sigh. "Come on in," he said, leading the way to the kitchen table. "So what's your name? Where you from?"

"Oh, you can call me... Beano," he said taking a seat across from Bruno. "I'm from here and there; mostly here. I lived in a cute little place on Wiley Drive for while, then on Cleveland Street. But mostly here."

Bruno's jaw dropped as Beatrice slowly placed a glass of water in front of the stranger. "You just named, in order, every place where Bruno and I have lived," she stammered.

"Actually I know everything there is to know about your relationship, and I need your help," he said with a smile. "You see... I AM your relationship!"

* * * * * * * * * * * * * * * * *

Environment - The Arena

What do you think you and your partner's relationship would say to you, if it could talk? Beatrice and Bruno are about to find out. They may have been intimidated and reluctant at first, yet at least for now willing to listen to what their relationship is trying to tell them. We're going to do the same thing here. We are going to explore what your relationship would tell you if it could. It all starts with knowing your Environment.

In this chapter, we will explore the "arena" of conflict resolution and the things to do before ever speaking a word. It's like all the preparations that are needed before ever playing a tennis match. Things like reserving the court, making sure the weather is fine, and before playing, knowing who your opponent will be.

Whose Side Are You On?

Imagine if one of the partners in a normal tennis doubles match were to suddenly leap over the net and play *against* their partner. That would be silly. That is not how the game is played. Doubles partners are on the same side of the net with each other, and remain there throughout the entire match.

In tennis, it's easy to see who your opponent is. They are the ones on the other side of the net. In conflict resolution, it is not so clear-cut.

You may go into a conflict resolution "match" not having a clear objective or goal in mind. All you know is your partner is, did, or believes something that you don't like. Or you are, did, or believe something that your partner doesn't like. Either way, you and your partner are on different sides.

On the other hand, you may go into conflict resolution knowing your partner is your ally, and who your opponent is. Yet even knowing this, there will be times when you believe that your partner has mysteriously changed sides and become your opponent. If this doesn't happen at all, then the conflict subject was not discussed or there wasn't any conflict to begin with.

The main goals of this chapter are to clearly show the one true opponent in conflict resolution, and that partners can work together on "the same side of the net," cleansing their relationship Environment of that common foe.

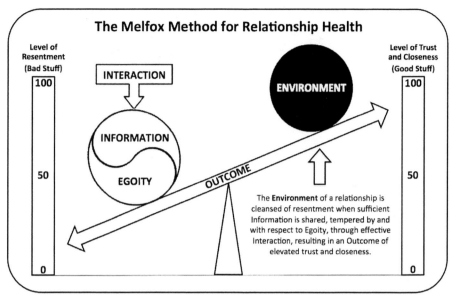

Diagram 3: *The Melfox Method* Model featuring Environment

The level of trust and closeness we have with our partner is dependent on the cleanliness or "lightness" of our relationship Environment.

We will be discussing the tools and process to clean and lighten this Environment in upcoming chapters. Before that, we need to know what is weighing it down in the first place.

The Root of All Relationship Problems

There are many terms to describe the "lack of attraction" you feel when you are having issues with your partner. We're going to bundle them all together and use one term in this book: *Resentment*. Resentment is the "paper" that comes between you and your partner. It is the reason you  don't feel as close as you could. It is the residual source of conflict within a relationship. It is the result of a real or imagined wrong done.

You may feel resentment more like bitterness, ill will, rankling, or bad blood. The physical manifestations or *expressions* of resentment include terms such as anger, hostility, rage, indignation, or hurt. Isolating and cleansing resentment from a relationship is the essence of conflict resolution.

Whacking at the Resentment Root

Think of the different relationship problems you've ever had or can think of. Money? Sex? Laziness? Even infidelity? These issues are not the problems. It's the *resentment* that you have *concerning* these issues that is the problem. Let's take money, for example. Let's say that both Beatrice and Bruno have jobs, yet Beatrice earns more money than Bruno. The difference in earning power is not necessarily an issue. It's only an issue if there is *resentment*:

Partner's Internal Feeling	Resentment?	An Issue?
Beatrice feels that Bruno is not earning enough	✔	✔
Beatrice feels Bruno's financial contribution is acceptable		
Bruno feels remorse or is jealous that Beatrice earns more than him	✔	✔
Bruno feels that Beatrice earning more than him is acceptable		

If a relationship is a road between two people, resentment is the fallen tree, the pothole, the stop sign, the foggy windshield, or washed-out bridge. It prevents us from clearly seeing, reaching, and "getting" the other person.

As we will discuss later, resentment may be multi-tiered or layered - with one issue causing another. It is also a shared experience. One person may have the resentment, but both share in the effect it has on the relationship. Identifying and clarifying resentment is the essence of *The Melfox Method*. The remaining chapters of this book deal with how to identify, expose, and eliminate the causes of resentment, and clear your relationship of obstacles that keep it from being a healthy ride.

Getting to Know Thy Enemy

Ever think about what a "relationship" is? We often say that we are "in a relationship" without giving any thought to what that really means. On the surface it may seem to be just two people together, that's all. Two entities. And when just two entities are involved in a conflict, it's only natural to assume that the conflict you have is with the other entity, right? But what if you're not alone? What if there is something else in the room besides you and your partner?

The Scent of Resentment

Imagine your relationship as a separate entity, like Beano. Imagine that the *resentment* you feel in your relationship is like *body odor* emanating from Beano. Get the picture?

You could figuratively douse it with perfume by walking on eggshells and keeping any conversation with your partner light and sweet. But this does not get rid of resentment.

You could wear virtual gas masks by avoiding conversations with your partner altogether. But this does not get rid of resentment.

You could even try to "scrub it clean" by compromising, or forgiving and forgetting. But even the best cleaning *outside* does not address the underlying issues that continue to reek with toxic resentment *on the inside*. You may forgive someone, yet the underlying resentment doesn't understand that concept. It will continue to wreak toxicity, even though you decide "the case" is closed and you stop talking about it. You can't just say a few words and wish it away. We will be discussing this more in the *Interaction* chapter.

Resentment is the Enemy of Relationships

For the purpose of this book, we will define resentment as follows:

> *Resentment: The feeling of distain caused by the non-acceptance that an individual presumably is, did, or believes something that does not match one's belief about or expectation of that individual.*

Yes, "presumably" is an important word here. As we will see later, upon adequate evaluation, resentment may be unfounded and meritless. But without the procedures to properly expose its irrationality, resentment, even when unjustified, will persist and adversely affect the relationship.

A critical theme that will run throughout this book is the idea that resentment is the enemy, not either of the two people in the relationship. This may seem self-evident, but experience has shown that most of us don't usually unite against this common foe. Usually it's our pride versus our partner's pride. It's our fears versus our partner's fears.

In this chapter, we will learn about the true enemy and nemesis of relationships – resentment:

1. First, we will explore three laws of resentment as they pertain to relationships.

2. Next, we will cover four reasons resentment develops and exists.

3. We will then learn why understanding is the key to exposing resentment, and how *The Melfox Method* goes about setting up the ideal conditions for conflict resolution.

Conflict Resolution Mindsets

As mentioned earlier, we traditionally see *conflict* resolution as a fight since we see *conflict* as synonymous with *war*. But two countries that have a conflict do not necessarily need to go to war. You don't need to bomb another country just because there is a conflict with fishing rights or a border dispute. Conflict can be resolved with *diplomacy*. Effective communication and conflict resolution is possible when we use *diplomacy* with our partner and work cooperatively to come to an understanding.

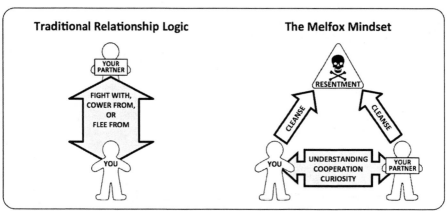

Diagram 4: Traditional Relationship Logic and The Melfox Mindset

It's only when we work together to unravel the mystery of our resentment that our relationship will have a clear road, and make it possible to restore our attraction to our partner. For this to happen effectively, constant attention must be paid to the primary objective: to understand each other. Not to win. Not to persuade. Not to cope. Not to forgive or compromise. The focus should be on *understanding each other*.

As you will soon see, resentment is simply caused by insufficient or faulty communication. Hiding away and coping with resentment prevents exposing its irrationality. Many times, the simple act of sharing resentment with your partner resolves the issue. Shedding light on an issue exposes its cause and thus weakens its power over us.

Exposure is the key to healing. Or as U.S. Supreme Court Justice Louis Brandeis once said: *"Sunlight is the best disinfectant."*

We must learn to swallow our pride and face our fears when it comes to sharing our feelings. By bringing resentment up to our awareness level and sharing it with our partner, the reasons causing it will be exposed. And like vampires in sunlight, once the cause of resentment is exposed and fully understood, it vanishes into dust.

This book will give you the tools you need to do just that.

Laws of Resentment

To better understand our "enemy" and how to defeat it, let's look at basic fundamentals or laws of resentment:

1. Resentment is cleansed and only cleansed from a relationship through the Interaction of the individuals who make up the relationship.

2. The effect that resentment has on the relationship of an individual has an equal effect on the other individual in the relationship.

3. Any resentment can be resolved to the point of acceptance by both individuals in a relationship.

First Law of Resentment

Resentment is cleansed and only cleansed
from a relationship through the Interaction of
the individuals who make up the relationship.

In other words, resentment is cleansed in the same manner that it was formed – through Interaction. Resentment is like toxic fumes that exude from a relationship that has not been properly maintained. You may place all the blame on your partner and feel they are the sole source of the toxicity. If this is the case, you may feel that they don't care, and that there is nothing you can do but leave.

Resentment is cleansed from the relationship when the cause of its toxicity is discovered and exposed. By effectively communicating with your partner, the cause of resentment will be discovered, leading to its elimination. Until this Interaction takes place, the resentment may fester, grow, and multiply.

What started as a simple misunderstanding may then grow into a major issue. No amount of self-talk or "wishing it away" will prohibit the growth and existence of resentment. Addressing its cause is a joint venture and the responsibility of both partners.

Remember, think of your relationship as a separate entity - an invisible and emotional entity - created by you and your partner. Working together is the only way to remove any toxicity and restore the health of your relationship. The magical thing about conflict resolution is the fact that it needs both people who make up the relationship to work on it at the same time in order for it to be successful.

In some banks, two keys are needed to open a safe deposit box. The bank has one key and the customer has the other. The vault will not open with just one key. The lock needs both keys to be used at the same time. Think of resentment resolution the same way. The "vault" will not open with just one person working on it. Remember, your resentment is a shared condition just like your relationship is a shared experience.

Talking With Other People

What needs to be understood at this point is that resentment is the killer of relationships. You can talk to your therapist about it. You can talk to your friends about it. You can even talk to yourself about it. But in order to *dissolve* resentment, you must tackle it head on with the person you have it with.

Talking about resentment with other people may make you feel better temporarily, but it's like paddling on one side of a canoe – you only go around in circles. The person or people you talk to are only getting one side of the story – your side. There is a strong possibility that the resentment you have toward your partner will not only persist, but also grow stronger.

How does talking to your friends or someone else help your *partner*? How do your friends know how your partner feels about the issue and its underlying circumstance?

A relationship is a living, breathing entity that is shared with another individual. Resentment needs to be discussed and hashed out *with that individual* if conflict resolution is to be achieved.

Using the lessons in this book, the fear of rejection and vulnerability will be replaced with solid, understandable, and powerfully effective communication. You will be working together to "clear the road" instead of pointing fingers and placing blame.

Trying to dissolve resentment without involving the other individual in the relationship is like breaking off a weed and leaving the root. It will grow back stronger than ever. It takes both individuals of the relationship to root out and resolve the entire resentment weed.

Second Law of Resentment

The effect that resentment has on the relationship
of an individual has an equal effect on the other
individual in the relationship.

This is similar to the first law of resentment in that it involves both individuals of the relationship equally. Understanding this symmetry is extremely important if the nature of resentment is to be fully understood. This is essential if the proper mindset and Environment for conflict resolution is to be established. In order to demonstrate this law, let's join…

Beatrice and Bruno's Anniversary

Beatrice was getting ready for her big anniversary date with Bruno. It was four months ago today that he gave her that flower. As she was brushing her hair and humming a happy tune, Beatrice was wondering what Bruno had in store for such an important occasion. Four flowers this time? Maybe four dozen! And, of course we will be going to the fanciest restaurant in town. She was feeling all giddy and her heart was all-aflutter. Bruno, being the stereotypical male, is completely oblivious to the "special" day. We now join the date in progress, as this grim reality is beginning to dawn on Beatrice...

BRUNO: What's wrong?

BEATRICE: (*solemnly, with her head down*) Nothing.

BRUNO: (*leaning forward*) Really, what's wrong?

BEATRICE: (*placing her paper napkin over her face*) Nothing.

BRUNO: (*touching her hand*) Was it something I said?

BEATRICE: No! Just leave me ALONE!! (*and storms off crying*)

BRUNO: (*staring down at his half-eaten Big Mac*) Grrrrr.

As you can tell, Beatrice and Bruno are sharing the same feeling of resentment, even though Bruno is clueless as to why it exists. The exact same feeling and level of separation from resentment exists for both Beatrice and Bruno. The only difference is the reason why.

If Beatrice feels that Bruno is not affected by the resentment, a feeling of animosity toward him is inevitable. If Beatrice understood that Bruno feels "just as bad" from her resentment as she does, a sense of balance is established and an atmosphere of cooperation naturally forms. With this, she would be much more likely to share with Bruno why she feels resentment toward him, which is the beginning step in the conflict resolution process, as we will learn later in this book.

Similarly, if Bruno is unaware of why Beatrice acted as she did, a feeling of animosity toward her is inevitable. If Bruno understood that Beatrice was feeling resentment, even not knowing the cause, a normal sense of balance is established and an atmosphere of cooperation naturally forms. He would actually want Beatrice to share her resentment with him, since he would know that is how his feeling of separation with her will be resolved.

Another way to understand this is to divide resentment into two flavors:

You feel resentment when....

1. Someone presumably is, did, or believes something you do not like, or
2. Someone does not like what you presumably are, did, or believe.

Let's take a look at the word "like" for a moment and see how it can help us understand conflict and resentment.

What It Means to "Like" Something

Have you ever thought about the meaning of the word "like"? We generally think of it as meaning pleasure or enjoyment. We can also look at it as being similar in nature. If you are "like" someone, you are "similar in nature." If they do something you "like," that means their action is "similar in nature" to yours. So when we don't like what somebody does, our defenses kick in and we, at least partially and for an instant, view them as a threat. This is because they have demonstrated something that is not part of our "nature."

Of course different things provoke our response in different ways. Sometimes when somebody does something we don't like, it's merely because we would've done something different. Other times, we don't like what somebody says because it threatens our "very nature." It is at these latter times that our defenses are most strongly invoked. After all, they are threatening our essence of existence by calling into question our very nature.

Third Law of Resentment

Any resentment can be resolved to the point of acceptance by both individuals in a relationship.

This may seem obvious at first, yet have you ever seen a divorcing couple on TV as they sit in an attorney's office? Most of the time they can't stand the sight of each other, and whenever they do speak to each other, it seems it's always in sarcastic tones or just plain yelling. It's hard to imagine them ever getting anything resolved, let alone having the desire to in the first place.

The encouraging part of this law is that if there's enough time and effective effort spent on it, **any** resentment *can* be resolved. Yes, "can" is the key word here. To dramatize this point, here's a different kind of fairytale...

The Island Nation of Bridgeway

Once upon a time, there was a tiny island nation of Bridgeway. It was made up of tiny little islands just big enough to hold one person. The only way to reach another island was to build a bridge, for the water was far too cold to swim, and the coastline was far too treacherous for boats. Each island usually had at least a simple rope bridge connecting neighboring islands, and if desired, a more substantial wooden bridge would be built replacing the rope bridge. To withstand the fierce tropical storms, the wooden bridges needed to be properly designed, built with a strong foundation, and regularly maintained.

One fateful day, a big storm raged and washed out the wooden bridge between Jack and Diane. Maybe the collapse was caused by a faulty design or foundation, or maybe it was not maintained properly. In any case, the bridge was gone and there was no way for Jack and Diane to reach each other. They tried to communicate by yelling, but the sound of the waves crashing on the rocky shore and bridge debris was too great for either to hear. Jack thought he was yelling loud enough, but since Diane didn't respond, he assumed she didn't care enough to rebuild the bridge. Diane was thinking exactly the same thing about Jack. After a while, they each gave up, walked away, and started building wooden bridges to other islands where at least there was the foundation of a sturdy rope bridge.

And they lived separately ever after.

Not exactly a warm and fuzzy story, but I hope you get the idea. Due to the lack of desire to reconcile, Jack and Diane had determined that it just *wasn't worth* rebuilding their relationship "bridge." If their desire were strong enough, they would have found a way, even if it had taken the rest of their lives. They *could* have... but they didn't.

Resolved to the Point of Acceptance...

To help explain this "resolved to the point of acceptance" part of the law, let's look at what happens when a tree falls, blocking a road:

1. A road crew is called out to remove the tree.
2. The main trunk is cut up and hauled away.
3. The broken branches are carried away.
4. The smaller twigs and leaves are swept away.
5. The remainder of the debris, *too small to matter*, is left on the road.

At some point, the road crew makes a determination that the debris is at an *acceptable level* for traffic to drive over safely.

Now the road crew could have come out with high-pressure hoses and sand blasters, and made sure every last particle of debris was removed before opening the road to traffic. But this would have been overkill, and a waste of time, energy, and taxpayers' money.

Resentment, like road debris, need not be dissolved completely for it to cease having an effect on a relationship. There comes a point in conflict resolution when an individual feels this has been accomplished. Their partner, however, may still need more Information and understanding before they sign off on the resolution. The conflict must be resolved to the satisfaction of both individuals if the toxic effect of underlying resentment is to be avoided. We will be discussing ways to ensure this in the *Interaction* chapter.

Acceptable Level of Value Compromise

Another way to explain the "acceptance" concept is to look at how much we are willing to sacrifice our value of something for the sake of convenience.

We may value "being green" yet ride around in a car using fossil fuel. We made a decision that adhering to that value has limits. We may carpool, limit joyrides, and have a car with a high MPG rating, and consider that to be acceptably "green." If we valued minimizing our carbon footprint more, we would take additional steps such as...

1. Buying an all-electric car (and charge it using solar power).

2. Riding our bike whenever the destination is close enough and the weather permits.

3. Growing sugar beets, using a distiller, and converting our car to run on less-polluting alcohol.

The point is, we all have limits when it comes to adhering to certain values. We make decisions to abide by those values to the point that it becomes too inconvenient.

The same is true with conflict resolution. We have a natural sense of resolution when the resentment is down to the point that continuing to talk about it is "inconvenient" and boring. We need to make sure it is sufficiently resolved with our partner, but anything more than that is overkill and a waste of energy.

Fundamental Reasons for Resentment

The following are four major reasons for resentment. The cause of most all resentment can be boiled down to one or more of these. It might move from one to another before the conflict is resolved.

1. Lack of Sufficient, Pertinent Information
2. Misunderstanding
3. False Assumption
4. Jumping to False Conclusion

1. Lack of Sufficient, Pertinent Information

Information that is omitted from conversation can easily be converted into resentment. Decisions made by yourself or your partner without adequate Information can lead to conflict and if not adequately exposed, resentment can easily set in. This is often the case when the relationship is new. Care needs to be taken early in the relationship to learn essential things about your partner's preferences, values, and idiosyncrasies.

Keep in mind that your partner does not know everything about you and what you like to see from them. You may choose to let certain things slide to avoid confrontation, especially early in the relationship. Resentment is often the result from this avoidance, even if you're not aware of it. As we will see later, identification of resentment is the first step in its resolution. By letting your partner know what you like or need, decisions they make can usually easily be adjusted accordingly.

Though many times the lack of Information is obvious and easily identified and resolved, at other times it persists and is buried. *The Melfox Method* then comes to the rescue by focusing in on the culprit and resolving the conflict.

2. Misunderstanding

There are two major areas of misunderstanding when comes to resentment:

a) Not hearing your partner correctly (thinking they said X when they said Y)

b) Not understanding your partner (not knowing or having different definitions of a word or phrase)

In either case, you or your partner innocently base decisions on inaccurate Information. It is easily seen how this can cause resentment. Just like in the case of lack of sufficient Information, identification and sharing of misunderstandings squelch any chance of resentment occurring.

An example of the first type was dramatized in the first season of *Saturday Night Live,* with Gilda Radner portraying commentator Emily Litella on Weekend Update. She mistook such things as "Violence on TV" as "Violins on TV," and "Natural Resources" as "Natural Racehorses." She would go on and on until the anchor would interrupt and point out the misunderstanding. She would then smile and finish with a sheepish "Never mind."

The other type of misunderstanding is being "on different pages" when it comes to a word or phrase. You may have something totally different in mind when your partner says something, or vice versa. This will cause resentment until you discover each other's meaning of the word or phrase and use better words that have *shared* meaning.

Again, if misunderstandings are not obvious when they occur, effective implementation of *The Melfox Method* brings them to light and eliminates the resentment they may have caused. The goal is for both partners to eventually smile sheepishly and utter "never mind" to each other.

3. False Assumption

One of the more common causes for resentment is the use of false assumptions. Reasons for this include expected patterns, social norms, past experiences, and laziness. To illustrate this, here's an example:

1	2	3	4	5	6	7	8
T	T	F	F	S	S	E	?

Assuming (pardon the pun) that you don't know the real answer (which is at the end of this section*), you could logically surmise that the next value would be an "E" since all the previous letters had come in pairs. But have you asked yourself why these particular letters? Why T, F, S, and E? Could they stand for something? By taking the time to discover or ask for the real pattern, you will see the real answer to be "N."

We often "fill in the blanks" with what we think is reasonable Information or a reasonable conclusion. Assumptions are like short cuts or macros in a computer program. They allow us to go through life without questioning every little thing we experience or believe. We make assumptions all the time; some valid, some not so much.

> *A 24-year-old looking out the train's window shouted, "Dad look, the trees are going behind!" His father smiled, and a young couple sitting nearby looked at the childish behavior with pity. Suddenly he again exclaimed, "Dad look, the clouds are running with us!" The couple couldn't resist and said to the father, "Why don't you take your son to a good doctor?" The father smiled and said, "I did and we are just coming from the hospital. My son was blind from birth and he just got his eyes today."*
>
> - Unknown

How often has this kind of thing happened with you? Of course, without making *any* assumptions, our lives would grind to a screeching halt...

As discussed in the previous sections, resentment can often be easily averted when you and your partner are both aware of the false assumption. Unlike lack of Information or miscommunication, false assumptions put the responsibility solely on the one making the assumption. This is not to place blame on them for the resentment, but rather to call to attention that care needs to be taken to avoid such resentment from reoccurring.

The Melfox Method attacks "false assumption" resentment by reconciling the difference between the desires of one partner and the actions of the other.

> * The "real" pattern in the sequence at the beginning of this section is the first letter of numbers beginning with two: (Two, Three, Four, Five, Six, Seven, Eight, Nine)

4. Jumping to False Conclusion

The basis for the conclusion in this case is protection. An event or series of events triggers you into "protection mode" or another automatic reaction. You literally "jump" over the idea of gathering additional Information to arrive at a conclusion that may or may not be the correct one. You skip to the end of the book after reading just one page.

Here's an example using a series of responses where you want your partner to reply to an email you sent...

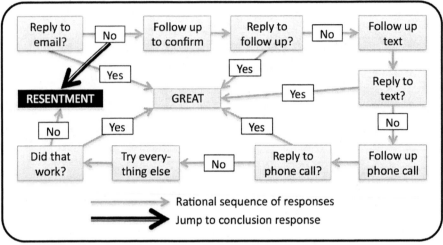

Diagram 5: Jumping to Conclusions Email

As you can see, by not going through a series of follow-ups and not giving one's partner the benefit of the doubt, resentment may form when it doesn't have to. By working through this resentment via *The Melfox Method*, this type of behavior can be easily identified and possibly eliminated in the future.

This type of short-circuited response may be caused by a painful past experience or by bumping up against a limiting or presuming belief. Only by sharing your resentment with your partner and revealing the irrationality of the response will the resentment be dissolved.

As we discussed earlier, exposing and eliminating limiting or presuming beliefs is one of the side benefits of proper conflict resolution. By having a totally open line of communication, your partner acts like a mirror to your unawareness. Things that have been holding you back for possibly years become demystified and readily apparent.

What makes this technique unique is that limiting or presuming beliefs naturally emerge as part of the process. By opening up to a truly caring and trustful partner, you can gradually bring limiting or presuming beliefs up to the awareness level and exposed to "sunlight." Unlike any other thing else that is irrational, once limiting or presuming beliefs are exposed to scrutiny, they naturally dry up and blow away.

Multiple and Consequential Issues

One of my favorite books growing up (and still today) is *A Fly Went By* written by Mike McClintock and illustrated by Fritz Siebel. The story is of a little boy who went on a journey of discovery. It started when he asked a fly why it was flying so fast. The fly said a frog was chasing it.

Now at this point the boy could have just said, "OK, thanks, just curious," plopped back down in the rowboat, and looked at the sky some more. Perhaps he already knew that frogs chasing flies isn't that unusual and *assumed* that was the end of the story. Thank goodness he didn't because that would have made for a rather short and boring book.

No, instead he asked the frog *why* it was chasing the fly. The frog said it *wasn't* chasing the fly. The frog said a cat was chasing *it*. Again, the boy could have stopped there since he knew cats chase frogs sometimes. But he didn't. Once again, he didn't *assume*. In fact the boy proceeded to spend the rest of the day asking chasers why they chased, and being told by the chasers they were being chased themselves.

SPOILER ALERT: At the end, we all discover a grown man with a gun started the whole mess by being spooked by a little lamb with a bucket handle caught on its leg. The man apparently thought the noise was something to run away from, which scared a pig and started the whole chain reaction that ended with the boy seeing a fly go by. Once the curious little boy pointed out to the man with a gun that the noise was just a bucket rattling and removed it from the lamb's leg, all was well and they all went home as friends.

Lessons learned:
1. Even grown men with guns can be scared.
2. Keep asking "why" to get to the root cause of anything.

In this book, we will be only focusing on the second lesson.

Resentment Could Be a Many-Layered Thing

Just like in the cat chasing the frog chasing the fly story, resentment can be composed of many consequential issues, each causing the one ahead of it.

And just like in the story, resentment (the "chasing") continues until the root cause is exposed and eliminated. Too often, during conflict resolution, we stop before we really understand the true reason for the resentment. And sometimes we don't even start.

> Her Diary:
>
> *Tonight, I thought my husband was acting weird. We had made plans to meet at a nice restaurant for dinner. I was shopping with my friends all day long, so I thought he was upset at the fact that I was a bit late, but he made no comment on it. Conversation wasn't flowing, so I suggested that we go somewhere quiet so we could talk. He agreed, but he didn't say much. I asked him what was wrong; he said, 'Nothing.' I asked him if it was my fault that he was upset. He said he wasn't upset, that it had nothing to do with me, and not to worry about it. When we got home, I felt as if I had lost him completely, as if he wanted nothing to do with me anymore. He just sat there quietly, and watched TV. I don't know what to do. I'm almost sure that his thoughts are with someone else. My life is a disaster.*
>
> His Diary:
> *Motorcycle won't start… can't figure out why.*
>
> - Unknown

One question to ask here is why didn't he just tell her he was having trouble with his motorcycle, and *that* was what was bothering him? When asked, why did he say, "Nothing"? What made him say that? Could it be that he had tried to talk to her about motorcycle stuff in the past and she wasn't interested? If that's the case, why isn't she interested? Could it be that her lack of curiosity about her husband's activities was caused by his lack of interest in *her* activities?

The Empathy Onion

It all boils down to the degree of understanding. Yes, the husband may explain why he didn't tell her when she asked what was wrong to the point that the wife "understands." Let's say that reason was he felt rejected by her when he talked about motorcycles. **But that is not the only thing that needs to be "understood" for the resentment to go away.** What hasn't been discussed and understood is *why* she rejected him in the first place. And that reason may be because he did something earlier that she didn't like.

This "peeling of issues" continues until you find the core reason for the resentment (lack of Information, misunderstanding, etc.). Once the core reason for resentment is fully understood by both you and your partner, there will be an automatic sigh of relief and a "Whew! OK, I get it and I trust you now!" by both you and your partner.

The challenge we face when resolving conflict is to *empathize* with our partner while *analyzing* the issue. There seems to be a tendency to avoid incorporating empathy into our conflict resolution toolbox. It's like mixing art with science, or chocolate with peanut butter. At first, we may have been taught or learned that combining things so different *can't* or even *shouldn't* be done. To effectively resolve conflict, we need to be able to have empathy for our partner as we delve into the reasons for resentment together. If you think that takes too much *work*, you are not alone.

Maintenance of Relationships

Let's try to rethink the whole idea of *working* on relationships or that relationships take *work*. That makes it sound like maintaining your relationship is a dreaded thing. Or worse yet, thinking that *anytime* a couple has to *work* on their relationship, it *must be in trouble* and that's something to avoid or be ashamed of. Would you consider taking care of the relationship with your child or pet as *work*? When you care about something, you naturally do the necessary things to take care of it. Why should it be any different with the relationship you have with your partner?

Man's Best Friend

Let's say you want a dog that catches flying disks, so you get a border collie named Sam. After taking Sam home and getting settled in, you begin to train him to catch flying disks. But let's say that Sam would rather just sit back and smile at the curtains all day. You assumed Sam would like to chase flying disks. Resentment would set in. You may be tempted to get another dog.

59

Now, let's put the shoe on the other paw.

You don't adopt a dog, then ignore it, and expect it to stick around. That's silly. When you take on the responsibility of dog ownership, you form a relationship with the dog that needs to be nurtured. Part of this nurturing is providing a healthy diet and clean Environment for the dog. If you do not provide these things sufficiently, the relationship you have with the dog will grow weak with resentment until the dog leaves in search of a better "relationship" (home) thus ending the relationship it has with you.

This same nurturing is required in the relationship you have with your partner. If this is not provided sufficiently, the relationship you have will grow weak with resentment until you or your partner leaves in search of a better "home." We need to keep it clean by washing away resentment as needed.

Cleaning Amnesia

Imagine a scenario in which you and your partner both get bonked on the head and begin suffering from "cleaning amnesia." You both simply forget the trash needs to be taken out, the floor needs to be mopped, and clothes need to be washed. After a while you would probably wonder why the kitchen is filling up with garbage, the floor is a dirty mess, and clothes can stand up by themselves. In this state of forgetfulness, you don't understand the world of  trash bins, mops, and washing machines. The way I see it, you have four choices:

1. Get someone else to clean up your mess.

2. Keep things as they are and grow weaker and weaker from the stench.

3. Leave your mess in disgust and start a new mess somewhere else.

4. Learn how to take out the garbage, use a mop, and run a washing machine.

Many of us are suffering from "cleaning amnesia" when it comes to relationships. We don't realize they need to be cleaned of resentment once in a while as a matter of course. So when the mess gets too great for us to take, what choices do we have?

1. We shouldn't try to get someone else to clean it, since resentment is only dealt with by those in the relationship (see first Law of Resentment).

2. We could decide to continue things as they are and suffer even more from an ever-weakening relationship.

3. We could decide to dispose of the relationship and begin building resentment in another (and eventually dispose of it...)

4. Or... we could choose to learn the ways and means of cleaning resentment from our relationship.

The Melfox Method provides instructions on how to use our innate "trash bin, mop, and washing machine" to clean up resentment. We need to see that there is a choice besides 1) continuing to suffer or 2) disposing of our relationship. We need to see that there is a third alternative.

Our Disposable Culture

Have you ever wondered about the extent to which our consumer life is based on planned obsolescence? It seems that things that used to be repairable and "last forever" are now exchanged for a new one at the first sign of trouble. For example, we used to have toasters that would last, and could be easily cleaned and repaired. Today, to keep the toaster manufacturers in business, the tendency is to sell at cheap prices cheaply made toasters that simply don't last. When we try to repair the toaster, we find we can't do it ourselves and the cost to repair is more than the cost to replace. When was the last time you read the care and repair instructions for a toaster? For many of us, we're lucky if we know how to clean out the crumb drawer.

Now let's say you like toast and see yourself liking toast for the rest of your life. Wouldn't it make sense to buy a quality toaster, one that can be repaired easily with available parts? The initial cost of the toast and any repair costs would surely be lower in the long run than buying a dozen or so cheap toasters over a lifetime.

Unfortunately, it seems that this "disposable culture" has infiltrated our view of relationships as well. We tend to look at relationships as "un-repairable" and disposable like the cheap toasters we buy today. Again, we need to see that this doesn't have to be the case. There is a choice besides 1) living with a "broken" relationship or 2) disposing of it. We can learn how to clean up the resentment and keep our relationship in fine repair.

Curiosity Kills the Spat

As you will learn throughout this book, one of the key concepts to resolving conflict in any relationship is to have *a burning desire to understand your partner*, a desire that outweighs your fear of vulnerability. And the best way to understand your partner is to ask your partner questions. But asking questions, as we have all no doubt experienced when resentment is involved, is sometimes asking for trouble.

Beatrice and Bruno - Then and Now

When Beatrice and Bruno first got together, their relationship was new and resentment was low. Once, when Beatrice was getting ready to go out, Bruno, being curious and all, simply asked:

BRUNO: Where are you going, Sweetums?
BEATRICE: Oh, just out to the store to look at some clothes.
BRUNO: OK, have fun and drive safe!
BEATRICE: I will. See you later, Honeypie!
BRUNO: Take care, Sugar Pie!

Later, after Beatrice and Bruno were seeing each other for a while, resentment naturally crept into the relationship. Now, when Beatrice would go out for the evening, Bruno, still being curious yet tainted with resentment, would ask:

BRUNO: Where are YOU going, *Sweetums*? [Insert slight sarcasm]
BEATRICE: Why should YOU care?
BRUNO: I don't care, actually. [Insert more sarcasm]
BEATRICE: Fine! Forget it!
BRUNO: Fine! Forget it!

So as you can see, when you mix in resentment, what starts out as innocent curiosity can turn into a Bud and Sissy scene from *Urban Cowboy*. Beatrice had interpreted Bruno's curiosity as passing judgment on her.

Speaking of movies, remember in *All The President's Men* when Woodward (Robert Redford) asks Bernstein (Dustin Hoffman) to discern judgment from curiosity?

> *A guy can come up to me on a street and he can ask me an address.*
> *Now is the man interrogating me, or is he lost?*

When someone asks us something, there always seems to be a decision we have to make when it comes to the motive. We can either see the questioner as curious for Information, or questioning our judgment on something.

Assuming Curiosity or Judgment

Of course, there is also a decision we make when it comes to what questions are asked and how we ask them. At that moment, do we honestly just want Information (curious) or are we a little on the critical side? This will determine what is asked and how it is asked.

We will go much more into the important role that inflection and the choice of words play in activating your partner's defenses in the *Information* and *Egoity* chapters. For now, let us look into the subtle difference between assuming curiosity and assuming judgment.

Why are you wearing that?
　　Curiosity: I feel like dressing up. Thank you for asking!
　　Judgment: Cause I want to. OK??? What's it to ya??

Do we have to go to your mother's tomorrow?
　　Curiosity: Why? Is something bothering you? Let's talk about it.
　　Judgment: Yes, you have to go, and you will pretend to enjoy it!

Why are you taking this route?
　　Curiosity: I enjoy going by the park on the way to mother's.
　　Judgment: If you don't like the way I drive, why don't you?!

This "curiosity or judgment" dilemma isn't limited to questions. With just about anything said, the listener needs to instantly discern it as either benign (curious) or with malice (judgmental). Among others, this instantaneous decision is based on three things:

1. The manner it was said (inflection, style, choice of words).
2. The level of our resentment at the moment.
3. Our awareness of the impact this decision will have on our level of resentment and the rest of the conversation.

By understanding the impact of what is said and how it is interpreted, we will be better able to "maintain control" and keep the conversation from eroding into something that adds to resentment. If you go into a conversation being judgmental, understand that this can only add to the conflict. Similarly, you may go into a conversation feeling judged. Understand that this too can only add to the resentment.

The Curiosity Mantra

In order to keep the conversation on the productive path to reducing resentment, you may want to have something like this Curiosity Mantra in the back of your head.

When I speak, I will always be curious, not judgmental.
The words I use and the way I say them convey a sense of wonder.
I have a burning desire to understand my partner.

When I listen, I will always assume my partner
is being curious, not judgmental.
If there is ever a question of the partner's motive, I will calmly ask.
I have a burning desire to understand my partner.

The Desire to Understand

One of the primary concepts of this book is the idea that resentment is resolved by having a big enough desire to understand your partner. This should be the mindset throughout any conflict resolution. In many ways, understanding is synonymous with love. There are few things in life that can compare to the pleasure we experience when we feel that somebody truly understands us. We feel "gotten." We feel totally connected to that person. Keep in mind that your partner wants to experience that feeling as well.

I Want to Understand You

In Dr. Gary Chapman's book *The Five Love Languages*, he lists the ways in which love can be expressed. We can view these same ways in terms of understanding.

1. Words of affirmation: I want to affirm that I *understand* you.

2. Receiving gifts: I want to show you that I *understand* what you value in the world.

3. Quality time: I want you to *understand* that I want to be with you.

4. Acts of service: I want you to *understand* that I know what you like done for you.

5. Physical touch: I *understand* that physical expression is important to you.

Remember our definition of resentment:

> *Resentment: The feeling of distain caused by the non-acceptance that an individual presumably is, did, or believes something that does not match one's belief about or expectation of that individual.*

It is only through the process of understanding that we will figure out the difference between our expectations of our partner and their actions. Without understanding, attempted conflict resolution becomes just a battle of defenses, and as a result, nobody wins.

If you don't have a big enough desire to understand your partner, conflict resolution would be like trying to clean your kitchen floor with bucket of mud. No matter how hard you try, the floor stays dirty and keeps getting dirtier as you scrub away with nagging, sarcasm, yelling, and moaning. You take out your frustration on your partner, instead of focusing on understanding your partner. Just like trying to clean the floor with mud, fighting with your partner puts the conflict resolution process in "reverse." It actually adds fuel to the fire and makes the resentment worse.

Not making understanding your partner the primary focus in conflict resolution is like saying you don't want to resolve the conflict. Focusing on understanding your partner transforms an argument into mutual cooperation. In other words, *it makes all the difference.* Once you internalize that concept, you are well on your way to understanding effective conflict resolution and restoring your relationship.

Identifying the Reason(s) for Resentment

The Melfox Method teaches concepts and techniques to help you and your partner understand each other better, and cleanse resentment:

1. It identifies missing Information withheld from you or your partner.

2. It identifies misunderstandings between you and your partner.

3. It identifies false assumptions made by you or your partner.

4. It identifies limiting or presuming beliefs that cause you or your partner to jump to conclusions.

The Melfox Mindset

I know the *secret* to working out *any* issue or conflict in a relationship.

Shhhh – it's a secret!

Know HOW to resolve conflicts. That way when an issue comes up, ANY issue, ANY time, you will know *how* to get rid of it.

> *Being happy doesn't mean everything is perfect. It means you've learned to deal with the things that aren't.*
>
> - Unknown

In the above quote, the word "deal" can be thought of as "cope," as in "learning to cope with something." That is not the Melfox way! We will learn how to *deal* with issues head on by resolving them, not surrendering to them and *dealing* with your despair.

The Melfox Mindset focuses on dissolving issues, not coping with them.

Hiding Your Love Away

Coping with issues is like hiding a rash on your face behind a veil of makeup. The rash is still there, but you've learned to "cope" with it. You feel that the only way to "deal" with the situation is to hide away part of yourself since you didn't know how to get rid of the rash. When you choose to "cope" with relationship issues, you hide away part of yourself, too. You protect yourself behind a veil of distrust.

It is only when we discover and eliminate the *cause* of the rash ("Oh, I'm allergic to strawberries!") that we are able to shed the makeup and reveal our true vibrant self.

The Melfox Mindset focuses on getting rid of the rash, not covering it up.

For the Colony, and Oppressed Ants Everywhere!

In the movie *A Bug's Life,* the ants at first thought the only way to deal with Hopper and the other grasshoppers was to just give in and give them what they wanted. You know, "cope" with the situation.

> Hopper: *"Now let me tell you how things are supposed to work: The sun grows the food, the ants pick the food, the grasshoppers eat the food..."*

So the ants spent most of their time gathering food for the grasshoppers and living pretty subservient lives. It was only when the ants learned to work together and face Hopper and the grasshoppers as *a united front* that they saw another option for dealing with the situation.

> Princess Atta: *"You see Hopper, Nature has a certain order. The ants pick the food, the ants keep the food, and the grasshoppers leave!"*

The Melfox Mindset focuses on fending off the grasshoppers, not appeasing them and coping with the consequences.

Let's Play Tug-Of-Trust!

Imagine playing a game with your partner called *Tug-Of-Trust*, in which you each hold the ends of a rope, put your feet against your friend's feet, and lean back. Unlike Tug-Of-War, the object is *not* to pull each other into the mud. It's quite the opposite. The object of this game is to keep each other from falling down. The more you lean back, the more exciting it is, since there is more danger of falling into the mud. Kind of like the excitement you feel when you ride a rollercoaster. Your excitement level (the distance you lean back) is dependent on your strength and the level of trust you have with your partner not to let go. The interesting part is that your partner is in the exact same situation.

Your partner is just as dependent on you, as you are dependent on them.

You soon realize that you can only lean back as far as your partner does, since the imbalance will cause one or both of you to fall. Also, you need to come back up the rope in sync, since a sudden pull or slip by one of you could cause the other to fall. The object of the game is for both of you to lean back as far as you can, hold it as long as you can, and then work yourselves back up without either of you falling into the mud. The farther down you go and the longer you hold it, the higher the score.

One thing that has not been accounted for yet is the condition of the rope. When the rope is new, it is strong, with no frays and no unraveling. After playing for a while, frays appear that weaken the rope, making it harder to grip. You may feel that there is nothing you can do about it, and concede to the possibility of losing your grip or the rope snapping at any time. "*Ropes just go bad after a while,*" you say to yourself. You *cope* with this by not venturing out on the rope quite as far as you could, ever fearful of the rope breaking or your grip slipping. Or you concede to the notion that sometimes you *lose* at Tug-Of-Trust through no fault of your own.

Of course, there is another way to deal with this "ropes-just-go-bad" issue. You and your partner may discover that if you regularly inspect the relationship rope, and work together to mend the frays as they occur, your trust in the rope will increase. This will allow you to "lean back" as much as you can, without the fear of it breaking or losing your grip.

The Melfox Mindset focuses on mending the rope, not coping with its frailty.

The Relationship Rope

When you think about it, playing the game of Tug-Of-Trust is very similar to being in a relationship…

Tug-Of-Trust Game	Relationships
Holding on to the rope, continuing the game.	Holding on to the relationship, as opposed to ending it. *"Let's hang on to our relationship."*
Letting go of the rope, allowing you or the other player to fall.	"Letting go" of the relationship, which ends it. *"If you let me go, I will miss you."*
Breaking your grip on the rope, allowing you or the other to fall.	Breaking up with your partner, ending the relationship. *"I would hate it if we broke up."*
Losing your grip and slipping down the rope.	Feeling your relationship "slip away." Losing your "grip" on the relationship. *"Don't let our love start slipping away."*
Strong grip on the rope.	Having a strong grip on the relationship. *"That's how strong my love is."*
Slipping down on a rope until it reaches the end.	After "slipping away," you come to the end of your patience in the relationship. *"I'm at the end of my rope."*
The rope has frayed down to a single thread.	The relationship has "frayed" to the point that it is ready to snap. *"My heart is barely hanging by a thread."*
The rope unravels at one end weakening the grip of both players.	The relationship is "unraveling" making it harder to "hold on." *"Our love is unraveling before us."*

The similarities between Tug-Of-Trust and relationships go on and on.

Repairing the Relationship Rope

At this point, let's concentrate solely on the rope. When playing the game of Tug-Of-Trust, taking time-outs to repair the frayed or unraveling rope is only possible if you know that the rope is in need of repair in the first place.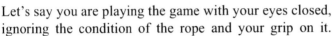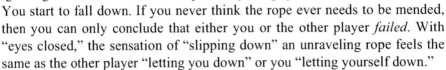

Let's say you are playing the game with your eyes closed, ignoring the condition of the rope and your grip on it. You start to fall down. If you never think the rope ever needs to be mended, then you can only conclude that either you or the other player *failed*. With "eyes closed," the sensation of "slipping down" an unraveling rope feels the same as the other player "letting you down" or you "letting yourself down."

Unfortunately, this is all too often how we see failing relationships as well. We blame and shame our partner or ourselves as if we deliberately tried to hurt the other person. The only thing that we *fail* at is tending to our relationship. We need to "open our eyes," see what is really causing our relationship to fail, and work together to mend it. Of course, if you don't trust your partner, you can "play it safe" and not "lean back." But this makes for a rather boring relationship.

Trust is how "close" you feel to a person. How close you feel depends on how much you feel you understand their feelings and values, and how much they line up with yours. It also depends on how much you feel a person understands your feelings and values, and how much they line up with theirs.

In fairytales and romance novels, the concept is generally conveyed that Relationship Ropes are magically indestructible and always in pristine condition. I think you realize by now that this is simply not true. During the normal use of a normal rope, breakages occur in the tiny fibers that make up the entire rope, causing frays and unraveling.

In relationships, these breaks represent resentment – tiny breaks of misunderstandings that, when not "repaired," eventually leave you and your partner "hanging by a thread." Our Relationship Rope needs to be periodically mended of resentment like a garden needs to be weeded and a driveway needs to be shoveled after a snowstorm.

Even when we are aware of resentment being the cause of our relationship woes, we are often too "afraid" to share it with our partner. We are fearful that our partner will attack us for blaming them or reject us entirely. Being "afraid" allows the "frays" and unraveling in our relationship to exist and "weaken our grip." We will talk much more about this fear of vulnerability in the *Information* and *Egoity* chapters.

Time-Out for a Joke

A rope walks into a bar and orders a drink. The bartender looks at it and says, "Sorry dude, we don't serve ropes 'round here." So the rope leaves disappointed.

The rope then ties itself into a knot, beats itself against a wall, goes back into the bar, and proudly orders a drink.

The bartender looks at him suspiciously and asks, "Hey buddy, aren't you that same rope who came in earlier?"

"Nope," the rope says confidently, "I'm a frayed knot."

Understanding, Trust, and Vulnerability

In a healthy relationship, you trust that your partner is not intentionally hurting you or intending to hurt you. No matter what they say, no matter how they say it, you know they didn't say it with malice in mind. The instant that is not true and you *feel* that what was said or done *was* intended to hurt you with malice, you're afraid the trust is gone and begin seeing your partner as "not on your side."

You may not think this is true and once you do think about it, it *isn't* true. All you have to do is think about it. Until we do, our unintentional reactions are in control, which means *we are not*. It is sometimes really easy for us to fear getting hurt and jump to the conclusion that somebody said or did something to purposely hurt us.

But how are we sure that this was their true intention? Did we ask them? Maybe they were teasing. Maybe they just misspoke. Maybe what they really meant to say was "I don't like that outfit on you" instead of "I don't like you in that outfit." We will get into language and its effect on another person's "defense system" in more detail in the *Information* chapter, and ideas on controlling the effect in the *Egoity* and *Interaction* chapters.

Regardless of what is said or how it's said, the sooner we stop *thinking* that our partner said it to intentionally hurt us, the sooner we are able to "take control" and ask questions to understand the meaning of what is said.

Having a Burning Desire to Understand Your Partner

At one point in the movie *Batman Begins*, Bruce Wayne (our hero) finds himself face-to-face with his nemesis, crime boss Carmine Falcone. Bruce purposely put himself in the vulnerable situation to show Falcone that he wasn't afraid. Falcone responded to this with the following statement:

This is a world you'll never understand.
And you always fear... what you don't understand.

So do you ever feel that "you'll never understand" your partner's world? How hard have you tried? How do you try? That's a good question. *How does one understand another person's world?* You could try to understand your partner by thinking about the relationship on your own and mournfully sing the song *I Just Don't Understand* to yourself.

Or you could simply ask your partner *why* they hurt or mistreated you and *genuinely* want to hear their answer. That's the tricky part. Once our partner starts telling us the reasons why they "hurt or mistreated" us, we often feel too vulnerable and stop wanting to understand.

When our vulnerability outweighs our desire to understand our partner, we become defensive. We defend by arguing (fight) or hiding away (fright or flight). But as long as our desire *to understand our partner* outweighs our vulnerability, progress is being made in dissolving the resentment.

Everything begins with understanding:

1. A lack of *understanding* leads to *resentment,* reducing *trust* and *closeness.*

2. The process of *understanding* dissolves *resentment,* increasing *trust* and *closeness.*

It's just a matter of overcoming your vulnerability, with a bigger desire to understand your partner.

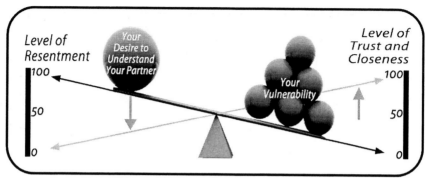

Diagram 6: Understanding/Vulnerability Model

As shown above, when your desire to understand your partner does not *outweigh* your vulnerability, resentment is high and trust is low. When your desire to understand your partner *outweighs* your vulnerability, resentment is low and trust is high.

Now that we know that the key to having a healthy relationship depends on having our desire to understand our partner outweigh our vulnerability, conflict resolution should be a snap, right? Well it's not that simple. We also need our partner's desire to understand *us* outweigh *their* vulnerability if resentment is to be dissolved.

Remember our second law of resentment?

> *The effect that resentment has on the relationship*
> *of an individual has an equal effect on the other*
> *individual in the relationship.*

If we try to press for understanding when our partner is not ready, an imbalance occurs that topples the conversation. We must be aware that our partner is a full half of the relationship and their vulnerability needs to be considered.

There Are Two Paths to Understanding

This concept can be dramatized with a teeter-totter. On the right side is the weight of your desire to understand your partner, and on the left side is the weight of your partner's desire to understand you. If you push down and your partner doesn't, the imbalance will tilt the board, upsetting vulnerability on the other end. If this happens and the conversation continues, defenses kick in and resentment can only increase.

Our partner's desire to understand us is just as important as our desire to understand our partner. We can drastically increase the probability that our partner will want to understand us by simply realizing that they want a healthy relationship just as we do.

If we see that our partner desires to understand us and we are aware of their vulnerabilities as well as our own, the relationship "board" will remain in balance and progress can be made in resolving conflicts.

Remember Our Curiosity Mantra

Whenever engaged in conflict resolution it is important to have a positive mindset, or at least know what it is.

> *When I speak, I will always be curious, not judgmental.*
> *The words I use and the way I say them convey a sense of wonder.*
> *I have a burning desire to understand my partner.*
> *When I listen, I will always assume my partner*
> *is being curious, not judgmental.*
> *If there is ever a question of the partner's motive, I will calmly ask.*
> *I have a burning desire to understand my partner.*

By being aware of what and how we speak, and by assuming your partner is being curious, not judgmental, we set a solid foundation for effective conflict-resolving communication.

Your Advantage – Two Against One

Most of us know there are two major types of tennis: singles (one versus one) and doubles (two versus two). There is another type of tennis known as Canadian doubles, in which one player goes up against two players. The two players usually have a distinct advantage since they can cover the court more effectively than just one player. They do, however, need to work together with strategy and cooperation, and be aware of the position of their partner to avoid running into each another.

This "two against one" type of tennis is rare, yet it should be the way we think when it comes to conflict resolution. Remember our communication mindset charts? Let's have some fun and put in some tennis nets to illustrate the difference between Traditional Relationship Logic (singles) and The Melfox Mindset (Canadian doubles).

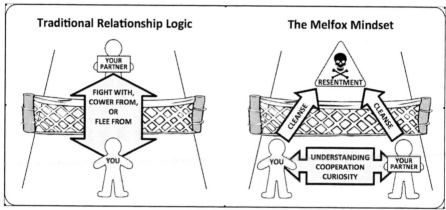

Diagram 7: TRL & TMM with nets

When you use Traditional Relationship Logic, it's you versus your partner. During attempts to resolve conflict, your goal is to win and your partner's goal is to win. You defend your beliefs tooth and nail, and try to convince your partner that you are right and they are wrong. Of course, your partner is doing exactly the same thing. In the end, one of you may win an argument, yet your relationship "loses" as it will continue to suffer with resentment. In this game, resentment is the real winner, by default.

When you have The Melfox Mindset, it's you and your partner *versus resentment*. You both have the common goal of defeating resentment by staying on the same side. You work together with strategy and cooperation to gain a better understanding of each other.

Just like in any team sport, you are constantly aware of your partner's "position" in order to avoid "running into" them, and work with them to achieve a desired result. This means paying attention to your partner and making every effort to understand them.

In the movie *Star Wars*, there is talk of a mysterious force that binds all living things. Throughout the movie you hear the saying:

> *The Force Will Be With You, Always.*

When talking with your partner, there is a similar "force" that binds the relationship you share. For a healthy relationship, you should "say" to your partner with words and deeds:

> *I Will Be On Your Side, Always.*

Defensive Reactions

Defensive reactions, as we will discuss in greater detail in the *Egoity* chapter, play a huge part in conflict resolution. They serve as a barometer of sorts, indicating the activation level of our sympathetic nervous system, which controls our fight-fright-or-flight response or what we will call Egoity.

Depending on who our partner is and other conditions, when our defenses are activated we either "fight" (lose our temper), "fright" (lose self-confidence), or "flight" (lose ability to continue the conversation).

1. We *FIGHT* by raising our voice, swearing, and taking other intimidating actions.

2. We *FRIGHT* by going into our "shell" of low self-confidence and protectionism.

3. We *FLIGHT* by literally running away from the conversation altogether.

In any case, the higher the level of reaction, the lower the quality of the conversation. Ideally, we want the level to be as low as possible, yet that is not always realistic. We all occasionally dip our toe in that pool, while some of us go for a swim every now and then.

Since we were just talking about *Star Wars*, let's revisit one of my favorite scenes from the movie:

If the Rebels Used Traditional Relationship Logic

When we last left our Star Wars *heroes on the Death Star, they had just jumped into a garbage masher to escape certain death on the detention level. After the masher walls began closing in, the rebels scrambled to find a way to prevent their demise. Let's pick up the dialog as Han makes an astute observation:*

ACTUAL SCENE (paraphrased)
HAN: One thing's for sure; we're all gonna be a lot thinner!
LUKE: (on comlink) Threepio! Come in, Threepio!
HAN: Get on top of it!
LEIA: I'm trying!
LUKE: Where could he be? Threepio! Will you come in?
C3PO: (on comlink) Whatz happenin?
LUKE: Shut down all garbage mashers on the detention level!
C3PO: You got it, dude. (Switches off the masher)
END: **The rebels escaped and went on to make two sequels.**

TRADITIONAL RELATIONSHIP LOGIC
HAN: One thing's for sure; we're all gonna be a lot thinner!
LEIA: This is some rescue! You guys make Darth Vader look good!
HAN: Well, you're the one that led us down here, princess!
LEIA: And YOU! (Looking at Luke) Talking with your girlfriend?
LUKE: (on comlink) Threepio! Come in, Threepio!
LEIA: I can't believe you get top billing for this movie!
LUKE: Well, at least I don't have cinnamon buns for ears!
LEIA: Oh yeah?? (Smacks the comlink from Luke's hand)
LUKE: URGHH!! The comlink broke!! WE'RE DOOMED!!
C3PO: Why haven't they called?
END: **They all got a lot thinner.**

As you can see, allowing your defensive reactions to take over can have dire results. The conversation begins to "go bad" the instant we see our partner "on the other side of the net." For whatever reason, we suddenly see them "trying to win" by defending their position or judging ours, so we do the same.

But what if we *didn't*? What if we learned to recognize when the conversation goes sour and simply refuse to see our partner as someone deliberately trying to hurt us?

Refusing to Win

Imagine a football game or any game in which the main objective was *not* to win. Silly, I know, but think about it. All the rules apply, yet no one keeps score, no one tries to score, and no one cares if the other team scores. Each team would "go through the motions" of plays and there would probably be a lot of delay-of-game penalties. In other words, having no desire to win would result in a rather boring game. Instead of yelling at each other across the line, there would be civilized talk and banter. Since there is no desire to be better than the other guy, there is no reason to try to hurt them. It would be like watching toddlers play football.

The same kind of thing can be said about drama on TV and at the movies. Think about how boring *All In The Family* would be if Archie actually got along with Meathead, didn't constantly ridicule Edith, and treated Gloria like an adult. We would see a boring family doing boring things and having boring conversations. That show would be cancelled after the first episode. Imagine any movie in which everyone got along, everyone helped each other, and no one ever tried to hurt anybody else. Not exactly a blockbuster plot.

In the areas of sports and drama, it's the whole idea of "trying to win" that creates the tension, drama, and adversity. In the area of conflict resolution, it's the whole idea of "trying to win" that activates our natural defenses and steers the conversation in a "me versus you" direction. The sooner we can take control and see when a conversation has turned confrontational, the sooner we can get the conversation back on a more peaceful and productive track.

It's only when we *individually* "refuse to win" and demand to stay on the same side with our partner that we are able to *mutually* "win" in the team sport of conflict resolution. There is still a *winner* since, like in tennis match, there needs to be a winner. Just remember we're playing doubles, not singles.

Your Defensive Circuit Breaker

Think about how a circuit breaker works. A circuit breaker is an automatically operated electrical switch designed to protect an electrical circuit from damage caused by power overload. If the temperature within the circuit gets too high, the circuit breaker "breaks the circuit" to prevent potential damage. The circuit breaker needs to be at the proper amperage so that it doesn't "trip" too easily (unnecessarily shutting down the system) or too late (causing damage). A proper circuit breaker ensures that the circuit is "warm" enough to allow work, yet not too "hot," which causes damage.

When our conversations get "too hot" (loss of temper or self-confidence), our "defensive circuit breaker" trips, yet often after damage is done. We storm out of the room or simply "shut down." The sooner we see a conversation has gotten "too hot" and take control, the less damage is done. Of course, the more mindful we are of the "temperature" of the conversation, the more likely we are at keeping it at a good "warm" setting in the first place. We will be talking more about this in the *Information* and *Egoity* chapters.

Mindset at Start of Interaction

In this chapter, we are dealing with the Environment going into the conflict resolution session or what we will call Interaction. In this section, we will be discussing your initial attitude toward your partner at the start of Interaction.

Remember Who Your Opponent Is

At the beginning of this chapter, we talked about how silly it would seem if at any time during a normal doubles match you or your partner were to suddenly jump to the "other side of the net" and play "against" each other. That is not how the game is played. Doubles partners are on the same side and remain there throughout the match.

Now imagine how silly it would be if at the very *start* of a doubles match, your partner was seen on the other side of the net. Talk about silly. The match would not even begin.

Being on the "other side of the net" should be seen as just as "silly" before Interaction as well. Grudges and anything else you "bring to the table" that indicates that your Egoity is already in control before the Interaction even starts make it impossible to resolve conflict.

Grudges Are Like Inherited Debts

Think about the concept of inherited debts. You weren't responsible for the debts, yet you were obligated to take them on. You haven't adequately processed the "grudge" from the last discussion, so it is still there at the start of the next. When I say processed, I don't mean the conflict has been resolved. By processed, I mean understanding that the grudge is just your Egoity still in control, and at least part of you metaphorically sees your partner on the "other side of the net."

Once you stop and think about it, you instantly take back control, know that defensive reactions are just a lack of understanding of your partner, and see your partner on the same side again. Your focus shifts from fighting your partner, to fighting the *resentment*. The resentment is still there, yet *it* becomes the enemy, not used as fodder in battling your partner. Grudges and other defensiveness toward your partner should be neutralized before Interaction begins, if effective communication (Interaction) and conflict resolution are to take place.

Disarming Your Resentment

One of my favorite cartoons growing up was *Underdog*. I remember an episode where the bad guy, "Electric Eel," had discovered a way to have electricity come out of his fingers, and he was going around melting stuff and causing all kinds of havoc. Underdog "neutralized" Electric Eel by putting him in a giant glass jar. The jar "encased" the harmful effects of the electricity so it wouldn't cause any more damage. After that, I assumed they worked on getting rid of Electric Eel's power at some point.

"Staying mad" or irritated at your partner causes all kinds of havoc in your attempt at conflict resolution. By shifting your attention away from how you feel about your partner to the resentment itself, you "encase" the resentment in a damage-proof "jar" where you and your partner can safely work on getting rid of it. The resentment is "harmless" until and unless we allow ourselves to see our partner as the enemy.

Environment During Interaction

When engaging in a conflict resolution conversation with your partner, your attention level and the surrounding Environment play important roles in its success. Any outside influences such as time limits and screaming kids keep us from being fully engaged in the conversation. When exploring and practicing *The Melfox Method*, especially at first, try to keep any distractions and distance between you to a minimum.

Calling Dr. Howard, Dr. Fine, Dr. Howard

Imagine going in for an operation and overhearing the surgeon talking to the nurse. "There better not be any complications. I have a 3 o'clock tee time and will not miss my golf game!" Right about then, you might choose to put off that nose job.

Time restrictions can cause havoc when undergoing an operation and when trying to resolve conflicts. The tendency would be to keep looking at the clock, which distracts you from your partner. All of your attention should be on understanding your partner, and the amount of time needed to do that is never known.

If there is a time limit, understand up front that issues may not be resolved at that time. We will be getting more into "time-outs" in the *Interaction* chapter. For now, understand that time limits should be minimized and be aware of their adverse affect on effective conflict resolution.

Ideally, choose a time with no time limits, and when both you and your partner are attentive. One o'clock in the morning is not the ideal time to start a conversation if your partner is a morning person, and six o'clock in the morning is not the ideal time if your partner is a night owl. Select a time that suits both parties.

Stop Da Music, Stop Da Music!

Now imagine that same surgeon trying to operate on you when a bunch of other activities are going on in the room. It would be like an episode of *M*A*S*H*. Needless to say, all of the doctor's attention may not be on you. The distractions most likely will cause mistakes and misunderstandings. Simple tasks may become hard to do or skipped all together. You may come out of the nose job looking more like Jimmy Durante, and less like Julia Roberts or Ryan Reynolds.

When it comes to conflict resolution, ideally choose a quiet, private place with a minimum of distractions. No TV in the background, no kids to worry about, and no noisy neighbors. It is also best to mute your cell phone, and turn off instant messaging. All of your attention should be on understanding your partner, and anything that distracts you from that lessens the chance for effective communication.

While some distractions are unavoidable, there is a big difference between distractions and avoidance. Remember the key to effective conflict resolution is to have *a burning desire to understand your partner*, not to avoid the issues and hope they go away.

Hello, Is There Anybody There?

As we all know, there are many ways that we can communicate. We may be tempted to resolve conflict without being face-to-face. The following are various ways of Information exchange and their drawbacks.

Face-To-Face - Sitting on couch or two chairs facing each other
  Drawback: None (OK, there may be bad breath)

Not Face-To-Face - Talk directly but not directly facing each other
  Drawback: No direct access to facial and body language

Video Conference - "Face-to-face" yet not in the same place
  Drawback: Electronic audio/video lessens the closeness factor

Telephone - Audio only
  Drawback: Same as above but without the video portion

Text Messages (Instant Messaging) - "Real time" written words
  Drawback: Same as above: audio is replaced with written words

Emails - Non-"real time" written words only
  Drawback: Same as above except any message is usually delayed

Physical Mail - Three-day delayed written words
  Drawback: Same as above except any message is always delayed

---

As you go down the list, the communication quality goes down as well. And with lower communication quality comes a higher chance for misunderstandings and assumptions, and all the other reasons that resentment is there in the first place. By trying to resolve conflict by any means other than face-to-face, you run a better risk of only adding to the resentment, not dissolving it.

To maximize the effectiveness of resolving conflicts, maximize the quality of communication. Misunderstandings and assumptions are plentiful enough in everyday conversations. The simple text message "Let's eat Grandpa" could be interpreted as inviting Grandpa to dinner, or inviting fellow carnivores to have Grandpa FOR dinner.

An Effective Way to Dissolve Resentment

Now that we've identified resentment as the true enemy of healthy relationships and the desire to understand as their greatest ally, the remaining chapters of this book will provide detailed concepts, techniques and benefits for exposing the reasons for resentment and facilitating understanding.

The *Information* chapter teaches techniques to clarify what is said and keep the conflict resolution on the right track. It concentrates on bridging the gap between your understanding and your partner's understanding of the resentment, by pointing out refutable statements and asking clarifying questions.

The *Egoity* chapter identifies the major obstacle in effective communication and teaches ways to "clear the road" by keeping our protective mechanisms at bay. It teaches the ways to control and retrain the Egoity when it comes to conflict resolution, by concentrating on its cause and purpose.

The *Interaction* chapter goes through the process of the actual conversation using the lessons from the previous chapters. It addresses the proper dialog pattern through the use of various techniques and props for effective conflict resolution. The cause, purpose, and management of interruptions are also addressed.

The *Outcome* chapter as well as the Epilogue chapter discusses possible results of the Interaction and their impact on the quality of your relationship. In addition to listing side benefits of using the techniques taught in previous chapters, subjects like deal breakers, delays, afterglow, and persistence are explored.

It is important to emphasize that proper conflict resolution begins and ends with effective communication with your partner. As we discussed in the *Introduction* chapter, self-reflection and discussions with other people may bring a particular resentment into focus, yet they are ineffective at actually resolving it. Establishing an open line of communication with your partner and focusing on the issue with effective Interaction will restore your relationship through conflict resolution. Having a burning desire to understand your partner is essential if true conflict resolution is the goal.

Environment - Recap and Review

In this chapter we have discussed the following:

Laws of Resentment

1. Resentment is cleansed and only cleansed from a relationship through the Interaction of the individuals who make up the relationship.

2. The effect that resentment has on the relationship of an individual has an equal effect on the other individual in the relationship.

3. Any resentment can be resolved to the point of acceptance by both individuals in a relationship.

Reasons for Resentment

1. Lack of Sufficient, Pertinent Information

2. Misunderstanding

3. False Assumption

4. Jumping to False Conclusion

Multiple and Consequential Issues

We learned that resentment can have many layers, and that issues need to be "peeled back" until the primary reason for resentment is exposed.

Maintenance of Relationships

We learned that the maintenance of a relationship could be seen as natural as caring for your child or pet, and not seen as "disposable" like a toaster. We just need to learn how to dissolve resentment like we learn to clean other things in order to restore our relationship.

Curiosity Killed the Spat

We looked at the difference between curiosity and judgment, and that the choice we make on either the delivery or interpretation of any sentence is based on:

1. The manner in which it was said (inflection, style, choice of words).

2. Our level of resentment at the moment.

3. Our awareness of the impact this decision will have on our level of resentment and the rest of the conversation.

The Desire to Understand

We looked at the similarity of the words "love" and "understand." We learned that focusing on understanding your partner transforms an argument into mutual cooperation.

"The Melfox Mindset"

We learned that the secret to working out the issues in a relationship is to know how to resolve conflicts, and that our mindset should be on resolving the issue at hand, not coping with it, if a healthy relationship is desired.

The Relationship Rope

We compared the relationship you have with a partner to a rope that needs to be maintained. Like a rope, a relationship develops "frays" and "unravels," and unless properly maintained, will weaken your "grip" or leave you "hanging by a thread."

Understanding, Trust, and Vulnerability

We learned that when your vulnerability *outweighs* your desire to understand your partner, resentment is high and trust is low; and that when your desire to understand your partner *outweighs* your vulnerability, resentment is low and trust is high.

Overcoming Your Vulnerabilities - Together

We learned that to press for understanding when our partner is not ready creates an imbalance that topples the conversation. We must be aware that our partner is a full half of the relationship and that their vulnerability needs to be considered.

Defensive Reactions

We discussed that when our defenses are activated during a conversation, we either fight or flight, and see our partner, not resentment, as the opponent. The sooner we see when a conversation has gotten "too hot" and "take control," the less damage is done.

Mindset at Start of Interaction

We learned that by shifting our attention away from how we feel about our partner to the resentment itself, we render the resentment damage-proof so our partner and we can safely work on getting rid of it.

Interaction Time, Place, and Method

We learned the ideal situation for effective conflict resolution is being face-to-face with no distractions and no time limits. This minimizes the chance for any misunderstandings and assumptions that may add to resentment.

****

Now that we have established that a relationship's only enemy is resentment and discussed its causes, it is time to learn how to reveal those causes. How do we do that?

> *How do we rectify an issue caused by a lack of sufficient, pertinent Information?*
>
> *How do we rectify an issue caused by a misunderstanding?*
>
> *How do we rectify an issue caused by a false assumption?*
>
> *How do we rectify an issue caused by jumping to a false conclusion?*

CHAPTER TWO - INFORMATION

Beatrice slowly sat down next to Bruno at their kitchen table. Sitting across from them was a man named "Beano" who claimed that he not only knew everything about their ailing relationship, but also was the relationship itself.

"Don't believe that I'm your relationship? That's fine. Doubt I would either, given the same situation." He then coughed and took a little sip of water. "That's OK. Let's just pretend for a bit."

Beatrice noticed stains under his arms and a foul breath. "Do you bathe?"

"I would, but bathing on the outside doesn't touch what's ailing me."

"How about deodorant?" Bruno smirked. "You know, common courtesy?"

"Aren't you tired of covering this up by masking the toxicity? I'm sick of it!"

"What are you talking about? What are we masking?"

"All the resentment between you two! It's killing me!" Beano said with a couple of big coughs. "You guys sweep things under the rug and hold your nose because you're being nice, and exposing the toxicity might not be pleasant. Meanwhile, I'm getting sicker and sicker!"

"Beatrice, it has taken you all this time to talk about your relationship, and you still don't know what to say! And you," Beano continued, pointing at Bruno, "You don't even know there are things that need to be said!"

"What things?" Bruno asked.

"Every time there's a bad assumption or a misunderstanding between you two, resentment forms like specks of dust inside my lungs and it's choking me!" Beano said with yet another cough. "And every time you guys fight or storm out of the room, it's like rubbing salt in the wound."

Beatrice sadly looked at Beano. "What can we do to make you better?"

Beano smiled eagerly. "I thought you'd never ask."

* * * * * * * * * * * * * * * *

Information - The Keymaster

"Beano" is about to share with Beatrice and Bruno the key to cleaning resentment from your relationship Environment. That key to conflict resolution is properly shared Information. Effective communication reveals the reasons for underlying resentment in a relationship.

> *"A **lack of communication** is the origin of most problems couples experience, often resulting in the breakdown of a relationship. Not understanding how to make feelings and wishes known to a partner in a non-threatening, non-combative fashion can lead to massive frustration and alienation from one another."*
>
> *- Norma Germain*

Due to bad experiences trying to resolve conflict in the past with our partner, many of us are tempted to give up. We may sweep resentment under the rug, yet there it is, still separating us and our partner. Ignoring resentment only makes our relationship sicker and sicker, just like "Beano." In order to resolve conflict, Information needs to be shared properly. Let's find out how.

Hitting the Ball

Tennis can be thought of in two parts: hitting the ball, and preparing for and reacting to a hit ball. Communication can be thought of the same way. It can be seen as two parts: what it communicated, and the reaction to what is communicated.

Like an ideal tennis shot, effective Information combines power and control to "straddle the line" between support (in-bounds) and conflict (out-of bounds).

When we get a bum call in tennis, we feel at least a twinge of outrage. We feel the same type of emotion when someone does something that we really don't like. We say or think things like:

"Hey, that was out-of-bounds!" or
"Hey, that's not fair!" or
"Hey, that's going over the edge!" or
"Hey, that's crossing the line, Mister!"

INFORMATION

In tennis, the balance of power and control determines the quality of the shot:

Three Possible Tennis Shot Results

TOO EASY: If the shot lacks power and is hit safely in the middle of the court, it does not reveal the weakness of the opponent.

TOO HARD: If the shot lacks sufficient control, it lands out-of-bounds and helps the opponent.

JUST RIGHT: If the shot has sufficient power while being controlled and hit in-bounds, it reveals the weakness of the opponent.

During normal Interaction, what is said (verbal language) and how it's said (nonverbal language) determine if and to what extent conflict is exposed in the conversation:

Three Possible Shared Information Results

TOO EASY: If the Information evokes no conflict, it's just small talk and pleasantries. It does not help reveal clues to the reasons for resentment.

TOO HARD: If the Information evokes too much conflict, an argument ensues or the Interaction ends altogether. This can only strengthen resentment.

JUST RIGHT: If the Information evokes conflict, yet doesn't cause Interaction to erode into an argument or end prematurely, clues to the reasons for resentment can be revealed.

It is solely the quality of shared Information that determines the effectiveness of conflict resolution during Interaction. When partners evade the conflict subject during Interaction, Information is "too soft," resentment will not be revealed, and it will continue. If Information goes "out-of-bounds" during Interaction by accusing and blaming each other, resentment can only build instead of being cleansed.

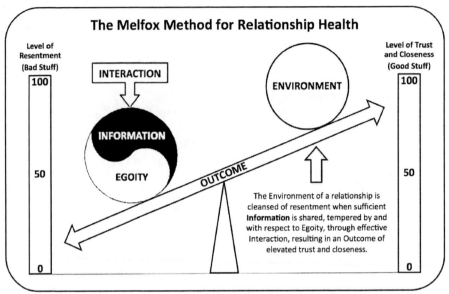

Diagram 8: *The Melfox Method* Model featuring Information

In this chapter, we will be focusing on relaying and requesting Information that is effective yet evokes a regulated defense response. Our goal is to hit the "sweet spot" between cold idle chitchat and a hot emotional argument.

What Is Information?

Information is the Keymaster. During Interaction, it's the Information shared that determines whether or not resentment is weakening or strengthening. Information is the stuff that can either bring a couple closer, or tear them apart. When you think about it, a relationship is nothing more than the continuous mutual exchange of Information between two entities. That shared Information can be heard, seen, felt... all our sensory perceptions.

If we learn anything new or change our opinion about someone, it's because new Information was shared. The impact of the quality of Information in resolving conflict cannot be overstated. Like billionaire Gordon Gekko said in the movie *Wall Street*...

"The most valuable commodity I know of is Information."

INFORMATION

Information is verbal or nonverbal communication that...

1. Is specific and organized for a purpose,
2. Has been verified to be accurate,
3. Is presented within a context that gives meaning and relevance, and
4. Can lead to an increase in *understanding* and decrease in uncertainty.

Let's examine each of these in context of conflict resolution.

Information Is Specific and Organized

Information has to be specific and organized if it is to help in resolving the conflict. In the heat of conversation, it is tempting to generalize feelings into absolutes. Specifics are needed to help pinpoint the cause of the feelings.

> BRUNO: You are always ignoring me.
> BEATRICE: Always?
> BRUNO: When you say, "I don't want to talk," I feel ignored.
> BEATRICE: Better.

Making generalized statements does not add Information to the conversation since there is not a basis for the subject discussed. Sentences need to be specific and organized so that you and your partner can *understand* exactly what is being discussed.

Information Is Accurate

In other words, if it ain't true, it ain't Information. As we will be taught in the *Interaction* chapter, sentences thought to be inaccurate are to be respectfully refuted. Until the question of accuracy is resolved, the effective exchange of Information relating to resolving the conflict has not really taken place.

> BEATRICE: I know you are cheating on me.
> BRUNO: Refutable.
> BEATRICE: OK, the way you ignore me feels like you are cheating.
> BRUNO: Better.

It is the responsibility of both people in the conversation to share accurate and timely Information, and to hold the other person responsible for sharing accurate and timely Information. It is impossible to *understand* each other when Information is refutable.

Information Is Meaningful and Relevant

The Information shared needs to be meaningful and relevant to the issue being discussed if it is to help resolve the conflict. If it is not, the confusion and frustration that could result adversely affect the quality of the conversation.

> BRUNO: When you say, "I don't want to talk," I feel ignored.
> BEATRICE: Oh, don't forget to take the garbage out tonight.
> BRUNO: What does that have to do with what I just said?
> BEATRICE: Nothing. Just remembered tonight is garbage night.
> BRUNO: (Grrrrrrr)

By staying "on task" and sharing relevant Information, the conversation stays focused on resolving the conflict. Any distractions, like unrelated sentences, splinters this focus, making it difficult for *understanding* to take place.

Information Increases Understanding

It seems that the previous parts of this definition of Information add up to simply making the sentence *understandable*. If a sentence is specific, irrefutable, and relevant, it adds to the *understanding* of one another. This is effective Information.

Conversely, by making an attentive and intended choice of *desiring to understand*, we can steer the flow of the conversation to make the sentences more specific, irrefutable, and relevant. The more we focus on understanding our partner, the more effective the Information, and the more effective the conflict resolution.

Just like in the previous *Environment* chapter, we are concluding that the *desire to understand your partner* is an essential mindset to have for resolving relationship issues. This chapter will delve into the "offensive" game plan of moving the conversation forward by sharing Information with your partner. It sounds simple enough, like crossing a bridge.

The thing is, as we will see in the next chapter, there is an old man guarding this bridge. As long as the sentences are Information, the old man will let the conflict resolution cross the bridge. If, however, he finds the sentence to be lacking in specifics, accuracy, or relevance, he may throw the conversation into the ravine of arguments, ill will, and further resentment.

We will divide this chapter into three main subjects:

1. The actual words used when making a statement or asking a question (*what* you say),

2. The manner in which the message is conveyed (*how* you say it), and

3. The impact that Information you share has on your partner.

In the next few sections, we will be discussing the actual sentences made during conflict resolution our verbal language. We'll see the importance that individual words, phrases, or whole sentences play in either generating or defusing a defensive reaction, and thus increase the levels of understanding and trust.

Controlling What You Speak

> *If words are to enter men's minds and bear fruit, they must be the right words shaped cunningly to pass men's defenses and explode silently and effectually within their minds.*
>
> - John Bertram Phillips

Sometimes the words you use don't allow your intended concept to "explode silently and effectually" in your partner's mind. Instead, at least for a moment, the words become weapons that your partner needs to defend against. Being aware of the impact that certain words have on either activating or defusing your partner's defenses regulates the conflict within the conversation and will "bear fruit" in the form of understanding and conflict resolution.

Trigger Words and Phrases

As we all know, individual words and phrases can be enough to invoke an adverse reaction and add conflict to the conversation. By being aware of the potential impact of these words helps us regulate their use.

Examples include:

> **All profanity** – indicates frustration in the conversation, possibly invoking defensiveness or submissiveness from the other person
>
> **Hopelessness** (can't, won't, couldn't) – sounds like you are "giving up" on the conversation and on understanding your partner
>
> **Indecisiveness** (I don't know, not sure, no answer) – puts the conversation "on pause" until resolved, possibly frustrating the other person
>
> **Lack of commitment** (try, perhaps, maybe) – puts into question the value of the conversation and conflict resolution efforts
>
> **Authoritative** (should, need to, must, have to) - invokes defensiveness or submissiveness (possible exception of preceding it with "we" instead of "you")
>
> **Generalization** (always, never, constantly) – when prefaced by "you," the lack of specifics could delay the conversation, possibly invoking frustration

By intentionally regulating these types of words and phrases, we can control their impact on the conflict level of the conversation.

Positive Words and Phrases

Certain words and phrases can also have the ability to keep the conversation "on course" and even reverse the effects of hurtful words and a defensive partner. By simply saying these "magic" words and understanding the meaning behind them, you can "reset" the overall tone of the conversation to the objective of resolving the conflict, keeping the two of you on the same side of the relationship net.

Examples include:

- *Please* and *thank you* (of course)
- *I'm sorry*
- *We can work it out*
- *I want to understand you*
- *I want you to understand me*
- *Let's help each other*
- *I will be on your side, always*
- *Let's get rid of this resentment, together*

These are like positive affirmations that help to remind both of you to "stay together" and resolve the resentment as a team.

Using the Correct Words and Hearing the Correct Words

It is possible for words to be said in error, or words to be heard in error, especially if vulnerability and defenses are high. The erroneous data can be enough to activate a defensive response from you or your partner that adds conflict to the conversation.

> *"The difference between the almost right word and the right word is really a large matter – it's the difference between the lightning bug and the lightning."*
>
> – Mark Twain

When you or your partner suddenly gets defensive from seemingly nothing, a good place to start is thinking about what was just said and seeing if there was anything that was said or heard in error.

For effective conflict resolution, it's important to not only "say what you mean" but to also "hear what was said." A good habit to get into is to echo back what each other said so that you both "are on the same page," which lessens the chance of misunderstandings. This will be discussed in more detail in the *Interaction* chapter.

Types of Sentences by Purpose

The following are different types of sentences by purpose, and below are their typical role in effective conflict resolution conversations:

Declarative Sentence – "I love *The Melfox Method*."

Conditional Sentence – "When you say you want to learn *The Melfox Method*, I feel you care about us."

Inquisitive Sentence – "Have you heard of *The Melfox Method*?"

Exclamatory Sentence – "I need you to learn *The Melfox Method*!"

Imperative Sentence – "Please learn *The Melfox Method*."

---

1. Declarative Sentences

We use declarative sentences to attempt to directly share Information and to give our partner the chance to understand us better. They are simple statements to share our world with our partner. As we learned in the previous section, Information can morph into attacking words if the words in the statement activate our partner's defenses. To prevent this, care needs to be taken to make the statement as accurate, specific, and relevant as possible.

2. Conditional Sentences

In order to tell how we feel about something, we use conditional sentences. Instead of declaring, "You hurt me," which could activate your partner's defenses, preface it with a conditional sentence like "When you laugh at me, I *feel* hurt." By adding the condition, we let our partner know when we feel what we feel. They can then use that Information to examine their intention and share their reality with "I was laughing with you, not at you" or something like that.

3. Inquisitive Sentences

Typically inquisitive statements are labeled as interrogative statements, but we do not interrogate during proper conflict resolution. Inquisitive statements are questions we ask in order to gain a better understanding of our partner. We are curious and ask our partner to define or clarify something we don't understand. To prevent defensive reactions, care needs to be taken to intentionally keep an Environment of responsibility and curiosity, not judgment. "Why did you do that?" becomes "Did I do something to make you do that?"

4. Exclamatory Sentences

Whenever we use exclamatory sentences in conflict resolution, it usually means that our defenses are activated or that we are frustrated. The exceptions to this are statements like "Wow! I really get you now!" or "Oh, now I get it!" Exclamatory statements usually carry with them trigger words like profanity and generalizations. When voices rise with exclamation, that's a good indicator that the conversation is, or is in danger of becoming, a battle of defenses rather than an effective Information exchange.

5. Imperative Sentences

Since they usually imply command and authority, most imperative sentences should be avoided during conflict resolution. They are sometimes accompanied with trigger words like "don't" and "must," which may cause the conversation to slide off track. When you remember to state something that you feel to be true as an opinion, any authoritative or commanding tone is removed from the statement. The imperative statement "Don't belittle me" becomes the conditional statement "When you laugh at me, I feel belittled."

Verbal Communication

Wouldn't it be great if we could all be like Spock from *Star Trek* and use the Vulcan mind-meld on our partner? Conflict resolution would be a snap. Just put a few fingers on their head and assess anything you want to know. Misunderstandings and false assumptions would vanish. Unfortunately, at least for now, mind-melds only exist in movies, TV, and other works of fiction. We need to base our perception of our partner's world through the comparatively primitive method of sharing and understanding words.

When resolving conflict, the whole focus should be on understanding your partner and making sure they understand you. You understand your partner when they tell you *whatever you need to hear* to see the issue from their perspective or "through their eyes." In order for them to tell you what you need to hear, you need to ask them to clarify their words and phrases, and ask them clarifying questions on things you're curious about.

Similarly, your partner understands you when you tell them *whatever they need to hear* to see the issue from your perspective or "through your eyes." In order for you to tell them what they need to hear, you share with them specific, irrefutable, and relevant statements.

So to summarize, here are primary reasons for talking during Interaction:

1. Requesting clarification of what was said (inquisitive)

2. Asking curious "Why?" questions (inquisitive)

3. Sharing specific, irrefutable, relevant (SIR) statements (declarative or conditional)

Requesting Clarification of What Was Said

When resolving conflict, the whole focus should be on conceptually understanding your partner and making sure they understand you. That need for understanding concepts within the conversation obviously extends to the individual words and phrases used as well. If the words used to make a concept are not understood, how can the concept be understood?

Many times, it is mishearing, or the difference of definitions of words or phrases that causes resentment in the first place. These types of misunderstandings are resolved only when we question what was said or the words and phrases that we suspect we don't understand. That reminds me of the old saying:

> *I know that you believe you understand what you think I said, but I'm not sure you realize that what you heard is not what I meant.*
>
> – Robert McCloskey

During effective conflict resolution, we should always ask our partner to clarify something we may have misheard, or words that either we don't understand or could have multiple meanings. Closing this gap of understanding is, in essence, dissolving resentment or preventing potential resentment. Since non-ambiguity and accuracy are essential components of the definition of Information, ignoring this gap can only add to the resentment pool.

Confirming What Was Said

Remember playing the telephone game? A written message would be whispered to someone, who would then whisper it to the next person, who would then whisper it to the next person, and so on. All along the way, the spoken message would be misheard or the relay message would be misspoken. The fun part was to see how much the last whispered message had changed from the original message.

What was fun playing as a kid demonstrates what can be devastating in a relationship. Words can be misspoken or misheard even in the most intimate conversation. Any defensive reactions caused by the subject discussed can also "change" the message spoken, or the message heard. Beliefs have a way of filtering and altering intended Information.

Even if you think you know what was said, confirming it reassures your partner that you are trying to understand them, which goes a long way to keeping them on "your side of the net." One way to confirm is to "echo back" to your partner what they said, and see if what you heard is what was actually said or intended. We will be getting more into conversation strategies in the *Interaction* chapter.

The Shared Meaning of Words and Phrases

A word or phrase by itself does not have value. It is only when you and your partner have a *shared meaning* of the word or phrase, that it adds value to the conversation. When our partner says something that we don't understand or is ambiguous, it is prudent for us to ask them to clarify it until we do understand. It is only then that it becomes

Information and is useful in the resolution of conflict. If we choose not to have the word or phrase clarified, we are just asking for trouble.

We will be getting into the importance of the manner in which you request word or phrase clarification from your partner in the *Interaction* chapter. For now, it is important to understand the need to ask clarifying questions when we are not clear on what was said, or what a word or phrase means.

Seeking to understand is a major component of effective conflict resolution, and one of the basic tenets of *The Melfox Method.*

Time-Out for Another Joke

Once upon a time there was a man from Poland who moved to the USA and married an American girl. Although his English was far from perfect, they got along very well until one day he rushed into a lawyer's office and asked him if he could arrange a divorce for him. The lawyer said that getting a divorce could depend on the circumstances, and asked him the following questions:

"Have you any grounds?"
"Yes, an acre and half and nice little home."

"No, I meant what's the foundation of this case?"
"It's made of concrete."

"I don't think you understand. Do either of you have a grudge?"
"No, we have carport, and not need one."

"I mean, what are your relations like?"
"All my relations still in Poland."

"Why do you want this divorce?"
"She going to kill me."

"What makes you think that?"
"I got proof."

"What kind of proof?"
"She going to poison me. She buy a bottle at drugstore and put in bathroom. I can read. It say: 'Polish Remover.'"

                - Unknown

Asking Inquisitive Questions

Even if we understand all the words and phrases used by our partner, there are other questions that need to be asked. They may tell us that they did something or believe in something that we don't like. Do we know *why* they did it, or *why* they believe it? Aren't we curious? Shouldn't we be curious? After all, this is the most important relationship in our life, *isn't it*? Besides, there may be an interesting reason why they chose to do it or believe it.

Doing What Needs to Be Done

You don't just buy a plant, ignore it, and expect it to live. You have a relationship with that plant. You are responsible for maintaining the relationship by watering it and making sure it gets adequate sunlight. Without performing this maintenance, the plant (and your relationship with it) will soon die.

Are you letting the relationship you have with your partner die on the vine? Are you less curious about them now than you were before? This is normal when there is resentment. Understand that it is the *proper asking and answering of questions* that lead to the *dissolving of resentment*. To understand our partner, we need to put in the effort to see past the resentment, train ourselves to be *curious*, and ask the questions that need to be asked.

Root Cause Analysis

In the previous chapter, we talked about multiple and consequential issues, and that we have to get down to the root cause of resentment in order to eliminate it. What typically happens in response to conflicts is that blame is thrown around, which builds resentment, then communication fails, which could lead to more resentment.

A different approach is to identify the root causes of resentment instead of what might be perceived as the cause. Perceived causes are most likely just symptoms and not the root cause, in which case the resentment was never really dissolved. In the business world, this approach to solving problems is called Root Cause Analysis.

Here is an example of an owner of a company using Root Cause Analysis to ask the general manager why the company isn't making money.

1. *Owner:* Why aren't we making any profit?
   Manager: Because not enough people are buying our product.

2. *Owner:* Why aren't enough people buying our product?
   Manager: Because they hear previous customers are dissatisfied.

3. *Owner:* Why are our previous customers dissatisfied?
   Manager: Because of the high number of defects in our products.

4. *Owner:* Why is there a high incidence of defects in our products?
   Manager: Because our products are shipped with defects.

5. *Owner:* Why are our products shipped with defects?
   Manager: Because there aren't clear quality specifications for our products.

6. *Owner:* Why are quality specifications for our products not clear?
   Manager: Because the people designing and managing the manufacturing process don't understand quality control.

7. *Owner:* Why don't the designers and managers understand quality control?
   Manager: Because we're not hiring people who have adequate experience with quality control.

The owner may have stopped asking after hearing the answer to question #1, thanked the general manager, and then wondered why customers weren't buying their products. Or stopped after the question #2 and wondered why the customers weren't satisfied. It was not until the owner got down to the root cause of the problem did an action item appear. If what the general manager told the owner is correct, hiring people who have adequate experience with quality control will resolve all the preceding issues, including the original one of not making money.

The Melfox Method uses the same type of approach to resolve relationship issues. Instead of seeking an "action item," the series of questions will eventually lead to the real reason for resentment (lack of Information, misunderstanding, etc.). It takes asking why over and over again until you get to the real reason. Otherwise, you're just left wondering.

It's Not Over Until It's Over

Let's say that you realize that you have resentment with your partner because they snore. You share that revelation with your partner that night when the two of you have some alone time. Your partner may shrug their shoulders, say that's just the way it is, and that there is nothing that can be done about it. You may agree and simply end the discussion. You may conclude that the snoring can't be helped and go on living with the resentment and maybe start sleeping in separate rooms.

Many of us do just that. We assume we have done all that we can do and there is nothing else to know about an issue. But what if you don't assume that? What if you asked your partner *why* they snored? They may not know immediately, yet asking your partner moves Interaction to the next level of understanding. You or your partner may come up with possible reasons for the snoring, like eating a pound of cheese an hour before bedtime. If that turns out to be the reason, your partner may decide to stop eating cheese before bedtime and the issue is resolved. It was the lack of Information (knowing) that cheese caused snoring, which was the real reason for the resentment. If, however, even when knowing it causes snoring, your partner decides to continue eating cheese before bedtime, the resentment remains. You may resign yourself to the fact that your partner will snore assuming they are doing it intentionally... just to hurt you. Does that sound familiar?

Yet again, what if you don't assume that? What if you ask your partner *why* they choose to continue to eat cheese when they know it causes snoring? Again, that brings the conversation to yet another level. It may turn out that your partner does it because they have resentment toward you for some unrelated reason and "not caring" about snoring is reflecting that. The back and forth aspect of asking and receiving Information will be covered more fully in the *Interaction* chapter.

For now, the point is if you stop asking "why" too soon, you won't get to the root cause of the resentment and your relationship will continue to suffer.

Being Curious, not Judgmental

To avoid having the "why" question come off as judgmental, choose words that show you're curious for the reason your partner did or believes something. Have a burning desire to understand your partner. It is easy to get into "defense mode" and allow yourself to begin judging your partner. As we will see later, your tone, inflection, and other nonverbal communication play a big role in how your partner will react to your questions. The words themselves could cause your partner to feel that you are being judgmental, which may invoke a defensive reaction.

> TYPICAL JUDGMENTAL: Why are you wearing THAT? [hissing cat sound]
>
> BETTER: Why did you choose to wear a jacket? Do you know it is 90 degrees outside?
>
> ANOTHER OPTION: [Just smile and be *curious* to see how long the jacket stays on]

During the conversation, remain curious. Make it your mantra. Whenever your partner says anything that you don't like, choose to be curious, not judgmental or defensive. Understand that they are simply sharing their world with you. That's all. They are letting you know what they did, how they feel, what they believe, and who they are.

Think about it. Unless they say something that is refutable, you have no right to "take exception" or dispute in any way what was said. You can refute (courteously, of course) something that your partner says YOU did, feel, or believe, but not what your partner says THEY did, feel, or believe.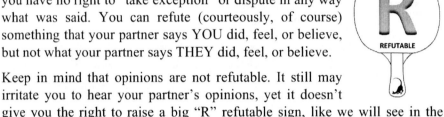

Keep in mind that opinions are not refutable. It still may irritate you to hear your partner's opinions, yet it doesn't give you the right to raise a big "R" refutable sign, like we will see in the *Interaction* chapter. There is, however, nothing preventing you from asking *why* they have their opinion.

BEATRICE: You are a jerk.
BRUNO: Refutable.
BEATRICE: Sorry... I believe you are a jerk.
BRUNO: That's better. WHY do you believe I am a jerk?

Instead of taking exception and saying something judgmental, choose to ask questions to clarify *why* your partner did something, or *why* they feel a certain way, or *why* they believe what they believe. When something they say rubs you the wrong way and the hairs start to stand up on the back of your neck, remain curious and *ask them why*.

By doing this, you help keep both you and your partner's defenses in check, and keep the conversation on the right track. We will be discussing more about keeping control of your defensive responses in the *Egoity* chapter.

Specific, Irrefutable, and Relevant Statements

When you are clear on the words and phrases used by your partner, and in the process of understanding your partner, you will want to add some of your own Information. You'll also be asked to provide answers to your partner's questions. When doing so, it is important to remember that a statement is not Information and useful in Interaction unless it's specific, irrefutable, and relevant. Anything else you say muddies the waters, delays the process of conflict resolution, and may invoke your partner's defenses.

It's a Two-Way Street

One key to effective conflict resolution is to have a burning desire to understand your partner. Another key is having a burning desire for your partner to understand *you*.

> *I want to see myself through your point of view.*
> - Unknown

When you have empathy, you realize that your partner wants to understand and be understood just like you want to understand and be understood.

Remember it's a two-way street. The ability of your partner to understand *you* is just as important as *your* ability to understand your partner. Anything that you can do to assist and support your partner in understanding *you* helps resolve the conflict.

Look like we need to enhance our Curiosity Mantra:

When I speak, I will always be curious, not judgmental.
The words I use and the way I say them convey a sense of wonder
so that I understand my partner, and my partner understands me.
I have a burning desire to understand my partner,
and for my partner to understand me.

When I listen, I will always assume my partner
is being curious, not judgmental.
If there's ever a question of my partner's motive, I will calmly ask
so that I understand my partner, and my partner understands me.
I have a burning desire to understand my partner,
and for my partner to understand me.

Remember "SIR Yes SIR"

To help your partner understand you, the statements you make should be "*S.I.R.*"... Specific, Irrefutable, and Relevant:

Specific

Avoid easily misunderstood words/phrases: "Let's eat Grandpa."
Better: "Let's go eat dinner, Grandpa."

Avoid vague words: "When you do that, I feel this way."
Better: "When you say you don't want to talk, I feel ignored."

Avoid generalizations: "You always yell!"
Better: "You usually yell when you are running late."

Irrefutable

Avoid opinions: "You are a jerk."
Better: "I believe you are a jerk."

Avoid unconditional accusations: "I know you are cheating."
Better: "When you ignore me, I feel like you are cheating."

Avoid falsehoods: "I haven't had a drink in a month."
Better: "OK, I might have had a few drinks last Friday."

Relevant

Avoid statements not dealing with conflict: "The handkerchief was nicely ironed and the perfume had a sweet, flowery scent."
Better: "The perfume on the handkerchief is not *mine*."

The above requirements for statements to be Information are especially helpful in evaluating statements already made. The lessons learned from mentally reviewing what was said (was it specific, irrefutable, relevant?) could be used for making adjustments in future statements. As opposed to thinking about all that before making a statement, you may consider simply concentrating on having *curiosity* and a *burning desire* for your partner to understand you and your world.

Just like asking questions helps you gain a better understanding of your partner, asking questions help your partner gain a better understanding of you. In order to keep the Interaction flowing smoothly, remember to keep your answers as brief and clear as possible, and consider the questions were asked in the spirit of curiosity, not judgment.

Thinking Before Speaking

We all know the adage "think before you speak" helps us to be more considerate, avoid "foot-in-mouth" disease, and organize our thoughts so our words make more sense. This is especially helpful when using *The Melfox Method*. Thinking through your relationship issues on your own, can help you and your partner resolve conflicts proactively.

The whole idea behind this book is to create an Environment in which you can better understand your partner and your partner can better understand you. It is through this understanding that conflicts are resolved. By thinking about what was just said and taking the time to fully evaluate it, you get a chance to see different ways to interpret the meaning of the message. The "thinking" part can help resolve issues all on its own. Calmly reflecting on the message gives us insights into what was said and a better understanding of it. And that's the whole idea, isn't it?

Thinking and "auto-correcting" before you speak also saves time and shows your partner you care. By taking a little bit of time to absorb and decipher what was just said, we have a much better chance of understanding and knowing what else to ask to get closer to understanding.

Nonverbal Communication

There is, of course, more to a conversation than the mere sharing of words. In fact, most social psychologists will tell you that nonverbal communication normally makes up about two-thirds of all face-to-face communication between two people. Long before there were words to say, our facial expressions and gestures conveyed to the other person what they needed to know. We instinctively interpret certain physical and vocal attributes to mean certain things at certain times.

Nonverbal communication may be done in lieu of the spoken word, like when we nod our head to indicate "yes." At times, its influence may totally override what is spoken or significantly alter the meaning. What we think we are conveying to our partner may be understood totally differently.

BRUNO: Good morning! (Big smile, cheerful expression)
BEATRICE: Good morning, Dear!

OR

BRUNO: Good morning. (Grumpy voice, solemn expression)
BEATRICE: (Someone's in a bad mood)

In other words, the way we say the words, our body language, our gestures, and other "non-word" communication may impact our partner's reaction more than the words themselves.

Loud and Clear

Prior to cell phones, folks would communicate from car to car via the same channel of their CB (Citizens Band) radio. Unfortunately, there are a limited number of CB channels. During the craze of the 1970s when *everyone* had a CB, it was not uncommon to have two or even three conversations at the same time on the same channel. The competing messages would make it very difficult to understand your CB partner and for them to understand you. The solution would be to jointly go to another channel and hope that it was not already being used.

Our nonverbal signals sometimes are like the other conversations going on at the same time on a CB channel. The difference is we are responsible for the other conversations on this channel. Fortunately, we can control these signals when we become aware of them. Many of us are simply unaware that we emit nonverbal messages that conflict with the spoken words. By intentionally taking control of our "non-word" actions, our intended message will be flawlessly relayed to our partner on a clear channel.

Nonverbal Communication During Interaction

During Interaction, nonverbal communication should only support the intention of the words spoken. Sarcastic tones, closed body language, overly excited gestures, and other external cues can alter the intended message and be interpreted as something completely different. Knowing the adverse affect that these other messages have gives us the impetus we need to want to control them. By becoming aware of them, we have the power to intentionally decide to eliminate them, instead of allowing them to impact the quality of our communication. Let's look at nonverbal communication by breaking it down into three groups:

1. Paralanguage (the way that you say your words)
2. Body Language (your body positions, gestures, and expressions)
3. Engagement (your eye contact and movement)

Paralanguage

Paralanguage refers to nonverbal elements contained in speech, such as the following:

> **Rate**... How fast you talk. The faster you talk, the more defensive you tend to be.
>
> **Pitch**... How high your voice is. The higher your voice, the more defensive you tend to be.
>
> **Volume**... How loud your voice is. The louder your voice, the more defensive you tend to be.
>
> **Voice Quality**... How clear your voice is. The less clear your voice, the more defensive you tend to be.
>
> **Rhythm**... How varied your rate of speech is. The more varied your rate of speech, the more defensive you tend to be.
>
> **Intonation**... How varied your pitch of speech is. The more varied your pitch of speech, the more defensive you tend to be.

The more you are able to control the defensive aspects of your words, the clearer your intended message becomes. Remember that the intent of Interaction is to share Information, and anything that distracts from the words spoken degrades the intended message. By keeping your speech rate, pitch, volume, and other paralanguage controlled, the words can be understood and the intended message conveyed.

Defending Your Word

If you have ever seen a TV defense lawyer prep a defendant before taking the stand, you've seen controlling paralanguage in action. The lawyer will constantly remind the defendant to relax and calmly answer the questions without getting too excited. The lawyer knows that the jury can interpret any sign of emotion as indication that the defendant may not be telling the truth or unsure of what they are saying. The prosecutor will try to rattle the defendant and use any emotionally charged paralanguage to discredit the defendant, or get the jury to interpret the message as something different.

We should look at conflict resolution in the same manner. During Interaction, we need to be our own defense lawyer. We need to constantly remind ourselves to remain calm and let only our words be communicated. We should look at any emotion during Interaction as a sign that our defenses have been engaged. We can then evaluate that defensive response and determine what it was that caused it. As we will see in the *Interaction* chapter, this self-evaluation is a key component of discovering the true cause of resentment.

Paralanguage During Interaction

We instinctively use paralanguage when we talk. We may raise our voice, pitch, and rate without really thinking about it. By understanding the impact it has on what we are trying to communicate during Interaction, we have a better chance of controlling it. This helps our partner only hear the words we say and not "read into" anything on how we say them.

During Interaction, we need to be aware of our paralanguage and control it as best as we can. This gives our words a fighting chance to be correctly interpreted by our partner as intended.

Body Language

Visual cues account for much of the message we convey to our partner. They can support the words spoken, or distract or totally alter their meaning. Just like paralanguage, being aware of the effects of our physical actions can help us control their effect on the conversation. There are numerous elements of what we call body language:

- Body positions and movements,
- Physical features, both changeable and unchangeable,
- Gestures,
- Connection with ourselves, our partner, and other objects,
- Facial expressions,
- Eye engagement, and
- The space between ourselves and our partner.

In other words, body language is anything you do, as opposed to verbal language, which is anything you say. The communication from you to your partner will be a combination of the two. Many of us don't realize the impact that our body language has on our partner's understanding of our spoken message.

Choosing Your Atmosphere

Let's say it is your anniversary, and you and your partner plan on having a romantic dinner to celebrate. If you were in charge of picking the restaurant, what kind would you choose? Would it be a busy cafeteria or a quiet formal dining establishment? Silly question. You would choose a place with a minimum of distractions so that you and your partner can focus only on each other and get lost in each other's eyes. The only sound you want to hear, not coming from your partner, is soft background music. Besides your partner, the only person you want to see is an occasional waiter or server.

If you had chosen the busy cafeteria, you would have a hard time understanding your partner with all the movement around you. It takes effort to tune out everything else, which affects your ability to "just be with" your partner. At least you know what you are trying to understand, and what you are trying to tune out.

Whether you know it or not, your body language sends messages to your partner that may be totally different from what you are saying. In this case, your partner may not know to try to "tune out" what is unspoken. The positions, movements, and gestures you make create an atmosphere not unlike the atmosphere of a restaurant. They can be defensive messages of judgment like crossing arms or a particular gesture. They may show signs of disinterest when you're actually deep in thought. Just like a busy cafeteria, your body language adds additional stimuli that your partner has to deal with during the conversation. The point is, when you are not aware of what your body is doing, it may be conveying messages you may not want to convey, *since you are not aware of it.*

Being Aware of Your Body Language

You may be simply unaware that you have struck a pose or made a face that "told" your partner something they might not like. Just like being aware of what we say and how we say it, being aware of and controlling our body language allows the true message to be conveyed as intended. Not being aware of our body language is like not being aware of our spoken language. Imagine not having control of what we say and just blurting out anything without thinking about it. That is essentially what happens when we are unaware of our postures, gestures, and expressions.

Here are a few examples of how body language sends messages:

1. Crossing of arms may indicate defensiveness or reluctance.
2. Rolling of eyes may indicate frustration.
3. Rubbing of eyes may indicate being upset or disbelief.
4. Scratching of nose may indicate concealing a lie.
5. Scratching of shoulder may indicate nervousness.
6. Shaking of head may indicate disagreement.

I say "may indicate" since there can be many reasons for you to unintentionally exhibit a certain posture or expression. Also, during Interaction, the receiver of the message might have learned to shut out any nonverbal messages and concentrate solely on the spoken words. This will be discussed in the *Egoity* chapter.

Body Language During Interaction

As much as possible, the condition of your body all during Interaction should be **relaxed**. Just like with paralanguage, understanding the impact that our body language has on what we are trying to communicate gives us a better chance of controlling it. This helps our partner to only hear the words we say and not "read into" any unwanted and conflicting visual communication.

- Legs when sitting should sit gently on the floor or may be casually flung out. They may be crossed, but are not wound around each other.

- The torso may sag slightly to one side (not be held there with irregular tension). It may also be well balanced, with the shoulders balanced above the pelvis. It does not curl up with fear, though it may curl up in a restful pose.

- Shoulders are not tensed up and generally hang loosely down.

- Arms hang loosely or move smoothly. They do not twitch and seldom cross each other, unless as a position of comfort. If arms cross, they hang loosely. Any crossing, of course, can indicate some tension. Folding arms may just be comfortable.

- Hands hang loose or are only used to enhance what we are saying. They are generally open and may shape ideas in the air. Gestures are open and gentle, not sudden nor tense.

- Mouth smiles gently or broadly without any signs of grimacing. Otherwise the mouth is relatively still. When talking, the mouth opens moderately, neither with small movements nor large movements.

- Eyes smile with the mouth, particularly in the little creases at the side of the eyes. A relaxed gaze will look directly at another person without staring, and with little blinking. The eyes are generally dry. Eyebrows are stable or may move with speech. They do not frown.

- Muscles in the face are generally relaxed. The forehead is a major indicator, and lines only appear in gentle expression. The sides of the face are not drawn back. When the head moves, it is with a smooth motion and in time with relaxed talk or other expression.

A relaxed body generally lacks tension. Muscles are relaxed and loose. Movement is fluid, and the person seems happy or unexcited overall.

Eye Contact and Engagement

The last type of nonverbal communication we will discuss is eye contact and engagement. They indicate how connected we are with our partner, and how interested we are in understanding their views or having our views understood. Essentially, engagement is how much direct attention you give to your partner. This, in turn, tends to play an important role in how much attention your partner is willing to give you. Engagement is a critical element of successful communication exchange.

In the classic 1951 science fiction film *The Day The Earth Stood Still*, an alien named Klaatu with advanced technology visits Earth. He talks with the "most intelligent person," which in this case is Professor Barnhardt. When the professor realizes he is talking with an alien, his eyes widen and he can't keep them off Klaatu. His expression may be interpreted as startlement or fear, like most everyone else in the movie, yet actually it is *curiosity*:

> *It isn't faith that makes good science, Mr. Klaatu. It's curiosity.*
> *Sit down, please. There are several thousand questions I'd like*
> *to ask you.*

The intensely wide eyes and constant eye contact revealed Professor Barnhardt's natural reaction of intense curiosity. He was begging for Information like a dry sponge begging for water. Due to his curiosity, he was fully engaged.

Now imagine being Klaatu at that moment. Wouldn't you feel important, respected, trusted, at-ease, and fully engaged yourself? Compare that with trying to have a conversation with someone who is closed up, and has little eye contact or engagement. If they continue to be disengaged, after awhile wouldn't you tend to feel disinterested and feel like giving up on trying? The conversation's engagement level is determined by the lowest common denominator – the one with the lowest engagement with the other. The lesser the engagement, the lower the amount of communication.

Now imagine being with someone who has the same expression as Professor Barnhardt, yet the attention is due to feeling defensive or vulnerable. It would be like trying to engage with a hissing cornered cat, ready to lash out its paw if you get too close. Wouldn't you tend to feel a little defensive and vulnerable yourself? Just because the engagement level is high, doesn't mean the conversation is a healthy one. Reasons for the attention may be diametrically opposed, like curiosity and judgment, or playing and fighting. Think about how we described conversation as like a tennis match. The game is being played regardless of whether you are seen on the same side of the net, or you are seen on the other side of the net.

Eye Contact and Engagement During Interaction

Eye contact and engagement are the most important type of nonverbal communication during Interaction. We can try to control our paralanguage and body language by intentionally forcing those elements to obey our wishes. That's a lot to focus on during conflict resolution. Instead we could just focus on forcing ourselves to be curious about our partner.

If we intentionally will ourselves to be curious, the nonverbal language we convey will naturally tend to be in accordance with that curiosity. Our voice and body will relax, and our eyes will be filled with wonderment. As long as we remain curious, our partner will tend to remain curious. It all goes back to our Curiosity Mantra:

When I speak, I will always be curious, not judgmental.
The words I use and the way I say them convey a sense of wonder
so that I understand my partner, and my partner understands me.
I have a burning desire to understand my partner,
and for my partner to understand me.

When I listen, I will always assume my partner
is being curious, not judgmental.
If there's ever a question of my partner's motive, I will calmly ask
so that I understand my partner, and my partner understands me.
I have a burning desire to understand my partner,
and for my partner to understand me.

The more we focus on being curious about our partner, the better the Information exchange, and the more effective the Interaction and conflict resolution will be. To root out resentment with your partner, be like Professor Barnhardt. Be curious.

Conflicting Nonverbal Communication

It is important to understand the effect that nonverbal communication has on the Information we are trying to convey to our partner. When communicating, nonverbal messages interact with verbal messages in four major ways: complementing, substituting, regulating, and conflicting.

Complementing: Nonverbal communication that supports the spoken words. Example: Saying you're curious while your body is facing your partner and making eye contact. When your verbal and nonverbal languages are in harmony, Information is easily and conveyed to your partner. This is the preferred function of nonverbal communication.

Substituting: Nonverbal communication that is used to replace spoken words. Example: Nodding your head instead of saying "I understand, go on." Care should be taken when substituting nonverbal for verbal messages to your partner, who may misinterpret them for something other than what you intended.

Regulating: Nonverbal communication that regulates communication and the flow of the conversation. Example: Gestures and expressions that indicate when to stop or start talking. Facilitates normal conversation with your partner.

Conflicting: Nonverbal communication that contradicts the spoken words. Example: Saying you're curious yet you're turned away or have trouble making eye contact. Stems from feelings of uncertainty, ambivalence, or frustration. Your partner will tend to disregard whatever you say in favor of your nonverbal message if they are conflicting. If ignored, progress of Information exchange will be impeded. Awareness of the conflict can become a valuable tool in identifying reasons for resentment.

We will be discussing how the awareness of conflicting nonverbal communication helps cleanse resentment in the *Interaction* chapter. For now, let's focus on the impact of conflicting nonverbal messages, why we convey them, and the effect they have on Interaction.

The Impact of Conflicting Nonverbal Messages

Remember our new best friend Sam, the border collie? Imagine taking him to the park for a walk. Let's say you are new at this "owning a dog" thing and don't realize you need a leash. Unless Sam is trained to stay, and without a leash, it will be pretty hard to keep him close after you open his car door. You'll probably spend the rest of your time in the park chasing Sam down and carrying him back to the car.

We already know we need to "leash" the words we speak to a certain extent. Most of us were taught to think before we speak and be somewhat careful with our words. If we were to let our words "run free" and let our defense reactions dictate what we say, it would probably be a short conversation.

> BEATRICE: I'm right. You're wrong. LA! LA! I can't hear you!
> BRUNO: Whatever. (And leaves)

Just like controlling what we say, we need to try to keep our nonverbal messages "leashed" and under control during Interaction. Like the owner of an untrained dog who doesn't know to have a leash, we may not be used to controlling our paralanguage and body language. To the extent we do, however, the clearer our intended message is conveyed.

Cause and Purpose of Conflicting Nonverbal Messages

Now you may be asking, "Why should I try to suppress how I am feeling, even during Interaction?" The simple answer is you shouldn't try to suppress your feelings, just be aware of them. Any unintentional conflicting nonverbal messages are in response to resentment, or a threat to a belief. Instead of seeing these messages as something to suppress or ignore, we could see them as insights to resolving conflict. They show us that something was just said or done that that we didn't like. We can use this Information to help pinpoint the issue causing the resentment.

Once you become aware of that, you could work on resolving that issue, or it may have to take a number and wait in line. Even though the Information given through conflicting nonverbal messages is valuable, the verbal conversation may be dealing with an unrelated subject.

To help dramatize this, here's another dog story:

Klondike of the Klondike

Once upon a time, there was a man named Klondike who lived up north of the Arctic Circle where the only means of transportation are walking and dog teams. He had a team of four dogs whose names just happened to be "Words," "Postures," "Gestures," and "Expressions." Unusual names for dogs I know, but stay with me.

Each dog was rather large, weighing almost as much as Klondike himself. Sometimes he would don a pair of skis and ride behind Words and let it go wherever it wanted. When business was needed in the nearby village, Klondike would attach all the dogs to a sled and take off. "Words," being the strongest dog, was always the lead. The other dogs were always supposed to follow "Words."

One day during a run, "Postures" started to pull the sled to the left. This slowed progress and made steering the sled difficult. Then "Expressions" started pulling in the same direction. This caused the sled to go so off track that took a lot of time and effort to rectify. It took them twice as long as usual to make it to the village.

After taking care of business and having a nice rest, Klondike and his dogs started heading home from the village. When they approached the spot where they derailed before, the other dogs all started pulling toward the right, and sure enough, the sled went off track again. Since it would have been very difficult to try to get the sled back on track and there still was plenty of daylight left, Klondike decided to order "Words" to go to the right with the other dogs to see what all the fuss was about. Riding the sled where there was no track was more difficult, but since all the dogs were pulling together, it wasn't that bad.

After a while, the dogs came across an old man lying in the snow. 'Thank goodness!" the old man beamed. "I went for a walk and got lost. I might have died out here if you hadn't come by!" Klondike helped the old man onto the sled and took him back home.

From that day forward, Klondike always paid attention when any of the dogs started pulling the sled in a different direction.

Just like the dogs in our story, instead of trying to suppress or ignore our conflicting nonverbal messages, we could use them to identify hidden issues. They may not be "on track" with the issue we are aware of and currently trying to resolve, yet are clues to unknown or unresolved issues. The key is to take note of such nonverbal messages so that they can be used immediately or at a later time to help identify and dissolve resentment.

It would be like explaining to "Gestures" or "Postures" that you understand there is some place they feel you should go; yet there is some place else you are going to first. Once they understand that, they will stop pulling the current verbal conversation sled off-track.

Impact of Controlling Conflicting Nonverbal Messages

It is easy to understand that our state of mind controls our physiology. When we are feeling a certain way, our bodies naturally exhibit postures, gestures, and expressions that support that feeling. When we feel defensive, our nonverbal language is closed and protective. When we are joyous and happy, the natural reaction is to smile with an open posture and inviting expression.

What may seem strange at first is that the inverse is also true. Our physiology controls our state of mind. To demonstrate this, next time you're in a depressed state, force yourself to hold your head up high, smile, and strut around briskly. You will find it impossible to remain in a depressed state as long as you are controlling your body like that.

So long as we have a relaxed, open physiology, we force our state of mind to be relaxed and open. When we hear something we don't like, the first instinctive reaction may be to cross our arms or turn away. This type of language tells everyone in the conversation that we are not open to or accept what was just said and that we are, at least for the moment, on the other side of the net.

By forcing ourselves to open up physically, we force our state of mind to be open to what was said and we are instantly on the same side of the net again.

Sharing Information During Interaction

As discussed earlier, our definition of Information is specific, irrefutable, and relevant (SIR) data shared during Interaction. Anything shared that is not effective Information delays the Interaction process and is not directly beneficial in our aim and goal of conflict resolution.

Difference Between Effective and Ineffective Information

Here's a quick review of what is, and what is not, effective Information during the process of Interaction:

Effective Information During Interaction

1. Requesting clarification of what was said

2. Asking curious "why" questions

3. Sharing specific, relevant, irrefutable (SIR) statements

4. Exhibiting nonverbal language that complements, replaces, or regulates #1-3 above

Ineffective Information During Interaction

1. Asking nonspecific or irrelevant questions

2. Sharing nonspecific, irrelevant, or refutable statements

3. Exhibiting nonverbal language that conflicts with other effective Information

Information is anything shared during Interaction that helps you to understand your partner better, and your partner to understand you better.

Ineffective Information is anything shared during Interaction that does not help you to understand your partner better, or your partner to understand you better.

Cause or Reason for Sharing Ineffective Information

If your sole goal were to effectively resolve conflict, you would strive to limit what you share to only Information. You would never intentionally share ineffective Information since you know that is counterproductive.

But why would you even unintentionally share ineffective Information? One reason you may go off the "Information track" is in response to something our partner shares. You may feel a sense of judgment or defense. It could be a slight twinge or a tidal wave. There may be a brief fuzzy vision of you and your partner moving toward opposite sides of the net, or a sudden reaction of temper.

Possible ineffective Information responses include:

- Adopting an accusatory or defensive voice (paralanguage)
- Faster rate
- Higher pitch
- Less controlled speaking style
- Less clear voice quality
- More varied speech rhythm
- More varied speech intonation
- Rolling or rubbing of eyes
- Scratching of nose or shoulder
- Loss of eye contact

Ineffective Information is the unintentional involuntary response to something displeasing or unacceptable. It's like the response from an automatic early warning system.

Yet Another Dog Analogy

You can visualize ineffective Information like the reactions of your pet dog when there is someone is at the front door. Depending on its nature and training, the dog may just lie there, calmly nudge you, or scream bloody murder. Regardless of its reaction, the dog does not answer the door. It can only inform you that acceptable company is at the door, or warn you of strangers.

Ineffective Information does not directly address an issue; it is an indication that there is something about an issue that is displeasing or unacceptable. As we will see in the *Egoity* chapter, the initiator of ineffective Information can be "trained" through understanding. When properly understood, ineffective Information can be seen as more useful, and less like a warning.

Ineffective Information is the expression of the defensive reactions we talked about in the *Environment* chapter. It is the physical manifestation of the "fight, fright, or flight" reflex. We "fight" by raising our voice and pitch, "fright" by crossing arms and looking away, and "flight" by leaving the conversation entirely.

Regulating and Utilizing Ineffective Information

Information is the sole ingredient we have to share during an Interaction session. Just like in many food recipes, care needs to be taken when adding ingredients if the dish is to a success. Adding in too much of an ingredient, adding it at the wrong time, or using the wrong ingredient (like salt instead of sugar) can ruin an apple pie.

Sharing too much Information or sharing it at the wrong time, or sharing ineffective Information can ruin or delay successful results from an Interaction. The key is to become aware and take control when the conversation has become too cold or too hot, and regulate the flow of the Information we share with our partner.

Science Experiment #2 – Circuit Temperature

Objective
To find the voltage setting to keep a wire at a warm, but not too warm, temperature.

Materials Needed
Power supply with rheostat control and voltage indicator, wire

Experimental Procedure
1. Connect the wire to the power supply with voltage at zero.
2. Put a few fingers on the wire.
3. Start putting power through the circuit by turning up voltage.
4. Continue increasing voltage and notice the wire getting warmer.
5. Increase the voltage until the wire is too warm to the touch.
6. Back off the voltage until it is comfortably warm to the touch.
7. Keep the voltage at that setting and note what that setting is.

Conclusion
By manually adjusting the voltage, we have determined the level that produces the ideal "warm, but not too warm," temperature.

During normal Interaction, the "temperature" of a conversation can change randomly. Unfortunately, many of us don't have our hand on the Information "control" or even know to use it. Ideally, we should have our hand on the regulator and instantly adjust the conversation temperature if it "feels" too cold or too hot.

In addition, some of us don't even have our fingers on the conversation "wire" to tell us if it's the right temperature. If we are not aware of the Interaction temperature, it will probably heat up until the wire burns up, ending the conversation with the smell of continuing resentment, like burnt metal, in the air.

Normal, Natural... and Expected

In addition to helping us regulate the conversation temperature, being aware of our own ineffective Information can also give us insights into the reason for resentment. When we catch ourselves speaking louder, using sarcasm, turning away, or saying non-SIR statements, the possibility exists for us to ask ourselves why we did it. Our internal dialog could ask things like:

> *"Why did my voice get louder just now?"* or
>
> *"Why did I feel the need to cross my arms just now?"*

When we are aware of our own expressions of ineffective Information, hidden clues to resentment get brought up to our awareness level for us to examine. This gives us a proving ground for identifying limiting or presuming beliefs, and effectively resolving conflict. This is discussed further in the *Egoity* and *Interaction* chapters.

Curiosity Kills Another Spat

As you know by now, much of this book centers on the Curiosity Mantra of resolving resentment by having a burning desire to understand your partner and for your partner to understand you. Part of this understanding involves being aware of ineffective Information shared by both you and your partner. Only by being aware of these messages can we use them to discover and dissolve resentment.

When I speak, I will always be curious, not judgmental.
The words I use and the way I say them convey a sense of wonder
so that I understand my partner, and my partner understands me.
I have a burning desire to understand my partner,
and for my partner to understand me.

When I listen, I will always assume my partner
is being curious, not judgmental.
If there's ever a question of my partner's motive, I will calmly ask
so that I understand my partner, and my partner understands me.
I have a burning desire to understand my partner,
and for my partner to understand me.

The more we stay curious about all conflicting messages, the more likely we are to discover new clues to resolve the issue, and the less likely the conflicting messages will be an obstruction to the conflict resolution process.

Curiosity Begets Awareness

Think of the allure of a haunted house. A small child may be too young to understand that all of the scariness is faked, and will not want to go in. Even though they see many other kids enter and come out unharmed, their curiosity is not great enough to overcome their fear. As they get older and more aware of the workings of a haunted house, their curiosity overcomes their fear and they go in. The thrill comes from experiencing the unknown, yet feeling safe enough from its perceived dangers. The more times we go through a haunted house, the more aware we become of each element of surprise and the less thrilling the experience. When we know what lies around every corner, the thrill is gone.

Just like a small child, we may be too fearful to go into our Interaction haunted house. We tell ourselves it is risking the very relationship itself to discover what is actually killing it. *The Melfox Method* helps us become "aware of the workings" of the conflicts we have with our partner, and utilize our own natural curiosity to overcome any fear of the unknown. Just like in a haunted house, *curiosity* is the driving force that turns unintentional demons into intentional peaceful understanding. Being curious about anything is the key to becoming more aware of it.

Tail Wagging the Dog?

It may seem counterintuitive to think that curiosity can help us control our ineffective Information and help create an atmosphere of mutual trust, closeness, and understanding. We tend to think that it's the trust and closeness we feel for our partner that permits us to have the sense of wonder we have for them. We see closeness as the dog wagging the tail of curiosity. Yet what if the reverse is true? What if it's the tail of curiosity that wags the dog of trust and closeness?

By intentionally forcing ourselves to be genuinely curious, we can instantly change the entire atmosphere of a conversation from argumentative to one of trust and cooperation. Now imagine if your partner did the same thing. When you ask questions and *have no expectation of the answer*, you are listening with pure curiosity.

When someone says or does something we do not like, our natural reaction is to take exception, feel they might see us on the other side of the net, and become defensive. If, instead, we maintain our "desire to inquire," we will wonder why they said what they said or did what they did, and try to understand the reason behind it. This goes back to our "curiosity vs. judgment" mindset we discussed in the *Environment* chapter.

Whether it's your partner saying or doing something we don't like, or the awareness of our own ineffective Information, we can choose to be curious.

Information - Recap and Review

In this chapter we have discussed the following:

What is Information?

We learned that Information is data shared with your partner that…

1. Is specific and organized for a purpose,
2. Has been verified to be accurate and timely,
3. Is presented in a context that gives it meaning and relevance, and
4. Can lead to an increase in *understanding* and decrease in uncertainty.

Controlling What You Speak...

Trigger words and phrases (i.e., profanity) can invoke a defensive reaction from your partner.

Positive words and phrases have the ability to keep the conversation "on course" and even reverse the effects of hurtful words and a defensive partner.

Verbal Communication

We discussed that Information is shared through:

1. Requesting clarification of what was said (inquisitive)
2. Asking curious "why" questions (inquisitive)
3. Sharing specific, relevant, irrefutable statements (declarative or conditional)

Nonverbal Communication

We discussed the different types of nonverbal language and their impact during Interaction:

1. Paralanguage (the way that you say your words)
2. Body Language (your body positions, gestures, and expressions)
3. Engagement (your eye contact and movement)

Ineffective Information

We also talked about conflicting nonverbal language and other ineffective Information, and their role during Interaction. We learned that regulating ineffective Information keeps the conversation from becoming to hot or cold.

Curiosity

We finished the chapter reiterating the importance of having a curiosity mindset and how that brings otherwise unknown Information to the intentional level.

****

Now that we have established that a relationship's only enemy is resentment and have discussed its causes...

And if properly shared Information is the key to revealing those causes...

What is stopping us from properly sharing Information?

CHAPTER THREE - EGOITY

"Beano" taught Beatrice and Bruno all about Information, and how properly sharing it is the essential component of conflict resolution. He explained it was through this proactive process that the reasons for resentment are revealed, dissolving its toxicity and clearing the relationship air. Beatrice listened attentively, while Bruno seemed more distant and skeptical.

"But you don't understand!" pleaded Beatrice. "I've tried to share my thoughts with Bruno in the past. He just throws it back in my face! Then I get all upset and things end up worse off than they were before."

"That's because all you do is complain, Bea!" Bruno interjected. "I'm willing to talk and all that, but not when I'm made to feel like everything's my fault! All you do is throw it back in MY face!"

"Don't I know it!" added Beano with a cough. "You both need to understand that just randomly sharing Information is not the answer. As you both know, sharing Information if done improperly can be painful and add even more toxicity to ME – your relationship!"

"So what can we do?" implored Bruno. "Why can't we share Information and resolve our conflicts?"

"Because you both keep blindly running into a closed door," Beano said with a smile.

"What door?" asked Beatrice. Bruno was curious as well.

"Are you sure you want to know?" Beano warned with a chuckle. "Because this is where things begin to get really interesting."

****

Egoity - The Gatekeeper

Beano made it clear to Beatrice and Bruno that simply sharing Information is not the answer to conflict resolution. It needs to be shared properly. Sharing Information haphazardly is the same as running full speed into a closed door – it never reaches its goal of resolving conflict and can only cause more resentment. Beatrice and Bruno are about to learn the secrets of the gatekeeper of Information – *Egoity*.

Think of Egoity like your watchdog, smoke alarm, malware security software, or other personal internal warning system. The trick is understanding its cause and purpose, and learning how to control it.

Preparing and Reacting to the Shot

Hitting a tennis shot is only one part of the game. The other part is preparation for and reaction to our opponent's shot. In much the same way, communication can be thought of in two parts. One part is sharing Information – what we learned in the previous chapter. The other part is the regulation of, preparation for, and reaction to, shared Information.

When a conversation is just small talk or idle chitchat, our reaction to what is said is "under control" and the conversation remains civil. If, however, someone says or does something we don't like, an involuntary defensive response can occur. This natural reactive response is what we call Egoity.

For at least that split-second, your sympathetic nervous system takes control of your thoughts and you are in "battle mode." Just as if someone jumped out at us from the shadows, our initial reaction is to flinch at the threat.

We continue to be in this hyperarousal state as long as the threat is real. Once we realize it is not a threat or the threat is gone, we settle down. This built-in reflex is a critical survival mechanism and should be highly valued and respected.

Egoity is the same type of reflex, yet not from physical threats. Any shared Information that threatens a preconceived understanding or belief evokes our Egoity. Understanding, controlling, and *using* our Egoity during Interaction allows us to effectively and civilly resolve our conflicts.

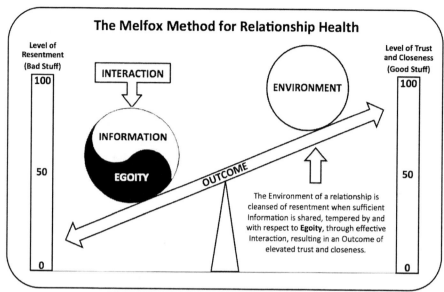

Diagram 9: *The Melfox Method* Model featuring Egoity

All of the chapters in this book, each being a portion of *The Melfox Method*, are important. Yet this one, Egoity, contains concepts that are the most novel and unbeknownst to most of us. Understanding the power of Egoity may be the one missing piece in your jigsaw puzzle of conflict resolution. Let's revisit an explanation from dating coach Norma Germain:

> *A lack of communication is the origin of most problems couples experience, often resulting in the breakdown of a relationship. Not understanding how to make feelings and wishes known to a partner in a **non-threatening, non-combative** fashion can lead to massive frustration and alienation from one another.*

By learning the cause and purpose of our threatening and combative reactions, we can learn how to regain and maintain control. This control keeps the conversation from eroding into an argument or prematurely ending, cultivating the proper Environment for conflict resolution.

To begin learning this vital concept, let's start out with something familiar.

Startlement and Hyperarousal

One of the vital built-in survival mechanisms we are all blessed to possess is our autonomic reaction to perceived threats. It is called the sympatho-adrenal response, the "fight or flight" response, or what we will call *hyperarousal*. After an initial startlement, hyperarousal instantly kicks in as long as we feel threatened, releasing adrenaline into our system. This causes an assortment of autonomic physical effects like our hearts to beat faster and our lungs to breathe deeper in preparation for responding to the threat.

When people are afraid, that fear can override their cognitive abilities so they're not really intentionally thinking through things. They're reacting in a defensive place, a fear-based place.

Proportional to the severity of the hyperarousal, that portion of our controllable awareness shuts down in favor of automatic emergency survival protocol. The higher the severity, the more out-of-control we feel. That part of us goes into "auto-pilot" and we lose total intentional control over our behavior.

As long as the threat is believed to be real, we will experience the autonomic involuntary impulse to fight with it, cower from it, or flee from it.

The Spark and the Fire

When you were very young, something walking toward you covered with a bed sheet and moaning "Boooo!" would most likely have frightened you. That frightened state would continue until the sheet was removed and you discovered the ghost was actually your laughing older brother. You had not yet learned the subtle clues that distinguish real from faked threats.

When encountering a perceived threat, there are two distinct responses:

1. Startlement (the initial, instantaneous, can't-help-it, "knee-jerk" reaction)
2. Hyperarousal (the sustained "fight or fright or flight" defensive mindset)

Both of these responses are autonomic reactions from our built-in sympathetic nervous system that vigilantly monitors our Environment for any sign of possible danger. It springs into action, automatically, when a perceived threat presents itself.

Startlement is the feeling of surprise ("Boo!") at the moment of awareness of the perceived threat. Startlement just gets the party started.

Hyperarousal is the lingering "out-of-control" defensive response that only exists when there is an insufficient lack of *understanding* of the perceived threat. The intensity of the hyperarousal and the duration of its activation depend on the individual's rudimentary respect and *understanding* of the perceived threat, including its motivation. The more we understand a situation, the more respect we have for it, or the less need for hyperarousal.

Startlement can be thought of as the spark, and hyperarousal as the fire. It is the lack of understanding and willingness to understand a perceived threat that serves as kindling and fuel to sustain the hyperarousal state.

1. **An unexpected tap on your shoulder from Ted**
   Startlement: Flinch for an instant, and then laugh about the surprise
   Hyperarousal: Scream like a little girl and mercilessly thump Ted with your umbrella (fight)

2. **Late night lightning and thunder**
   Startlement: Awake briefly, and then peacefully return to sleep
   Hyperarousal: Dive under the bed shaking, or crawl in bed with mommy and daddy (fright)

3. **Accidently touching a hot stove**
   Startlement: Jerk your hand back, then rinse it with cold water and get back to cooking
   Hyperarousal: Run out of the kitchen crying and swearing that you'll never, ever step foot in the kitchen again (flight)

Observing the hyperarousal reactions reminds us of children before they are accustomed to their surroundings. As we grow up, we learn to not break into hyperarousal just because someone unexpectedly taps us on the shoulder, thunder goes boom, or we accidently touch a hot stove. In each case, hyperarousal is the effect of not *understanding* the reason why the perceived threat triggered the initial startlement.

The more you understand something, the less effort it takes to put out the hyperarousal fire, take control of the situation, and *accept the situation.*

1. If you absolutely know it would be Ted sneaking up behind you to try to scare you, hyperarousal is nonexistent. The less you know about who tapped you on the shoulder, the greater the hyperarousal and effort it takes to let your guard down and *accept the situation.*

2. If you totally understand that thunder is just the sound caused by the sudden collapse of the vacuum created by lighting, hyperarousal is nonexistent. The less you understand about thunder, the greater the hyperarousal and effort it takes to relax and *accept the situation.*

3. If you understand that touching hot stove elements will burn you and accept the consequences of touching them, hyperarousal is nonexistent. The less you understand about stove elements, the greater the hyperarousal and effort it takes to *accept the situation.*

Acceptance Means Understanding

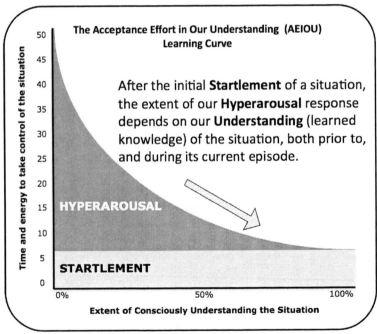

Diagram 10: AEIOU Learning Curve

In the Acceptance Effort in Our Understanding (AEIOU) diagram on the previous page, we borrow the learning curve concept to explain how our degree of understanding a situation determines the effort to bring hyperarousal under control and acceptance. Each episode of the same situation type brings greater understanding, reducing the reaction time and energy required to take control of subsequent episodes.

To help demonstrate this, let's go back to our "brother and bed sheet" analogy with him pulling the same prank once a month. After a few times, you may be startled at first, but the actual time feeling scared would more than likely be getting shorter, since you've "seen this movie before" and we are very adaptive creatures. Over time and experience, your reaction to the same type of stimulus changes. It evolves from a constant state of fear to a brief display of startlement. In essence, we learn.

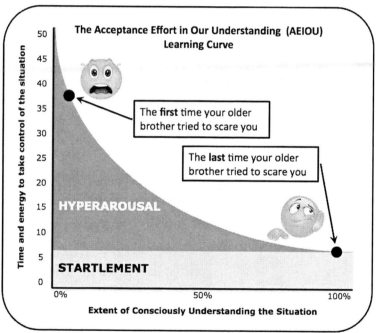

Diagram 11: AEIOU Learning Curve – Brother Prank

By intentionally focusing on understanding the perceived threat and through experience, we learn to quickly assess the startlement "spark" and rein in our hyperarousal "fire." The only reaction you had the last time your brother ever tried to scare you with a sheet over his head was an eye roll.

Hyperarousal Patterns

After the initial startlement, there are three basic patterns of hyperarousal:

---

1. **Minimum Hyperarousal**

    An expected tap on your shoulder by a friend

2. **Intermediate Hyperarousal**

    An expected tap on your shoulder by a stranger

3. **Maximum Hyperarousal**

    An expected tap on your shoulder by a grizzly bear

Each reaction is dependent on the level of understanding one has of the perceived threat and the desire to understand. To help visually explain the different patterns, below is the Level of Alert Based On Understanding and Recovery (LABOUR) chart:

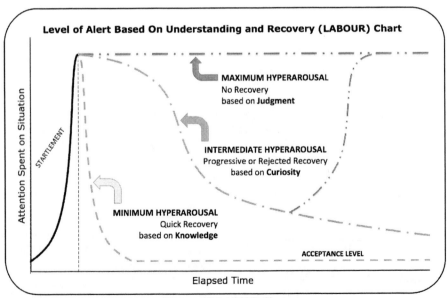

Diagram 12: LABOUR Chart

Minimum Hyperarousal

After the initial startlement, *prior or instantaneous knowledge of the situation* diffuses the hyperarousal. The attention spent on the situation quickly dissipates, and the level of alert returns to its pre-startlement acceptance level.

Intermediate Hyperarousal

After the initial startlement, a lack of prior knowledge of the situation sustains the hyperarousal, yet *curiosity of the situation* helps provide a better understanding of it. This either...

1. Confirms the threat and escalates attention level back to Maximum Hyperarousal, or

2. Continuously lowers the attention needed on the situation, reducing the alert level eventually to the point of acceptance.

Maximum Hyperarousal

After the initial startlement, *judgment of the situation* perpetuates full hyperarousal. At the given level of awareness, there is no doubt that the threat is real, and no possibility of acceptance. Full attention is spent on one of three things:

1. Destroying or repelling the threat (fight)

2. Cowering until the threat goes away (fright)

3. Running away from the threat to safety (flight)

It may seem obvious, but the more we understand something, the more instinctive the engagement with it becomes. When you first get a dog, you have to spend a lot of effort getting to know its wants, needs, and personality. After a while, you and your dog settle in to a predicable routine, basic Interaction becomes more instinctive, and the attention required for basic Interaction with the dog diminishes.

With anything new and not understood, that feeling of being on guard is very high. As we learn more about the situation, our trust and acceptance grows, and we spend less intentional energy (attention) protecting ourselves from it.

Perceived Threats

Let's now focus our attention on only threats that we may *perceive* as real, yet, in reality, are not. Pranks, fear of thunder, things like that. If we are unable or unwilling to interact with and learn of the perceived threat, there is no chance of reducing our fear of it, and thus our hyperarousal state.

Even if the perceived threat quickly reveals itself as harmless, it may be too late to ever accept the situation. Bob may take off the bear mask and say it's him, yet by then you may already be three blocks away.

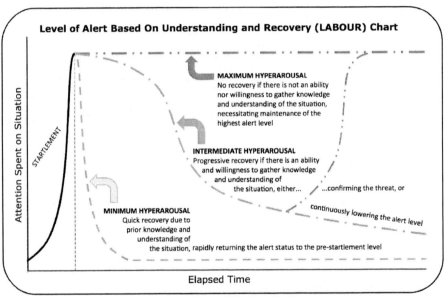

Diagram 13: LABOUR Chart Part 2

It is only when we have the ability and willingness to gather knowledge and understanding through curiosity that progress can be made to return the alert level back to an acceptable level.

Physical Threats and Threats to Beliefs

Thus far, we have discussed the cause and purpose of hyperarousal in dealing with perceived physical threats. Big brothers covered in bed sheets, unexpected taps on your shoulder, thunder, and touching hot stoves all produce, or threaten to produce, physical harm.

Startlement and hyperarousal, however, are not only activated when our *physical* survival or integrity is at stake. A conversation, even with a trusting partner, may trigger hyperarousal. In this case, the same type of fight, fright, or flight response may be provoked, yet it is not your physical self that is threatened. It is a *belief* that is threatened. Some examples:

- It is your *belief* that all the walls in your house should be painted off-white. Your partner would like to paint the kitchen yellow. Your partner has *threatened* your *belief*.

- It is your *belief* that your partner will like the birthday present you gave them. Your partner gives indications that they don't like their present. Your partner has *threatened* your *belief*.

- It is your *belief* that your partner should not get all upset just because you forgot their birthday. Your partner got all upset because you forgot their birthday. Your partner has *threatened* your *belief*.

- It is your *belief* that you agreed to meet your partner at the movie theatre at 8 p.m. It's 8:10 and they still haven't arrived yet. Your partner has *threatened* your *belief*.

When someone directly or indirectly shares Information that we perceive as contrary to our expectation, the integrity of a belief is suddenly threatened. As long as we hold fast to that *belief*, we will protect it *as if our physical selves* were threatened. Yet it is *not* our physical selves that are being threatened; it is our *beliefs*. This protective reaction to such belief-threatening Information is what we call *Egoity*.

Introduction to Egoity

The dictionary definition of Egoity is simply "personality" or "selfhood." For the purposes of *The Melfox Method* and this book, we will define Egoity as the following:

> *Egoity: The startlement and possible hyperarousal response caused by interpreting Information as a threat to a belief.*

The potential for Egoity exists in the entire spectrum of relationships. Here are a few examples:

- A verbal altercation with a stranger
- Enragement at what someone online posted in a chat or comment
- An argument with your boss or subordinate
- That awkward first dinner with the in-laws
- Managing a conflict with your intimate partner

While this Egoity-inducing list could be much longer, in this book, we will be focusing primarily on the last entry – managing a conflict with your intimate partner. Simply put, if you have the belief or understanding that your partner is "A," yet they say something that indicates they are *not* "A," your Egoity may be evoked.

Egoity Manifestations

While the extent of Egoity depends on numerous factors, any hyperarousal manifestation will be the same as if caused by a physical threat – fight, fright, or flight. Here is a chart listing these three ways that Egoity is expressed, and how they are typically manifested:

Egoity Manifestation #1: **FIGHT** (The Lion)

1. State of mind: Aggravation, aggression, hostility
2. Main sports strategy: Offense
3. Boxing style: Sting like a bee
4. Driving style: Foot on the gas
5. Movie role: Protagonist
6. War strategies: Blitzkrieg, ambush, trench raiding
7. Typical inner voice: "I'm right and you're wrong... ROAR!!"
8. Nonverbal communication: Loud voice, direct eye contact, high-pitched voice
9. Typical method for protecting a belief: Intimidate the messenger
10. Egoity goal: Destroy or repel the threat

Egoity Manifestation #2: **FRIGHT** (The Turtle)

1. State of mind: Intimidation, passive-aggression, victimization
2. Main sports strategy: Defense
3. Boxing style: "Rope-A-Dope"
4. Driving style: Foot on gas *and* brake
5. Movie role: Antagonist
6. War strategies: Trench warfare, disinformation
7. Typical inner voice: "I'm under attack! Batten down the hatches!"
8. Nonverbal communication: Hunched body, wary eye contact, crossed arms
9. Typical method for protecting a belief: Antagonize the messenger
10. Egoity goal: Cower until the threat goes away

Egoity Manifestation #3: **FLIGHT** (The Deer)

1. State of mind: Avoidance, noncooperation, aversion
2. Main sports strategy: Doesn't play
3. Boxing style: Takes a dive
4. Driving style: Foot on the brake
5. Movie role: Walks off the set
6. War strategies: Camouflage, retreat, cease fire
7. Typical inner voice: "Change the subject!" or "I'm outta here!"
8. Nonverbal communication: No eye contact, annoyed, antsy
9. Typical method for protecting a belief: Avoid the messenger
10. Egoity goal: Run away from the threat

In each case, the motivation for Egoity is the *protection of a belief.* The Lion protects a belief by offensively dominating and intimidating the messenger of Information that challenges the belief. The Turtle protects a belief by shielding it from Information that challenges the belief. The Deer protects a belief by fleeing from Information that challenges the belief.

Bear in mind that these Egoity manifestations are not to be confused with one's inherent personality. The Lion, Turtle, and Deer simply represent the style of Egoity someone has at any given time based on the given circumstance. Some factors that determine this Egoity manifestation include the following:

Type of relationship you have with the other person (spouse, boss, parent, child...). Generally, the more authoritative person will play the role of the Lion.

Subject discussed. Whoever has the bigger problem with the current situation is more likely to play the role of the Lion.

Information exchanged. For example, during the conversation, Information may be shared that shifts the balance of power. This may cause the swapping of Lion/Turtle Egoity manifestations within the same discussion.

OK. So Egoity is only evoked when beliefs are threatened. What can we do about that? Aren't we supposed to defend our beliefs? Weren't we taught that? Shouldn't we *stand up* for what we believe? "If you don't stand up for something, you'll fall for anything." Right?

We will go about finding the answers to these questions about beliefs in the same way we answered questions on Egoity – by learning and understanding it. Let's begin our exploration into the mystical world of *beliefs* – where I am always right and you are always wrong.

The Power of Beliefs

Since Egoity is only evoked when a belief is threatened, it is important to understand what is meant by a *belief*. If we can control whether or not we *believe* something, we can control our Egoity associated with that belief. When we control our Egoity, we can control the flow and quality of Information. And it is the effective sharing of Information that leads to the identity of resentment and the discovery of the reasons for it, thus resolving the conflict and strengthening the relationship.

Wait a minute: That sounds pretty important. Let's go over that sequence again in reverse and call it our Resentment Cause Analysis:

RESENTMENT CAUSE ANALYSIS
1. In order to strengthen your relationship, you need to be able to resolve conflicts.
2. In order to resolve conflicts, you need to be able to discover the reason(s) for resentment.
3. In order to discover the reason(s) for resentment, you need to be able to identify resentment.
4. In order to identify resentment, you need to be able to effectively share Information.
5. In order to effectively share Information, you need to be able to control Egoity.
6. In order to control Egoity, you need to be able to stop feeling a belief needs protection.
7. In order to stop feeling a belief needs protection, you need to be able to **transform the belief into a postulate**.

So bottom line, it is only when we are *able* to transform underlying beliefs into postulates that can be scrutinized that we are *able* to ultimately strengthen our relationship.

Definition of Belief

For the purpose of this book, the definition of *belief* is:

> *Belief: Confidence in the truth or existence of something that is neither susceptible to, nor constantly scrutinized by, rigorous proof.*

In other words, beliefs are shortcuts. Beliefs enable us to function without having to rigorously verify and validate everything. Beliefs are *assumptions* of truth or existence. The strength of a belief in the truth or existence of something is proportional to the confidence one has in it.

1. The upside of a belief is that there isn't the constant burden of proof.

2. The downside of a belief is that it may be wrong, yet, *as long as it is seen as a belief,* we will defend it from threatening Information *instead of resolving the conflict.*

Let's say you create a computer program that calculates temperatures accounting for the wind chill factor. You test it thoroughly and tweak it until you have a real strong *belief* it is totally accurate. Then one day, your friend Linus tells you that he thinks a result from the program may be wrong. At that moment, *and as long as you still have that belief,* you are defending it from Linus and his threatening Information instead of cooperatively resolving the dispute.

Like every other belief you have, you defend it with Egoity by some type of fighting, cowering, or fleeing. The moment you can admit to yourself that your *belief may be wrong*, you stop defending it with Egoity, make it available to scrutiny, and are then able to work cooperatively with Linus to figure out what really is the issue.

Belief Rating

At any moment in time, we have an internal rating for every belief we have. It is like opinion polls we are sometimes ask to participate in by marketing companies. They usually look something like this:

Please rate your belief in the following statement:

My partner will love all the birthday presents I will ever give.

○ Strongly Agree (very high confidence that the statement is **true**)
⊗ Somewhat Agree
○ Slightly Agree
○ No Opinion or Neutral (no belief either way)
○ Slightly Disagree
○ Somewhat Disagree
○ Strongly Disagree (very high confidence that the statement is **false**)

Be mindful that this rating is just a snapshot in time. New Information can instantly change whether or not we believe in something, and the strength of that belief. A good way to look at the rating is that it is based on what you know RIGHT NOW. "Based on my present level of awareness, this is what I believe."

In many cases, we are not aware we have a belief about a certain subject, nor its rating. We automatically evaluate our experiences against such beliefs without thinking about it. They are like sets of rules that work behind the scenes so we don't have to spend any intentional energy contemplating and defending them.

Now let's view the same belief rating on our Belief-O-Meter® below:

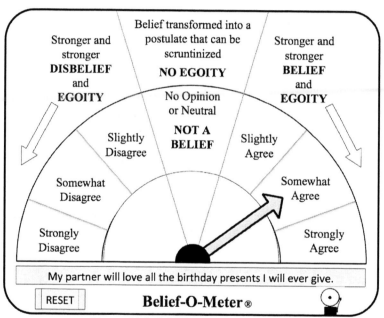

Diagram 14: Belief-O-Meter® Somewhat Agree

As you can see, the *stronger* the belief or disbelief in something, the *stronger* the Egoity protection when threatened, and the *further away* you are from effectively resolving the conflict.

However, regardless of how strongly you agree or disagree with a belief, as long as Information shared *does not* conflict with it, Egoity associated with that belief *is not evoked*.

Whenever belief-threatening Information *is* shared, a choice is instantly made in regards to our reaction:

A. Should I transform my belief into a postulate that is susceptible to scrutiny?

OR...

B. Should I continue to defend my belief by fighting, cowering, or fleeing? (Default)

As long as the choice is **B**, we view the sharer of the belief-threatening Information on the opposite side of the net, causing the conflict resolution process to stall or reverse. It is the *strength* of the belief that determines the effort needed to change the answer from **B** to **A**.

Belief Strength

Each belief has a strength factor. Some beliefs are easily challenged and dismissed while others seem to be set in stone. Think of the strength of a belief as how stiff or rigid the needle on our Belief-O-Meter® is if we tried to move it. As long as a belief remains a belief, the imagination will explain away or deflect any conflicting Information. Two factors that determine the strength of a belief are:

1. The amount of **investment** you have with the belief.
2. The degree of **identity** you have with the belief.

Belief Investment

Let's say you believe that all frogs are green. You were told that all frogs are green as a child and nothing has ever come up in your life to ever challenge that belief. Then one day you see a picture of a *Phyllobates terribilis* also known as the golden poison dart frog. This frog is native to Colombia, South America, and definitely yellow in color, not green. Since you have never really contemplated the color of frogs and have little vested on the subject, you will more than likely "change your mind" and easily abandon your belief that all frogs are green. The strength factor for this belief was low since it was so easily transformed into a postulate that could be scrutinized, challenged, and changed.

Now let's say that you *do* have a vested interest in the color of frogs. In fact, you wrote a non-fiction book titled *All Frogs Are Green* and give talks on the subject at the local library. In this case, when you see a picture of a yellow frog, you will *less* than likely "change your mind" and abandon your belief that all frogs are green. Your belief may be strong enough to encounter such conflicting Information and still remain rigid. You may defend your "all frogs are green" belief by deducing that the picture was Photoshopped to make the frog look yellow, and that there must be a worldwide conspiracy to make us think that not all frogs are green.

The investment you have in your belief may be in money (sales of *All Frogs Are Green*), reputation (your status in the Biology community), time ("It took 2 years to write that book!"), or simply pride ("What will my mother think?"). The bigger the investment in a belief, the bigger the price you may have to pay if it is wrong. As long as you feel that the price is too high to pay, you will continue to defend the belief.

> *To accept our own fallibility is to embrace the permanent*
> *possibility of someone having a better idea.*
>
> - Richard Rorty

Belief Identity

Another factor that determines the strength of a belief is how much we *identify* with it. In other words, how much we feel a belief is *part of us*. The more we identify with a belief, the more we will defend it as if it were a *physical* threat. When we identify with a belief, it is unthinkable to not protect it from scrutiny. Opening the belief up to scrutiny would feel like walking out in sub-zero weather wearing only a T-shirt and gym shorts. It is totally contrary to our basic survival instincts.

Think of beliefs like things we wear. They may be easy to take off, like earrings or underwear, or a bit harder to remove, like tattoos. Yet even though they are attached to the skin, tattoos are still not part of us. You may identify so much with some beliefs that they feel like they are encrusted on you... but they are NOT you.

Let's say one late summer day, you lend your lawn edger to your neighbor Carlos. You wait a day. No return. You wait a week. No return. If you don't ask Carlos for it soon, you might forget to. But you don't ask for it. Next thing you know, it is fall and winter and you forget all about it. The longer you wait, the stronger the possibility that Carlos might actually forget you lent him the edger, and think it is HIS edger. Haven't you ever lent something to a friend and then later on had to ask for it back? Unless it's very distinctly yours, there might be a question over who really owns it.

Beliefs can be thought of like that edger. We could think that a belief is part of us, like Carlos thinking the edger is his property. Or we could see that all beliefs are "lent out" for the sake of convenience, and that they are not "part of us" and at times need to be open to scrutiny.

Science Experiment #3 - Clean Residual Milk From Glass

Objective
To graph the relationship between milk dry time, and the effort it takes to clean it out.

Materials and Equipment Needed
Glass with flat bottom, milk, straw, pencil and paper, and throw in the kitchen sink.

Experimental Procedure
1. Splash a bit of milk in the glass, enough to cover the bottom.
2. Sip out as much milk as possible with the straw.
3. Set the glass aside for 15 minutes.
4. Depending on severity of milk dryness, rinse or wipe out glass, or put in dishwasher.
5. Record effort level needed to clean out the glass.
6. Repeat the above procedure 13 more times, adding 15 minutes each time to step 3.

Conclusion
The longer time passes, the more encrusted the milk becomes in the glass and the greater the effort needed to clean it.

If you actually did this experiment, your results may look like this chart:

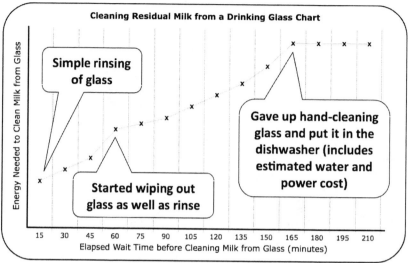

Diagram 15: Science Experiment – Dried Milk Clean Time

The lesson learned with this experiment: In time, something (milk) that is *not* part of something else (the glass) may begin to act as if it *were* part of something else.

In much the same way, as time goes on, we tend to *identify* more and more with a belief. Just like with the edger we lent to Carlos, the longer time passes, the more he *identifies* with the edger, and the *stronger he believes* that it belongs to him. The longer we allow a belief to remain unchallenged, the harder it may be to see it is not *part of us*.

Egoity in Action

To give you the feel of Egoity, let's take a look at it in action in everyday life. We will also see how Egoity is interconnected with resentment and Information.

Typical Egoity Battles

The following are snapshots of typical Egoity battles during Information exchange attempts:

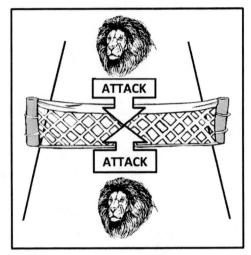

LION VS. LION: Both partners attack each other. Shouting matches. Name-calling. Finger-pointing. If mutual Egoity persists, Interaction usually ends with one "giving up" or feeling outmatched, morphing into a Deer, and leaving in a huff, complete with door slam.

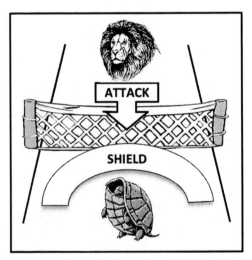

LION VS. TURTLE: The Lion attacks while the Turtle shields. The Turtle feels distrust toward the Lion and inferior in regards to the subject discussed. If mutual Egoity persists, Interaction usually ends with either the Lion "giving up" or the Turtle "not able to take it" anymore.

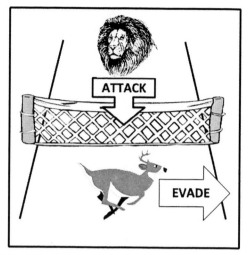

LION VS. DEER: The Lion attacks, yet the message is not received. The Deer evades, ignores, or escapes from the conversation. As long as one partner is in "Deer mode," conversation is not effectively taking place.

It can be said that "Turtle vs. Turtle," "Turtle vs. Deer," and "Deer vs. Deer" are nonexistent since you need an antagonist (Lion) to create a battle.

Here's a snapshot when both partners are in non-Egoity mode:

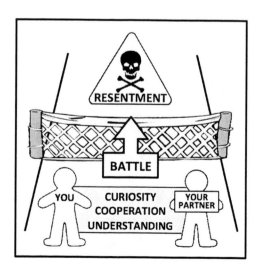

As discussed in the *Environment* chapter, resentment is the cause of all relationship issues, and can only be addressed through understanding and cooperation between the people in the relationship. When our Egoity ceases to control us, we take back control and see our partner "on the same side of the net."

Of course that doesn't automatically mean your partner sees YOU on the same side. Even though your words and actions are shared with curiosity, your partner may still feel the need to fight, cower, or run. We will discuss how to deal with this situation in the *Interaction* chapter.

The extent of pride, sacredness, or value in a belief is a factor that determines the extent of Egoity. As long as the idea of being wrong about our belief is off the table, our Egoity will continue in top gear. It is only when we allow the possibility of being wrong about our belief to creep into our awareness, do we start to rein in our Egoity.

The Idea of "Being Wrong"

When you think about it, being wrong about a belief is not a reflection on you as a person, nor does it mean that you have ashamedly made a wrong decision about something. It simply means that something you believe turns out not to be true. Through no fault of yourself or anyone else, a belief you have may not be true and there was nothing you could have done to prevent adopting it – with the limited Information you had *at the time*.

Conflict exists when two people do not share the same belief about something and at least one person finds that unacceptable. When Information is shared that resolves the conflict and the dust settles, it will be evident that at least one person was wrong about their belief.

So, on average, people in conflicts are wrong about their threatened belief at least half the time. Those who have a "resolution disposition" (The Melfox Mindset) are not at all concerned about winning arguments and find that "being wrong" about half the time is acceptable. Their energy is spent on finding the cause and reason for resentment, regardless of who needs to change their belief.

Those who maintain a "me versus you" disposition (Traditional Relationship Logic) feel that belief conflicts are battles to be won or lost and find "being wrong" unacceptable. "You have to stand up for what you believe" is their motto. Their energy is spent fighting, cowering from, or fleeing from any Information that threatens their belief, regardless of the evidence available. We will be getting more into these opposing mindsets in the *Interaction* chapter. The reason that a belief turns out to be wrong may be boiled down to four primary possibilities. Do these look familiar?

1. Lack of Sufficient, Pertinent Information
2. Misunderstanding
3. False Assumption
4. Jumping to False Conclusion

That's right. The reasons for a belief not being true *are the same reasons for* **resentment**.

Egoity and Resentment

Simply stated, Egoity is evoked when our partner shares something that we don't like. If this rings a bell, in the *Environment* chapter, it was stated that we feel *resentment* when:

1. Someone presumably is, did, or believes something you do not **like**.
2. Someone does not **like** what you presumably are, did, or believe.

Resentment and Egoity are very close in nature. Resentment is the *condition* of conflict and Egoity is the *expression* of the condition of conflict. Resentment is the underlying constant feeling of non-acceptance, while Egoity is the real-time hyperarousal response to Information that exposes the resentment. Even our definition of resentment is similar to our one for Egoity:

> *Resentment: The feeling of distain caused by the non-acceptance that an individual presumably is, did, or believes something that does not match one's belief about or expectation of that individual.*

Resentment is the oily rags and leaky kerosene containers in our relationship garage. A dangerous condition exists, yet resentment doesn't reveal itself until there is the fire of Egoity. We can try to prevent Egoity by closing up our relationship garage from our partner, or we can prevent the Egoity fire by cleaning up resentment.

Egoity and Information

If resentment can be thought of as the *fuel* and Egoity as the *fire*, then the sharing of Information is the *spark*.

Let's say you are sensitive to pine pollen and live in Atlanta. Every March, your eyes water and you sneeze a lot. If you move to a place free of pine trees, your allergic reaction to pine pollen may never be triggered, although you remain susceptible to pine pollen. As long as you stay away from triggering your allergic reaction to pine pollen, your natural susceptibility to pine pollen is not revealed.

Resentment can be thought of as the *susceptibility* to pine pollen, while threatening Information is the *pine pollen* and Egoity, the *allergic reaction*. Like pollen sensitivity, resentment is a pre-existing condition. As long as we stay away from (and don't think about) belief-threatening Information, our Egoity will not be triggered. The threatened belief and associated resentment will not be revealed.

Here are some interesting analogies to describe our concept of Egoity with respect to Information:

If Information is...	Then Egoity is...
The Novice Diaper Changer	The Nervous On-looking Spouse
An Action	An Opposite and Equal Reaction
A Bookkeeper	An Auditor
An Employee	The H.R. Department
An Automobile Driver	A Traffic Cop
A House	The Home Security System

The item listed as "Information" is either regulated or protected by the item listed as "Egoity." The same type of autonomic response occurs during conversations, including Interaction. Egoity, like any other hyperarousal response, is activated when our instinctive self senses a threat.

Egoity Factors

As discussed earlier, the amount of pride or sacredness we have in a belief is one ingredient in our Egoity chili. Here are four of the primary factors that determine the intensity and duration of our defensive response:

1. The extent to which we value the threatened belief (investment and identity)

2. The extent to which we value the relationship with the sharer of the threat

3. The extent to which the belief is threatened

4. The extent to which we understand the fundamentals of Egoity

---

1. Value of Threatened Belief

As illustrated above, how much pride or sacredness we have in the subject of the threat plays a critical role in how much and for how long our Egoity is engaged. The more investment or identity we have with a belief, the less tolerant we will be with threatening Information.

2. Value of Threatened Relationship

The intensity and duration of our Egoity depends greatly on the value we place on the relationship. Criticism from a random stranger we can either take or leave; yet it holds a much greater weight when coming from our intimate partner.

3. Intensity of Threat

Naturally, the greater a threat is to a belief, the more intense our Egoity protective response.

4. Understanding of Egoity

It is this last factor that we can control and is the subject for the remainder of this chapter.

Laws of Egoity

To better understand Egoity, let's look at some basic fundamental laws:

First Law of Egoity

Extent of Egoity is inversely proportional to the desire
for understanding the situation causing the Egoity

The more you desire to understand something instead of battling against its existence, the less extent of Egoity. Once you stop playing "battlin' beliefs" and resume the desire to understand your partner, your Egoity is turned off like a switch.

This law is similar to what was displayed in our AEIOU chart. After initial startlement, the extent of ensuing hyperarousal depends of the understanding of the situation. The more we understand a situation, the closer we come to accepting it, which ceases the need for Egoity.

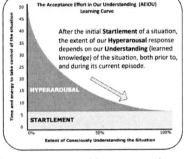

This law asserts that it's the simple desire to understand a situation that defuses the need and extent of Egoity. You may not totally accept something, yet as long as you desire to understand it, you are not fighting it.

Think about how this law of Egoity is demonstrated during conflict resolution. Conflict exists when there is something that we don't accept about our partner. As long as we desire to understand and accept it, our emotions stay in check.

When we shut off the desire to understand our partner, we automatically shift into some form of Egoity. Curiosity has turned to judgment and our inner Lion, Turtle, or Deer emerges.

> *Knowledge and ego are directly related.*
> *The less knowledge, the greater the ego.*
>
> - Albert Einstein

Second Law of Egoity

Extent of Egoity is inversely proportional to being "in control"
(fully responsible and aware of your actions)

In other words, the more intense our Egoity, the less voluntary control we have of our actions. We use terms like "losing our temper" or "feeling panicky" when we recall these instances of lack of control. The more we lose our temper or panic, the less intentional control we have and the more involuntary our actions become.

Think about how you would feel if you were so mad you wanted to break dishes, so scared you wanted to cower in a corner, or so scared you fled like being chased by a madman. You could then imagine just how more out of control our actions are, when our Egoity is more in control.

This law is dramatized metaphorically in stories like *Dr. Jekyll and Mr. Hyde*, or in movies like *An American Werewolf in London* and many other horror films. The premise is essentially the same: Some "outside force" temporarily changes human nature, causing "irresponsible behavior" and memory lapses. The plot usually centers on trying to eradicate the mysterious "outside force" (or the afflicted) before it causes (more) out of control damage.

Think of these "outside forces" like imaginary Egoity pills that turn people into their full-fledged Lions, Turtles, or Deer.

When a belief is directly threatened and you choose to defend that belief, it's like taking an Egoity pill that temporarily releases your inner Lion, Turtle, or Deer. To a certain degree, you are "irresponsible" and not intentionally aware of your actions. The thing to remember is that the Egoity pill is only effective so long as you defend the belief that is threatened. Once we stop defending it, our Egoity retreats back to its cage.

How often have you looked back "in horror" at the things you've done and said during moments of Egoity? But what if you could take control whenever you start to lose control? How would you like that "looked back" time to be *instantaneous?* By understanding and being aware of your Egoity tendencies, you can train yourself to take back control as soon as you feel it start to slip.

Third Law of Egoity

Extent of Egoity engagement is directly proportional
to the extent you are battling with your partner or
seeing them as an opponent

The instant your Egoity is evoked and for the duration it is evoked, you are at odds with your partner. You are fighting with your partner, cowering from your partner, or fleeing from your partner. It may just last a second, yet in that second, you see your partner as the enemy.

When you are having just "a little disagreement" with your partner, your Egoity is "little." You may see your partner as having just one toe on "the other side." But when a polite disagreement turns into a major ruckus, there is no doubt. Your partner is not on your side.

Even during minimal hyperarousal, there is a period of time when you see your partner on "the other side" or, in other words, as the enemy. This is a normal and natural reaction to belief-threatening Information. The sooner we control our Egoity by accepting the fact that our belief may be wrong and turning our attention from our partner to the issue, the sooner we can begin effectively resolving it.

Fourth Law of Egoity

Extent of Egoity engagement directly reflects the extent
of the underlying resentment

This law demonstrates the tight correlation between Egoity and resentment. The intensity of Egoity displayed when talking about an issue tells us the impact the resentment surrounding this issue is having on the relationship. Big Egoity means big resentment.

Think of the effect that different wattage levels have in an electrical circuit. The higher the wattage, the faster the toy goes and the brighter the light. The toy and light are expressions of the wattage, just like Egoity is the expression of the resentment. The amount of "emotional charge" surrounding an issue dictates the amount of "emotional charge" displayed as Egoity.

Egoity is caused by resentment. If there were no resentment, there wouldn't be Egoity. Yet presence of resentment doesn't mean Egoity is displayed.

A Brief History of Egoity

Once upon a time, we didn't have the advancements we enjoy today. The relative lack of language, recorded history, and mass communication made it very difficult for us to effectively understand our world and each other. Just relaying the sentence "I am going to walk to that big rock over there and sit" to someone right next to you may take five minutes to convey. This lack of understanding one another made for a rather fearful place to live. We were constantly "on-guard" and often severely. We were almost exclusively in hyperarousal every waking second.

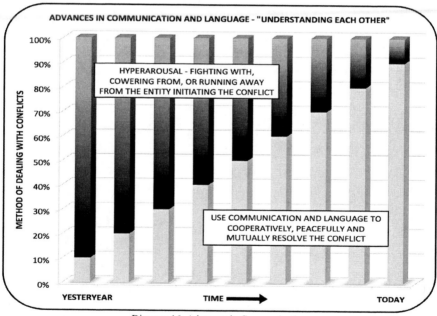

Diagram 16: Advances in Communication

When there are insufficient language skills for effective communication, conflict resolution is impossible. Therefore, any physical threats are dealt with by fighting with, cowering from, or running away from the entity (person) initiating the physical threat.

Similarly, whenever a *belief* is threatened and there is insufficient Information shared, Egoity runs the show and never lets up. All belief conflicts were dealt with just like physical threat conflicts – by fighting, cowering, or running away.

It is through the increased level and expansion of language that we are equipped to communicate effectively, thus eliminating the need to fight, cower, or run away. The incredible calm of community cooperation that we sometimes take for granted was unfathomable back when language and communication skills were insufficient for conflict resolution. For example, in business we have learned how to deal with contractual conflicts peacefully and effectively. Disputes are usually resolved cooperatively without the urge and need to fight, give in, or give up.

With our advanced level of language and communication, we can use peaceful means to resolve belief-threatening conflicts. We can learn to resolve these disputes without fighting with, cowering from, or running away from the person sharing the belief-threatening Information. Egoity can be thought of as just a friendly message helping us expose and remove resentment, not the opening bell of a boxing match.

Cause and Purpose of Egoity

As discussed earlier, belief-threatening Information is the spark that sets off the Egoity fire. It remains engaged as long as we can't accept or believe the shared Information. The sole cause of Egoity is the sharing of belief-threatening Information:

> The Information upsets us by the notion that our partner presumably is, did, or believes something that is contrary to our understanding of our partner (threatens a belief we have of our partner)
>
> OR...
>
> The Information upsets us by the notion that our partner presumably thinks that we are, did, or believe something that is contrary to our understanding of ourselves (threatens a belief we have of ourselves)

The threatening Information causes or *triggers* Egoity into protecting the belief, and it will continue do so for as long as it remains a belief. Here are some examples of Egoity triggers...

You have a Belief that...	Egoity Triggering Information
Your partner is not political.	You see a campaign sticker on your partner's car.
Your partner thinks you are their financial hero.	You overhear your partner asking *someone else* a finance question.
Your partner respects your privacy.	You see your partner barge into your room uninvited.
Your partner is considerate.	You see your partner text and check emails *constantly* during a romantic dinner.

There are, of course, countless other situations in which Egoity is triggered, yet all stem from threatening a belief with new Information. Egoity is evoked whenever our partner says or does something we don't like, and we are unable or refuse to change our belief about it.

The Rise and Fall of Egoity

1. You have a belief.

2. Your partner shares Information that threatens that belief.

3. At this point, your Egoity springs into action, causing you to fight with, cower from, or flee from your partner.

4. As long as the belief is held as unquestionably true, the only possible thing that would explain why your partner would ever share such Information is that, for some reason, *they are deliberately trying to hurt you*. Someone trying to force you to question and possibly denounce your belief feels the same as someone trying to force you to question the worthiness of your family, home, liberty, or life. At this point, you feel that the belief is *part of you*. Your Egoity will protect it as long as you (your belief) feel threatened by your partner.

5. The instant you are able to transform your belief into a postulate that can be scrutinized, the desire and need to protect it vanishes, eliminating the need for Egoity. You no longer feel your partner is trying to hurt you, and instead see them on the same side of the net. It is now the *belief* that is challenged.

Here are the three ways Egoity helps protect your belief:

1. Attacking your partner **protects** your belief.

2. Shielding from your partner **protects** your belief.

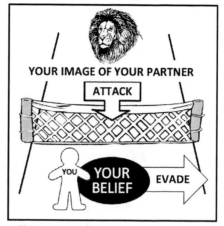

3. Evading your partner **protects** your belief.

When you stop feeling the need to *protect* a belief from scrutiny, your Egoity stops. At that point, you stop seeing your partner on the other side of the net and begin working together, not against each other.

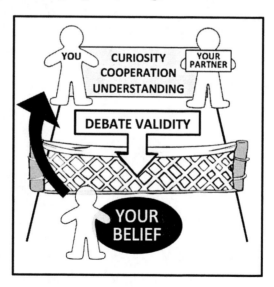

Your Egoity, like any other autonomic response, is only there for protection. When you relinquish the need to *protect* a belief, the Egoity tasked to protect it *naturally and automatically vanishes.*

Reaction to Belief-Threatening Information

Let's say you decide to wear an accessory and your partner feels that it doesn't go with your clothing. If your partner elects to confront you on your selection, your Egoity may engage – *for protection*. You may not have too much vested in your pride of fashion sense and be totally open to its criticism. Yet the more pride you have in your fashion sense, the more likely you will dislike the criticism, causing your Egoity to sound an alarm. You may silently admit to your wardrobe malfunction and hold a grudge - flight, vehemently defend our choice - fight, or protect your belief in some other way.

We all know that feeling. Our partner says something that rubs us wrong. We feel that sudden change in our own attitude as we get that "hairs-standing-upon-the-back-of-our-neck" sensation. As described at the beginning of this chapter, for at least that brief moment, our Egoity takes control and we are fighting with our partner.

By understanding the cause and purpose of that one moment of startlement, we arm ourselves with the knowledge needed to regain control and prevent the conversation from eroding any further.

When we protect our beliefs, we are only protecting them from scrutiny. It's like becoming a world champion boxer, and then *protecting* the title by not accepting any challenge bouts. To protect the title from the "scrutiny" of others, any contenders wishing for a title match may be verbally abused (fight), accused of badgering (fright), or ignored (flight).

Egoity, the Watchdog

Egoity is the reaction (protection) to Information that threatens an understanding or belief. Think of the job of a watchdog. When a perceived threat draws near, a watchdog starts barking. For our own protection, we want this to occur. Our dog is warning us that an unknown entity is approaching our front door. At this point, if we were curious about what was out there, we would pat the dog on its head, whisper "I'll  take it from here," take control of the situation, and answer the door.

Yet what if we allowed our dog to continue barking as we closed our eyes, covered our ears, trembled in fear, and did nothing? By our not taking control, our watchdog would continue to ward off whatever was out there. It may be a friend, a thief, or even a representative from Publishers Clearing House holding a giant check. We will never know until our curiosity overrides our vulnerability, and we take control and answer the door.

Remember our Understanding/Vulnerability Model?

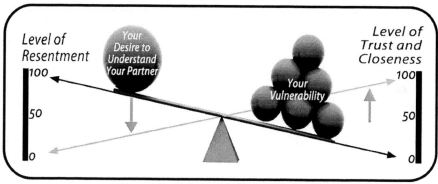

Diagram 17: Understanding/Vulnerability Model

Once our desire to understand (curiosity) is great enough, our vulnerability is outweighed and we take control. Until then, we are too afraid to face "what may be out there." Instead of trying to understand, we close our eyes, cover our ears, and let our Egoity run the show.

Our Egoity is very much like the actions of a watchdog. It warns us that Information has been shared that is not congruent with a current understanding or belief. Our Egoity springs into action, taking control, and will continue to "bark" until we figuratively pat it on its head and *take back* control. We take back control by being *curious* about what was said or done, overriding our initial reaction of judgment and vulnerability.

Egoity Is the Messenger, Not the Problem

Yes, this point was made earlier, yet it cannot be overemphasized. Egoity is simply a "messenger boy" for resentment. Resentment is the problem, not Egoity. Egoity is the normal, natural, self-preservation, and knee-jerk reaction caused by the condition of resentment.

When you hear belief-threatening Information, the first twinge of Egoity is to notify you that there has been a disturbance in your belief universe.

Wouldn't it be nice if you were to interpret that initial twinge of Egoity like someone politely tapping you on the shoulder and quietly whispering...

> *"Excuse me... but something was just said that is not in accord with something you believe."*

All your Egoity is doing is letting you know that something is wrong, like a smoke alarm or watchdog. Yet without understanding Egoity, and allowing it and our imagination to run wild, our interpretation of the *exact same feeling* could be like someone jumping around and frantically screaming...

> **"WE'RE UNDER ATTACK!!! FIGHT, HIDE, RUN!!! DO SOMETHING!!!"**

In either case, Egoity is only a messenger of the problem, not the problem itself. Without this understanding, Egoity is vilified and shunned, just like the proverbial messenger of bad news. Conversations that may evoke Egoity are avoided since fighting, cowering, and fleeing are generally unpleasant for both you and your partner. Yet purposely evading Egoity does not make the issue go away, nor let you know the real problem.

Don't Blame the Messenger!

Suppressing Egoity is like shunning and verbally abusing a mail carrier just because they deliver bills and credit card statements. Having an attack dog in your yard to keep the mail carrier away does not eliminate the issue of mounting debt.

In fact, willful ignorance can only make the debt problem worse by keeping you in the dark as to the severity of the issue. Evading the message of debt will not and does not keep the bank from repossessing your car or home.

Letting Egoity deliver the message of resentment reveals to us the source of the issue, which can then be properly addressed. Whether or not you allow the Egoity message to be delivered, the underlying resentment will still cause havoc with your relationship.

Discovering Your Relationship "Leak"

Let's say you find out your car has a tire with a slow leak. You take it to your friendly neighborhood service station to see if the tire can be repaired, hoping you don't need to buy a replacement. To find the hole in the tire, the service person might inflate it to normal pressure, spray it with water, and see where air bubbles come out. Once the leak is 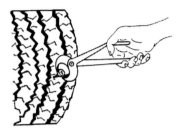 pinpointed, the spraying of water is stopped. The tire is sprayed with water just long enough to locate the leak – no more, no less. Based on the location and severity of the puncture, the tire may or may not be repairable, yet the spraying did show the location of the leak.

Resentment is like a tire leak. We can choose to ignore it, limp on down the shoulder on the rim, and eventually ruin our relationship like driving on a flat tire. Or we could choose to be responsible and experience the uneasiness of discovering our relationship "leak" by "spraying" it with Egoity. Egoity should be evoked just long enough to pinpoint the resentment – no more, no less.

Warnings Are to be Heeded, not Disabled

Another way of looking at Egoity as "just the messenger" is thinking of it like you would a home security system. When the alarm goes off, it is meant to be disruptive. The disruption warns us that something is threatening our home's security. Once the alarm has our attention, we can turn it off and address the issue.

The alarm is only the messenger, not the issue. Disabling the security system to avoid getting disrupted does not prevent intruders from invading our home. In order to feel secure and be responsible when an issue arises, we should *want* to be disrupted. In the case of a home security system, you know why you want to be disrupted.

Similarly, for effective Interaction, we need to know why Egoity happens and why it needs to disrupt. It is warning us that a belief is being threatened like a security alarm warns us that our house is being threatened. Without this knowledge and seeing this as a warning, we might be tempted to "disable" our Egoity since it would be seen as the problem itself. The resentment lives on as we try to stifle the warning.

The Little Town of Obliviousville

Once upon a time there was a little town named Obliviousville where the people all lived peacefully. The biggest industry and building in town was the Owell paper factory. Just for kicks, an evil spell-caster cast an evil spell upon the entire town. This spell made everybody forget the purpose of fire alarms. They simply didn't know or remember why fire alarms existed.

One morning, the alarm on the side of the building started blaring. A crowd gathered and everybody stared at the alarm in amazement. After all, they didn't know why the alarm was making all that noise.

"You know what," said Mildred. "I think it is just in its nature make all that noise. We're just going to have to put up with the noise until it goes away, and move when we can't take any more."

"I think we should shoot it," said George, loading his shotgun. "Something that makes that much racket needs to be shut up."

"Hold on, hold on," pleaded Phil. "We don't have to be destructive. If we put a blanket or two over it, maybe the noise can be muffled."

Just then little Tommy shouted to the crowd. "Maybe we should ask Professor Nesbitt! She's the smartest person in town!"

Professor Nesbitt was summoned to the paper factory and carefully assessed the situation. After a few minutes, she walked up a ladder to the alarm, lifted up a weather guard, and unplugged the alarm's power cord.

The crowd cheered as the alarm fell silent. The noise, at last, was gone. Soon, the crowd dispersed and everyone in Obliviousville went back to their regular way of life.

****

Oh, by the way, later that day, the Owell paper factory burned down to the ground.

As you can see, ignoring, silencing, stifling, or disabling a warning alarm can have devastating results. The people of Obliviousville paid the price for not knowing the difference between a warning and a nuisance. Understanding this difference can help you see Egoity for what it really is. The more you ignore, silence, stifle, or attempt to disarm your Egoity, the less aware you are of the resentment fire that is threatening to destroy your relationship.

Disabling a smoke alarm only increases the chance of a fire destroying a home. Similarly, avoiding conversations that may evoke Egoity only strengthens the underlying resentment, since it is allowed to continue to fester and grow. Any attempt to dismantle or ignore our Egoity only increases the chance of resentment destroying our relationship.

Avoiding Egoity by not communicating is like choosing not to cook just to make sure the smoke alarm doesn't go off. We understand that there is an acceptable degree of smoke and heat that can occur without the fear of setting the alarm off. And even if we do burn up the bacon and set off the alarm, at least we know what caused it and how to clear the air.

By understanding that there is an acceptable degree of "smoke and heat" that can occur during conversations, we can freely express ourselves without fear. The more we know about Egoity, we more we can respect its presence and recognize its purpose. When our Egoity alarm goes off due to the smoke of burning resentment, we will know what caused it and what needs to be resolved to "clear the air" in our relationship. Of course that assumes our Egoity alarm is properly set so that it alerts us when the resentment smoke is sensed, and not before.

Lack of Egoity Control Extremes

To better understand the nature and power of Egoity, let's look at the inherent dangers that exist when it is allowed to be totally out of control. In this section, we take a look at the effects of Egoity when its lack of control approaches its extremes – all the way off, or all the way on, all the time.

Think of the effects of watering a houseplant: If you don't know how to control the faucet and how much water to use, it's very likely that you will either water it too little, or water it too much. Of course, either option is harmful to the plant.

The same thing is true when it comes to Egoity. If we don't know how to control it and how much to use, it is very likely Egoity will not react properly, causing harmful effects in our relationship. Let's look into what happens when...

1. Our Egoity fails to evoke when it normally would – Infatuation
2. Our Egoity evokes when it normally wouldn't – Abhorrence

Infatuation: Egoity Is Always OFF

When belief-threatening Information is shared and our Egoity does not warn us, we are experiencing **infatuation**. It's what happens when our Egoity smoke alarm fails to goes off when it normally would. Depending on its intensity and your point of view, infatuation can have different names, such as obsession, adoration, spellbound, smitten, in-love, beguiled, puppy love, and lust.

For whatever reason, for a particular person or thing, we override or ignore our normal Egoity response. It's like we unplug or take the batteries out of our Egoity smoke alarm. We choose to discount, disbelieve, or justify the belief-threatening Information, or alter our conflicting belief ("change our mind") to agree with the new Information. We do whatever it takes to avoid conflict and confrontation.

You develop a belief that the person you are infatuated with is "perfect – just the way they are" and you accept everything that person is, does, and believes. This belief overrides all conflicting Information.

Infatuation Responses - Example #1

Belief: My partner will NEVER insult me in front of my mother.

Belief-Threatening Information: Your partner insults you in front of your mother.

Discount/Disbelieve Response: "My partner didn't mean it. My partner must be joking."

Justified Response: "Everyone's entitled to their opinion."

Agreement Response: "My partner WOULD insult me in front of my mother."

Infatuation Responses - Example #2

Belief: My partner will not get drunk every night.

Belief-Threatening Information: Your partner gets drunk every night for a week.

Discount/Disbelieve Response: "It's just a phase. This will be the last time my partner does that."

Justified Response: "My partner works so hard and needs to unwind."

Agreement Response: "It's OK if my partner gets drunk every night."

Although your Egoity does not get engaged with the person or thing that you are infatuated with, it is evoked when outside Information threatens your overriding infatuation belief. For example, family and friends may try to point out that your partner is rude and a drunk, and that you shouldn't accept that. Your Egoity immediately springs into action and protects your belief by fighting with, cowering from, or evading the source of the threatening Information.

Infatuation can be thought of like a stuck needle on a gauge. We even have expressions like "I am stuck on you" or "I can't help myself" when we are infatuated with someone. All the trouble in the film *The China Syndrome* stemmed from the fact that there was a stuck needle in a coolant level gauge at a nuclear power plant. The supervisor took actions that he felt were best based on the level as indicated on that faulty gauge. When enough conflicting Information made him doubt the reading, he tapped his finger on the gauge, dislodging the stuck needle, and revealing the REAL coolant level, which was dangerously low.

Infatuation means the needle on our Egoity gauge is stuck on "OFF." When our Egoity needle gets unstuck, our natural and normal reactions to threatening Information resume.

Abhorrence: Egoity Is Always ON

When our Egoity is evoked without the presence of belief-threatening Information, we are experiencing **abhorrence**. It's what happens when our Egoity smoke alarm goes off when there isn't any smoke. Abhorrence can have different names, such as hatred, loathing, detestation, and repellence. For whatever reason, for a particular person or thing, our Egoity always seems to be evoked. Our Egoity smoke alarm blares constantly or at the slightest hint of smoke, and we can't turn it off. At its extreme, everything this person or thing does is seen as hostile.

Abhorrence, like infatuation, can be thought of like a stuck needle on a gauge. This time, the needle is stuck in the "ON" position. Until we dislodge the needle, we are unable to see the issue through curious eyes. Again, when our Egoity needle gets unstuck, our natural and normal reactions to threatening Information resume, and we are able to address the conflict rationally.

Effective Egoity Control

Your Egoity control may be set to be totally passive and trustful, and allow anyone to get close to you. Or your Egoity control may be set to not trust anyone, and growl and snap at anyone who gets close to you. Each extreme is dangerous in its own way. Like watering a houseplant too little or too much. Somewhere in between is a healthy medium.

In the World of Heating Systems…

Infatuation is… Setting the thermostat too low so that the heater is never on.

Abhorrence is… Setting the thermostat too high so that the heater is always on.

Effective Egoity Control: Setting the thermostat so the heater goes on and off when it should.

In the World of Houseplants…

Infatuation is… Not watering enough.

Abhorrence is… Watering too much.

Effective Egoity Control: Watering the right amount.

In the World of Watchdogs…

Infatuation is… Sleeping through a home invasion.

Abhorrence is… Barking at and biting a postal carrier.

Effective Egoity Control: Warning its owner only when there is a threat.

We take dogs to obedience school so that they can have better social behavioral skills. Yet it is mostly the OWNERS of the dogs who are getting trained at these schools, *not* the dogs. WE are trained how and when to discipline or reward to get a desired behavior from our dog. It is our hope that little Spunky will eventually learn *on its own* not to bark at mailman  Mario. Until such time, at least *we* know what to do to calm down Spunky and regain control of the situation.

Effective Egoity control means it is evoked when a threat is detected, yet not before. Just like a properly trained watchdog, Egoity is properly trained when it warns us when it should, and settles down on our command. Before any of that is possible, we need to train ourselves and learn how to get our Egoity under control. Welcome to The Melfox Egoity Obedience School!

Regaining Control of Egoity

As discussed earlier in this chapter, Egoity is a built-in, critical animal survival reflex that should be highly valued and respected. Any shared Information that threatens a preconceived understanding or belief evokes our Egoity. Understanding, controlling, and *utilizing* our Egoity allows us to effectively engage in Interaction and civilly resolve our conflicts.

Effective conflict resolution requires us to allow the door to our Egoity room to open, even though there are scary things lurking inside. Many of us simply feel too vulnerable to let that door open. We'll do anything *to avoid conflict*. When we have allowed that door to swing wide open in the past, it has caused nothing but arguments, bitterness, and more resentment.

By not understanding the nature of Egoity, we don't know how to control it. As a result, we have learned to avoid saying or doing *anything* that might open that door. Ironically and tragically, it is *those very things* that need to be shared if the conflicts surrounding them are to be resolved. By understanding Egoity, we learn how to control it. Effective conflict resolution is not preventing the door to our Egoity to open; *it's learning how to close the door.*

Learning to Take Control

One of a parent's objectives is to gradually relinquish control of their child's life as they steadily learn to control themselves. Take playing outside, for example. At a certain age, we were trusted to play outside without Helicopter Mom constantly looking over our shoulder. Then later on, we didn't need Mom to be around at all. Of course there may not always be an agreement on when certain freedoms should be granted. There are times when a child wants to take control of something, yet the parent still feels the need to be in control. You know she's just trying to help, yet there comes a time when it can be embarrassing for your Mom to hold your hand when crossing the street, especially in front of your date. Hopefully long before that, you learned how to take control of the responsibility of walking across the street from your Mom by showing and advising her that you could do it yourself.

Think of Egoity as a mother who never ever stops looking out for you. Like a responsible parent, Egoity is concerned with your safety and survival, and will warn you and *take control* if it ever feels you are threatened. We should welcome any warning from our Egoity; we just don't need it to take control. You may not be able to prevent Mom from warning you to look both ways before crossing the street; you just need to let her know you don't need her to hold your hand.

So how do we calm Egoity down and take control again? It's not like we can magically regain control with a simple push of a button. But wouldn't it be cool if we could? Remember our Belief-O-Meter® from earlier in this chapter? Imagine having a machine that instantly shows your internal rating for any belief, from "Strongly Agree" to "Strongly Disagree." Now imagine that same machine can instantly have you regain control with a push of a button.

Beatrice and Bruno's Birthday

One day, as Bruno's birthday was fast approaching, Beatrice went to Jim's T-Shirt-A-Rama and picked out the perfect gift. After carefully wrapping it, she gave the gift to Bruno.

At that moment, if asked, Beatrice's rating for the belief statement: *"Bruno will love the birthday present I got"* would be around "Somewhat Agree." She was giddily optimistic that Bruno would *just love* the lime-green T-shirt she got for his birthday. Let's see how that registers and what it looks like on her Belief-O-Meter® seen here:

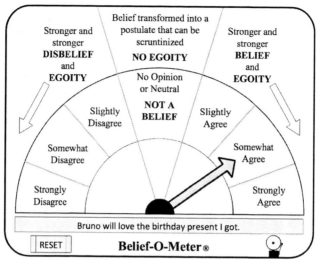

Diagram 18: Belief-O-Meter® Initial Beatrice Belief

All was well and Beatrice smiled while Bruno unwrapped the tissue, opened the box, and lifted up a lime-green T-shirt. Through nonverbal language and words, Beatrice began to realize that maybe Bruno wasn't all that keen with the present. At that moment, the Information Bruno shared with Beatrice threatened her belief that "*Bruno will love the birthday present I got.*":

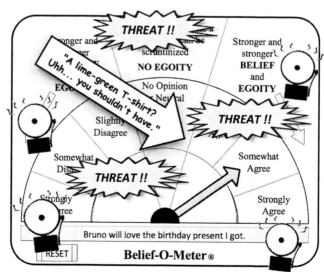

Diagram 19: Belief-O-Meter® Beatrice Belief Threat

From this point on, and until Beatrice changes her belief, her Egoity is evoked and she will fight with, cower from, or flee from Bruno and his belief-threatening Information. Here are a few examples of Beatrice's words, actions, and attitude:

FIGHT (The Lion)

Intimidation: "Oh, you hate everything I give you, don't you?"

Belittlement: "You have no taste when it comes to fashion."

Authoritativeness: "Lime-green is in!" (Don't cha know)

FRIGHT (The Turtle)

Victimization: "Oh, I never give you the right gift." (Sniffle)

Sensitiveness: "I have great taste in fashion; go ask my friends!"

Antagonism: "Go ahead; just throw it away!" (See if I care)

FLIGHT (The Deer)

Elusiveness: "Alrighty then… uhhh… Let's have cake!"

Escapism: "That's it. I'm outta here!" (Cue door slam)

And so it goes. Resentment builds up from the conflicting beliefs. Beatrice's Egoity is evoked whenever Information is shared that threatens her belief that Bruno loves the present she gave. Meanwhile, her Belief-O-Meter® is flashing lights and blaring alarms.

As long as Beatrice holds onto that belief, she is figuratively placing the "battle-line tennis net" squarely between herself and Bruno, *not* between them and resentment. The belief is strong enough to overpower her desire to understand Bruno and respect his honest opinion. And, of course, resentment caused by this conflict will grow and affect their relationship indefinitely.

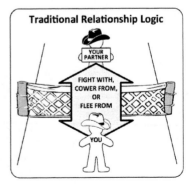

At any time, Beatrice could recognize her

Egoity was evoked and ask herself why it was. When Egoity is evoked, it's sometimes difficult to break its spell. But what if Beatrice's Belief-O-Meter® had a reset button? What if she could simply push a button, and the rating for her belief would reset? Just for fun, let's visually see what that would look like:

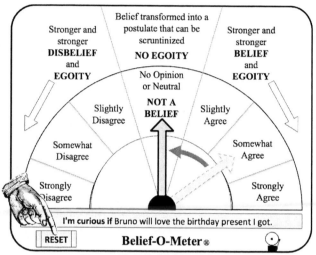

Diagram 20: Belief-O-Meter® Reset

As well as the rating, you may have noticed that the statement on the Belief-O-Meter® has magically changed. It now reads: "*I'm curious if my partner will love the birthday present I got.*"

Beatrice's belief was magically changed into a postulate that can be challenged. The statement needed to be altered so that it could be evaluated and scrutinized with Bruno's new Information. After the evaluation, the new postulate can then be changed back into a belief statement with a rating based on the impact of the new Information.

If Beatrice misunderstood Bruno and he *does* love the gift, the belief rating would revert back to the "Agree" side. If Bruno confirmed his dislike for the shirt, then the same belief would have a "Disagree" rating.

In either case, the new Information is used in the evaluation of the belief, instead of seen as a threat. This is the essence of effective conflict resolution. The quality of our Interaction is dependent upon our ability to convert threatened beliefs into postulates.

Resetting Your Belief

In order to reset your internal Belief-O-Meter® and regain control of Egoity, you need to either change the threatened belief statement, or change the way you look at it. You could alter the statement to be an inquiring phrase introducing a hypothesis like these:

> *"I'm curious if ... my partner will love the birthday present I got."*
>
> *"I wonder if ... my partner will love the birthday present I got."*

Or you could change it into a conditional statement like these:

> *"Based on the Information I have so far...*
> *my partner will love the birthday present I got."*
>
> *"My partner will love the birthday present I got...*
> *based on my current level of awareness."*

Or simply add a statement at the end of the original belief that makes it a challengeable postulate. Something like:

> *"My partner will love the birthday present I got. **I wonder if that is so.**"*

You can only scrutinize a postulate of curiosity, not a statement of absolute.

Taming Egoity

In the previous section, we discussed how to regain control of your Egoity by changing a threatened belief into a postulate that can be scrutinized. If there were just one belief threatened one time, this would be all we needed to do. However an Interaction is likely to contain a multitude of threatened beliefs that are each threatened multiple times. We learned how to settle a startled horse. In order to *tame* a horse, we need to calm it down every time it is startled, until eventually it feels that there is nothing to fear and learns to trust us.

Defending the Belief: "My partner will love the present I got"

1. Thinking you need to "win" the argument by holding on to the belief

2. Thinking you need to be "right" by maintaining that your belief is "right"

3. Thinking you need to be superior to your partner by holding onto the belief

4. Thinking that abandoning a belief would somehow tarnish your reputation

5. Thinking you should never offend nor be offended (activating your inner Deer)

For Interaction and conflict resolution to proceed effectively, we have to figuratively push the reset button on our Belief-O-Meter® every time a belief is threatened. This is what we will call *taming* Egoity. Each time we "push reset" on a belief and change it into a postulate, we at least temporarily overcome the concerns in our internal dialog that are associated with the original belief.

Scrutinizing the Postulate: "*I wonder if* my partner will love the present I got"

1. Curious whether the postulate is correct or incorrect, not caring who "wins"

2. Curious whether the postulate is correct or incorrect, not caring if it's "right"

3. Curious whether the postulate is correct or incorrect, not really caring who is "better"

4. Curious whether the postulate is correct or incorrect, not caring what anyone will think

5. Curious whether the postulate is correct or incorrect, knowing that "offending" is possible

Horse Sense

Taming our Egoity is similar to taming a horse, or anything else that is wild or easily startled. A bona fide horse trainer knows not to *fight with, cower from,* or *run away from* an untamed horse just because it rears up. Spooked horses may flare up, but *trainers* don't. They know that flare-ups from untamed horses are normal and natural. How quickly they can settle a horse is what matters. The trainer knows  to calm down the horse as quickly as possible, and as often as needed.

My Last Time on a Horse

I don't have much experience with horses. With one blaring exception, I've been content with those controlled vacation trail rides. On the last one, my steady steed and I were toward the back of a group of around twenty. I was enjoying the average run-of-the-mill ride when a loud crack of a branch suddenly sounded above the trail leader.

The lead horse was spooked and took off at a gallop. The second horse ran too, yet not as much as the lead. The third one even less, and so on. The horses back in the pack were noticeably startled, yet few ran at all.

The moment my horse got scared, I could feel the fear beneath me. With my inexperience, it was rather intimidating to be on something that is fearful for its life, even for a split second.

Soon the excitement was over, and we all got back in line and resumed our relaxing ride.

Looking back on my horse adventure, it is interesting to ponder the reactions each horse had when the branch cracked. For the most part, the horses closest to the branch reacted the most. But proximity to the perceived threat is only one variable.

Another factor of how much a horse reacted might have been their experience with falling branches. If a horse had experienced the pain of a branch falling on them in the past, the threat would be perceived as more real and have more strength than for other horses. Still another factor for how much a horse reacted might have been the relative experience of the rider. One could tell how experienced the riders were by how quickly and confidently they settled their horse.

Think of Egoity as the actions of a startled horse. As listed earlier, here are some factors that determine the strength and extent of Egoity in the story:

1. **Extent to which we value the threatened belief:**
   How much do we have invested in or how much do we identify with the belief? The horse is VERY invested in the belief, since falling branches may be fatal. Someone on the back of a horse should want the horse to be instinctively startled at a cracking branch, since running away could be the very thing to that saves them both.

2. **Extent to which we value the sharer of the threat:**
   What is the relationship worth to you? If you don't really care to be riding on a horse, after the spooking you may be tempted to end "your relationship" by getting off and walking. In this case, the value placed on the relationship is low. It might be slightly higher if the nearest sign of civilization is 50 miles away.

3. **Extent to which the belief is threatened:**
   What is the immediate degree of danger from the threat? Horses and their riders closer to the cracking branch have a higher probability of getting hurt. Those of us farther away had a much lower degree of danger.

4. **Extent to which we understand the fundamentals of Egoity:**
   How well can you control your Egoity? How quickly can you turn a belief into a postulate? Trained and seasoned riders can settle a startled horse more quickly than newbies. By learning the nature of horses and with experience, anyone can learn to quickly and confidently control a startled horse.

Just like with horses, by learning the nature of Egoity and with experience, anyone can learn to quickly and confidently control it. We can learn to tame our Egoity by changing the threatened belief into a postulate, yet we have to know when to hit the "reset" button. The reaction we need to have with Egoity is the same type of reaction we already have when we touch something too hot.

The Human Circuit Breaker

Remember the science experiment in the *Information* chapter in which we demonstrated the "right" temperature for a conversation? Not so cold that the conversation is meaningless; yet not so hot that it exceeds the breaking point.

When you get "hot-under-the-collar" or "hot-tempered" with your partner, what is your breaking point? How soon can you tell that Egoity has taken over since a belief has been threatened? Do you know what to do when you reach your breaking point?

Arguments and other Egoity displays can heat up a conversation to the point that it's "too hot" and causes damage. As soon as you realize that your Egoity has been evoked, internally hit the Belief-O-Meter® reset button, take control, and change whatever belief being threatened into a postulate. Doing that is like tripping the circuit when it gets too hot.

Sometimes the simple act of *knowing* that you are in Egoity takes effort. The sooner you realize you are in Egoity, the sooner you can cool the conversation. Once a candle is lit, blow out the match or risk burning your finger. You are sometimes too close to the situation to know when you are in Egoity.

Wouldn't it be nice if loud music would play and a toy duck would drop down from the ceiling every time your Egoity was evoked? That way you would instantly know a belief was being threatened and change it into a postulate to be scrutinized. As we will see in the *Interaction* chapter, there are many ways to recognize something, once you know what to look for.

SPOILER ALERT: Many involve your partner!

Training Egoity

In the first part of this chapter, we discussed the overall concept of Egoity: its definition; its history; its cause and purpose. Before that, you may have only thought of Egoity as something that needed to be avoided and shunned. It probably has always been thought of like a big, ugly monster-dog that needed to be kept locked up in the cellar. As if horrific stories are told at bedtime and around campfires of times when Egoity was allowed to run amok scaring small children and the elderly. We all have stories of damage caused by unrestrained Egoity. We may try to keep it locked away, out of fear. After all, you always *fear* what you don't *understand*.

After learning about and *understanding* Egoity we may feel comfortable enough to open the cellar doors and peek inside. We learned to hit the "reset" button, and settle Egoity down when it growls and barks. The lesson continued with teaching that taming Egoity is the continuous process of settling it down whenever it gets evoked. Congratulations! You have completed the classroom lessons of The Melfox Egoity Obedience School. Your Egoity is now more or less housebroken, at least on paper (pardon the pun). In this section we will learn how to *use* Egoity. We will revisit the *purpose* of Egoity and see how exposing Egoity can help us discover the underlying resentment in our conflicts.

Understanding Radiators

I spent my senior year in college living with two roommates in *The Ship's Inn* room of an old fraternity house. When the temperature dropped low enough, it was time to turn on the room's heater, which was an old steam radiator. My roommates and I tried to turn on the heat by opening the valve. This caused an unpleasant odorous gas to escape, so we quickly shut it off.

Admittedly, none of us knew much about steam radiators. I figured the valve was to a gas line that shouldn't be opened. Needless to say, after awhile the room got pretty cold. I remember putting a sign on our door renaming the room *The Ice Palace* and spent as little time in there as possible.

We must have gone at least a few days in that room as the temperature dropped. Eventually, someone came into the room who *understood* steam radiators. He went right over to it and opened that same valve we were fearful to open. The gaseous odor escaped like before, yet after awhile the hissing stopped and the valve was closed. He said that air sometimes collects in the pipe that needs to be bled out.

Once the air was allowed to escape, steam filled the radiator, which heated the room. *The Ship's Inn* was soon toasty warm and stayed that way throughout the winter.

Egoity is like that radiator. If we don't understand Egoity, we are hesitant to "open its valve" since it is, at first, unpleasant and seemingly dangerous. We would rather have cold conversations with our partner, or no conversations at all, than experience displeasure and risk burning our relationship down to the ground.

It is only when we sufficiently *understand* Egoity that we feel safe enough to open up its valve and warm up the Interaction enough to resolve conflict. Avoiding Egoity may turn your relationship into *The Ice Palace:* a place where you want to spend as little time as possible.

It is now time to see your Egoity put to work. It is time to see your tamed yet unemployed housedog as a helpful watchdog. You still have to maintain a strong grip on its collar, yet that doesn't mean it can't be helpful. Welcome to The Melfox Egoity Training School!

Bruno Being Bruno

Imagine you are Bruno in our birthday present episode. If you fear the reaction that Beatrice might have if you don't *just love* the present she gave, you may suppress your true feelings and only share Information that doesn't conflict with her belief that you *will* love it.

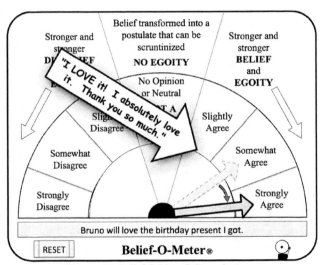

Diagram 21: Belief-O-Meter® Strongly Agree

In this case, Bruno has decided to *avoid conflict* by acting like he loved the lime-green T-shirt. Of course this only *transfers* the primary feeling of resentment from Beatrice to Bruno. In essence, Bruno is just *deferring* conflict to a later time. Eventually that resentment will rear its head when Beatrice notices Bruno never wears the shirt, or if Bruno finally admits he doesn't love it. Until such time, the resentment Bruno feels for receiving an unwanted gift and for having to pretend that he loved it will be just another piece of paper between Bruno's magnet and Beatrice's steel.

Cause and Purpose of Egoity Review

As discussed earlier this chapter, the purpose of Egoity is pretty simple. It is to point out when shared Information threatens a belief. Period. The moment we comprehend that our Egoity has been evoked, we should settle it down by identifying the threatened belief and take back control.

Allowing Egoity to continue after that point is not only useless; it is harmful to the conversation. Letting Egoity continue after realizing it has been evoked is like continuing to engage your car's starter after the engine has started. It serves no purpose, makes a lot of noise, and is harmful to the car.

Remember that Egoity is just the spark that exposes the belief threatened and the underlying resentment that threatens the relationship. A barking watchdog is just the spark, which identifies the intruder, which threatens its domain. Not taking control and allowing your watchdog to continuously bark can only interfere with your investigation of the intruder. Allowing your Egoity to "bark" can only interfere with your investigation of the resentment.

Congratulations! You have just completed the classroom lessons at The Melfox Egoity Training School. We have learned how to settle and tame your Egoity, and how it is useful. It is now time for a field trip. Let's get on Egoity's back and go for a ride.

Controlling Egoity During Interaction

As stated at the beginning of this chapter, the concept of Egoity as something *useful* may be a very difficult thing to comprehend. You have probably been told your whole life to "control your temper" and "don't lose your cool" without knowing how to effectively do that or even what it really means. So instead, you may resort to avoiding any conversations that *may* get heated.

And these conversations, ironically, are exactly the ones that need to take place *to resolve conflict*. If you go your whole life being afraid of something, it would be a difficult task learning to trust it. We have all experienced the pain and frustration of letting our defensiveness get the best of us during our attempts to resolve conflict. It is our lack of knowledge of Egoity that makes us fearful of it.

Imagine if you didn't know anything about controlling fire. You go out and build a nice log cabin somewhere complete with fireplace, and move in. Your first meal is going to be baked beans so you start a fire and begin adding logs. Since you don't know that the fire needs to be *controlled*, you put too many logs on the fire. The heat and fire will  get bigger and bigger as you add more logs, until the whole log cabin burns to the ground. You need someplace to live so you build another log cabin, and proceed to burn that one to the ground. After a while you may be hesitant to build fires at all. You may just end up shivering in a cold log cabin and settling for cold baked beans.

Just as we need to know how to control fire, we need to know how to control Egoity. Without this control, we risk either burning up our relationships, or settling for rather cold ones.

Controlling Egoity – The Show So Far

If we don't *understand* something, we naturally *fear* it. Without understanding Egoity and how to control it, we naturally fear (and have experienced) its destructive powers. Whenever we have allowed Egoity to run wild during moments of conflict, it always seemed to end up causing *more* conflict.

Many of us *want* to talk to our partner and resolve conflict, yet the closer we get to talking about resentment, the more our wild Egoity seems to burn up the conversation. We may think the only other option is to see our Egoity as something to be kept hidden away. We purposely avoid or trivialize any conversations that might evoke our wrath.

If Egoity were a horse, it would be seen as something so wild, it should be kept in the barn out of fear of hurting itself and others. Let's review what we have learned so far in regards to controlling Egoity. We'll begin by listing some basic steps in taming a horse. I'm sure this list doesn't match one that might be offered by *Horse & Hound* magazine, but it serves our purpose:

1. Open the barn door, walk up to the horse, and grab the reins.
2. When the horse rears, pull down on the reins and regain control.
3. Take the horse for a walk, regaining control as needed.
4. The horse is tamed to the extent that you can walk around the barn and maintain control.

Now, let's review the same type of steps needed to tame *Egoity*:

1. Have a confident understanding of Egoity fundamentals (cause, purpose, definition, etc…).

2. As soon as you realize Egoity has been evoked, change the threatened belief into a postulate that can be scrutinized, thus regaining control. *"What belief was just threatened?"*

3. During Interaction, each and every time you realize Egoity has been evoked, "reset" the threatened belief and regain control.

4. Egoity is "tamed" to the extent that you can have a conversation revealing conflict and still maintain control.

Of course, just like horse training, it takes more than just reading a list in a manual to know how to control Egoity. Learning from the manual means nothing if it's not applied. Real learning comes from practicing and experiencing what the manual says.

And as we all know, experience is the best teacher. A manual can only tell you what you are *going* to learn. A book on dancing may show you the different steps and tell you what foot goes where when, yet it is only through practice and experience that you train yourself to do the dances described in the book. I doubt that someone who has never danced before could just read a book and instantly qualify for *Dancing with the Stars*.

In the next chapter, *Interaction*, we will go outside the classroom with step-by-step advice for effective conflict resolution with your partner. It is only through practice and experience with your partner that you train yourself to apply *The Melfox Method*. Practicing effective Interaction is like dancing the tango; it takes two.

Riding Your Egoity Horse

Now that we've reviewed how to control your trusty steed, it is time to learn what it feels like to actually get on your Egoity horse and put it to use. Here is where we "break in" and ride Egoity. Some of this is a preview to what the next chapter is all about: engaging in Interaction with your partner and practicing all the lessons you have learned.

1. **Where and When?**
   As discussed in the *Environment* chapter, care should be taken when choosing the time and place for Interaction. It would be counterproductive, as well as inconsiderate, to jump on and try to ride a horse when it is sleeping, eating, driving, or on the phone with its mother.

2. **Interaction Initiation**
   Interaction begins. You get on the horse. You may encounter resistance at first, especially if your partner is not familiar with Egoity and how to control it. This is where you can put into practice the lessons learned in resetting your Belief-O-Meter®, changing your threatening beliefs into postulates, and regaining control.

3. **"Get Off My Back"**
   Throughout Interaction, there will be spats of Egoity from both sides. Just like a horse that is uncomfortable with a rider, when beliefs are threatened, there could be an urge to scream "GET OFF MY BACK!" from either partner. Effective Egoity control means overcoming that urge and realizing it's the *belief* that is doing the screaming.

4. **Using the Carrot, Not the Stick**
   You cannot use force and be successful using *The Melfox Method*. Aggression, frustration, and pleading are all signs of Egoity, and allowing it to fester can only create fear and hurt any attempts at effective conflict resolution. When riding a horse, compassion, patience, and a little TLC helps it to trust you, not fear you.

5. **Keeping Your Eye on the Prize**
   The entire *Outcome* chapter details many of the enormous benefits of effective conflict resolution. Controlling your Egoity throughout Interaction is a pivotal skill for its success, yet like with anything new, it requires practice and patience. If a horse knows the trail ends in a meadow of sweet clover, it may be more willing to put up with the hassle and this thing on its back.

Curiosity Kills Yet Another Spat

We are almost done with describing Egoity, and how to control and use it. There is a shortcut that, if properly and diligently applied, can help tremendously in controlling Egoity. We have discussed it before, yet it deserves repeating. It is the heart and soul of The Melfox Mindset – *Curiosity*.

As you know by now, much of this book centers on the Curiosity Mantra of resolving resentment by having a burning desire to understand your partner and for your partner to understand you. Part of this understanding involves being aware of Egoity evoked by both you and your partner. Seeing it as a helpful warning instead of an evildoer can help keep the conversation on track toward resolving conflicts.

Again, let's start out with our Curiosity Mantra:

When I speak, I will always be curious, not judgmental.
The words I use and the way I say them convey a sense of wonder
so that I understand my partner, and my partner understands me.
I have a burning desire to understand my partner,
and for my partner to understand me.

When I listen, I will always assume my partner
is being curious, not judgmental.
If there's ever a question of my partner's motive, I will calmly ask
so that I understand my partner, and my partner understands me.
I have a burning desire to understand my partner,
and for my partner to understand me.

The more we stay *curious* of Egoity, the more likely we are to discover new clues to resolve the issue, and the less likely it will be an obstruction to the conflict resolution process.

Your Belief on Trial

Whenever your Egoity is evoked, a threatened belief is put on the defense. Imagine at that moment, a mini-courtroom appears in your mind, with the belief in the witness box. It has been put on trial and accused of the crime of *being wrong*. Where are you in the proceedings? As long as your Egoity is evoked, you are the *defense attorney* and your partner is the *prosecuting attorney*. You conjure up supporting evidence and plead your case for your client, the belief. It is your job to spend all of your energy defending your belief and countering conflicting evidence from your partner.

Having *curiosity* about your belief helps to free you from defending it. It helps you hit the "reset" button and turn the threatened belief into a postulate that can be examined. You instantly see yourself and your partner in the *jury box*, working together with factual Information to resolve the conflict, instead of being on opposite sides in a court case.

Remember Beatrice

Let's go back to the Beatrice's Belief-O-Meter® for a second. The reset button not only changes her belief rating from "Somewhat Agree" to "Not A Belief," it also changes the belief statement to the challengeable postulate: *"**I'm curious if** Bruno will love the birthday present I got."*

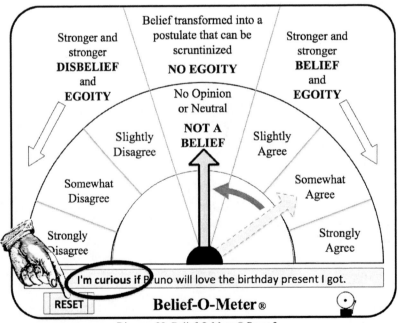

Diagram 22: Belief-O-Meter® Reset 2

Curiosity is a very powerful word and mindset. When the desire to *know* exceeds the desire to *defend*, Egoity is controlled. Curiosity can serve as the glue that keeps you and your partner on the same side of the net.

Your Anti-Resentment Security Software

Let's say that a belief is a free computer program that you download from the Internet. This program may or may not contain a virus, but if you *believe* it to be clean or don't even know to check, you will ignore any warnings and install the program. When you run the program, you will ignore or close out any irritating pop-up window from your built-in antivirus security software that warns you of an impending virus attack.

If you start to have computer problems, blaming it on the new program will not even be considered. At any time you could question your program's cleanliness, test it for viruses, discover it is the culprit, and purge it and its effects from your computer.

This "program-is-fine" *belief* at the time of the installation and beyond prevents you from even considering it could be the source of your computer issue. You may even give up and throw away your computer before ever considering it was the new program you installed that was causing the problem. Think of how differently your actions would be if you were *curious* about the virus warnings, instead of just seeing them as a *nuisance*.

So long as you think that your computer is maintenance-free and impervious to malicious programs, any "conflicts" you experience will be blamed on a faulty computer, not the programs. Imagine how many computers you would go through if you discarded them at the first sign of trouble. Yet isn't that what many of us do with our relationships?

Just like unverified software should be tested for viruses, beliefs should be tested for accuracy whenever Egoity warns us of a threat. Think of Egoity like your own built-in anti-resentment security software. *Curiosity* and respect of the warning help you overcome the desire to disable it. As long as you ignore or disable Egoity, the underlying resentment will continue to wreak havoc on your relationship until you give up and throw it away.

Egoity - Recap and Review

In this chapter we have discussed the following:

Introduction to Egoity

We learned that Egoity...

- Is a natural sympatho-adrenal response, just like ones to physical threats

- Overrides cognitive abilities to the extent of its intensity, just like ones to physical threats

- Is the startlement and possible hyperarousal protective response caused by interpreting Information as a threat to a belief

- Is evident by fighting with, cowering from, or fleeing from the source of the belief-threatening Information

- Varies in intensity and duration, depending on the type of relationship one has with the source of the belief-threatening Information, the subject discussed, and the Information exchanged

The Power of Beliefs

We learned that a belief...

- Is confidence in the truth or existence of something that is neither susceptible to, nor constantly scrutinized by, rigorous proof

- Has the upside of not having the constant burden of proof

- Has the downside of maybe being wrong, yet defended

- Has strength factors that include the amount of investment and the degree of identity you have with the belief.

- Needs to be changed into a postulate that can be scrutinized before Egoity can be controlled and effective conflict resolution can take place

Egoity in Action

Possible Egoity battles include:

1. Lion (fight) vs. Lion (fight). Shouting matches. Name-calling. Finger-pointing.

2. Lion (fight) vs. Turtle (shield). The Turtle feels distrust toward attacking Lion and inferior in regards to the subject discussed.

3. Lion (fight) vs. Deer (escape). The Lion attacks, yet the message is not received. The Deer evades, ignores, or escapes from the conversation.

When our Egoity ceases to control us, we take back control and see our partner "on the same side of the net."

Reasons for a belief being wrong are the same as the ones for resentment:

1. Lack of Sufficient, Pertinent Information
2. Misunderstanding
3. False Assumption
4. Jumping to False Conclusion

Resentment is the *fuel,* Egoity is the *fire,* and the sharing of Information is the *spark.*

Laws of Egoity

1. Extent of Egoity is inversely proportional to the desire for understanding the situation causing the Egoity

2. Extent of Egoity is inversely proportional to being "in control" (fully responsible and aware of your actions)

3. Extent of Egoity engagement is directly proportional to the extent you are battling with your partner or seeing them as an opponent

4. Extent of Egoity engagement directly reflects the extent of the underlying resentment

A Brief History of Egoity

When there are insufficient language skills for effective communication, then conflict resolution is impossible. Increased level and expansion of language enable us to communicate more effectively thus decreasing the need to fight, to cower, or to run away.

Cause and Purpose of Egoity

Egoity triggers include:

1. Sharing Information that upsets us by the notion that our partner presumably is, did, or believes something that is contrary to our understanding of our partner.

2. Sharing Information that upsets us by the notion that our partner presumably thinks that we are, did, or believe something that is contrary to our understanding of ourselves.

You use Egoity to protect a belief by:

1. Attacking your partner (Lion)
2. Shielding from your partner (Turtle) or
3. Evading your partner (Deer)

When you stop feeling the need to protect a belief from scrutiny, your Egoity stops.

Egoity Is the Messenger, Not the Problem

Egoity is the normal, natural, self-preservation, and knee-jerk reaction caused by the condition of resentment. The more you ignore, silence, stifle, or attempt to disarm your Egoity, the less aware you are of the resentment that is threatening to destroy your relationship.

Egoity Control Extremes

1. When belief-threatening Information is shared and our Egoity does not warn us, we are experiencing *infatuation*. For whatever reason, for a particular person or thing, we override or ignore our normal Egoity response.

2. When our Egoity is evoked without the presence of belief-threatening Information, we are experiencing *abhorrence*. For whatever reason, for a particular person or thing, our Egoity always seems to be evoked.

Effective Egoity control means it is evoked when a threat is detected, yet not before.

Regaining Control of Egoity

By understanding Egoity, we learn how to control it. By not understanding the nature of Egoity, we fear it, and have a tendency to avoid saying or doing anything that exposes the underlying conflict. Ironically and tragically, it is *those very things* that need to be shared if the conflicts surrounding them are to be resolved.

We control Egoity by changing the threatened belief into postulate that can be scrutinized. We can do this by:

1. Adding words to the beginning of the belief statement like "I'm curious if..." or "I wonder if..." or "Based on the Information I have received so far...".

2. Adding an amendment statement behind the belief like "I wonder if that is so."

Taming Egoity

For Interaction and conflict resolution to proceed effectively, we have to change the threatened belief into a postulate that can be scrutinized every time the belief is threatened.

Training Egoity

When you are able to control Egoity, you can then start using it for its intended purpose of exposing and identifying the underlying resentment.

Controlling Egoity During Interaction

Review of steps needed to tame Egoity:

1. Have a confident understanding of the basics of Egoity.
2. As soon as you realize Egoity has been evoked, change the threatened belief into a postulate that can be scrutinized, thus regaining control.
3. Each and every time you realize your Egoity has been evoked, "reset" it and regain control.
4. Egoity is "tamed" to the extent that you can have a conversation and maintain control.

Things to keep in mind during Interaction that can help you control and use Egoity:

1. Care should be taken when choosing the time and place for Interaction.
2. Resistance may be encountered at first, especially if your partner is not familiar with Egoity and how to control it.

3. Effective Egoity control means overcoming the urge to fight with your partner and realizing it's the threatened belief that should be scrutinized.

4. Aggression, frustration, and pleading are signs of Egoity, and allowing it to fester can only create fear and hurt any attempts at effective conflict resolution.

5. The *Outcome* chapter details many of the enormous benefits of effective conflict resolution.

Curiosity

We finished the chapter reiterating the importance of having a curiosity mindset and how that can help you turn beliefs into postulates, and thus control Egoity.

****

Now that we have established that a relationship's only enemy is resentment and have discussed its causes...

and that properly shared Information is the key to revealing those causes...

and that controlling Egoity enables Information to be shared properly...

How do we use Information and Egoity to reveal the causes of resentment and resolve conflict?

CHAPTER FOUR - INTERACTION

Beatrice and Bruno listened attentively as the personification of their relationship, "Beano," explained the concept of Egoity. He described how it is a normal natural response that gets triggered whenever a belief is threatened. "It just like a watchdog," he said. "You have to get it tamed, or it'll make a lot of noise and tear up the furniture. However, when it is properly trained, it is a resentment detection machine."

"Wow, this really makes sense," Beatrice said. "Our defensive outbursts are just ways of dealing with threatened beliefs. It is our beliefs that need to be challenged, not each other."

"No wonder we could never resolve anything," Bruno added. "We were focusing our attention on defending beliefs, not resolving the issues."

"Exactly!" Beano coughed into his jacket sleeve. "Egoity is the protective door that you two kept ramming into every time you tried to talk. Egoity does not allow you to enter the room of understanding when a belief is threatened." He coughed again and took a sip of water.

"The real trick to controlling Egoity is simply understanding what it is," Beano added. "By understanding its cause and purpose, you can use it to find the reasons for resentment, resolve conflicts, and restore your relationship."

Beatrice and Bruno were beginning to see what they had been sorely missing in their relationship: an effective way of maintaining it.

"Now that you understand the concepts of Information and Egoity, let's put them together, and put them to work," Bruno said, rubbing his hands together. "So far, it's just been talk. It is time to take some action."

****

Interaction - The Solution

Here and now is where the rubber meets the road. Some say that "Knowledge Is Power" is a misnomer and that it should be "Applied Knowledge Is Power." Well, if the previous chapters were knowledge, this chapter is where you apply it. Like Beano said, Interaction is the integrating of Information and Egoity. The last two chapters are the ingredients, and in this one we will measure them out, mix them up, and make an effective solution.

Cooperation, Teamwork, and Common Goals

A winning team knows that working together harmoniously brings out the best in everyone and gives them the best chance for success. Yet what is seen as success, the goal, may be different from person to person. This holds true in business, sports, and personal relationships.

When people work together to achieve a common goal and keep their collective Egoity in check, the results can be amazing. Businesses use mission statements and periodic meetings to help everyone stay in sync toward a common goal. Sports teams use signals before and during plays, to ensure everyone is on the same page.

On the other hand, constant bickering between co-workers with cross-purposes creates an uncooperative workplace, and productivity suffers as a result. In doubles tennis, the more out of sync the partners are, the lower their chances for success, and the less enjoyable their experience.

When attempting conflict resolution, how often are you out of sync, have your signals crossed, or not on the same page with your partner? You have the common goal of resolving conflict, yet that is not enough. After all, you may feel that the conflict will be resolved only when the other person "gives in" and admits they were wrong. In that way, the conflict can be resolved without the need for you to ever examine any of your beliefs.

It may be true that your partner is wrong about some of their beliefs, yet as we discussed earlier, it is just as likely *you* are wrong about some of *your* beliefs. For effective conflict resolution, you need to work together as a team. You need to see that resentment is the enemy, and have the common goal of getting to its root cause and restore the relationship.

For that to happen, you need effective Interaction.

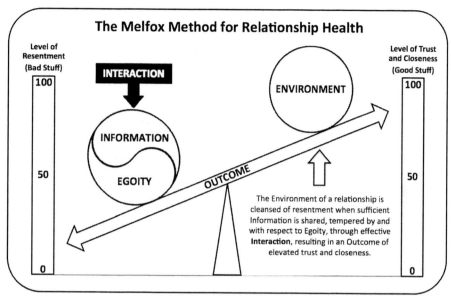

Diagram 23: *The Melfox Method* Model featuring Interaction

In this chapter, we will be exploring the melding of Information and Egoity in action. Effective Interaction, like any other skill, requires knowledge, patience, and practice. Do not expect to be an expert the first time you do it.

Learning a new skill or achieving any worthy accomplishment has its moments of pain, discomfort, and messiness. But when it's done, it's done, and the reward is sweet. Learning effective Interaction is no different. Paraphrasing the words of author Art Williams:

> *I'm not going to tell you it's going to be easy.*
> *I am telling you it's going to be worth it.*

Effective Interaction

An important concept to understand is that the quality of Interaction depends on the quality of Information shared *and* the extent to which Egoity is kept under control. Effective Interaction is impossible if shared Information is not proper *or* Egoity is not controlled.

The Product of Proper Information and Controlled Egoity

Interaction is the product of Information and Egoity. In other words, it can be thought of like a multiplication expression: Information times Egoity equals Interaction. Properly shared Information shared, along with controlled Egoity, creates the opportunity for effective Interaction.

If Proper Information is:	And Controlled Egoity is:	Then Effective Interaction is:
Clean Water	Quality Soap	A Clean Face
The Color Blue	The Color Red	The Color Purple
Two Atoms of Hydrogen	One Atom of Oxygen	One Molecule of Water
The Number Three	The Number Three	The Number Nine
Mass	Velocity	Momentum
An Eager Student	A Competent Teacher	Quality Learning

If the quality of Information shared *or* the extent to which Egoity is controlled is *lacking*, the effectiveness of Interaction will be *lacking*.

> When you wash with dirty water, you will end up with a dirty face, regardless of the quality of soap you use.
>
> If you wash with dirt instead of soap, you will end up with a dirty face, regardless of how clean the water is.

The last two chapters (*Information* and *Egoity*) discussed the components of Interaction. This chapter will deal with the effective utilization of these components during conflict resolution. After all, even if you have clean water and quality soap, you can't clean your face if you don't know how.

The Power of Mutual and Voluntary Exchange

A partnership is a voluntary arrangement in which individuals agree to cooperate to advance their mutual interests. "I'll scratch your back, if you'll scratch mine." A business transaction is like a temporary partnership. The participants agree to an exchange of goods for *both* their benefit. Each has what the other wants, whether it's bread, money, time or Information. When a business transaction is mutual, voluntary, and honest, both participants are *wealthier* since they are better off than they were before. They wouldn't do it otherwise.

If the transaction isn't voluntary or either participant feels taken advantage of, it shouldn't take place. A transaction that involves stealing, lying, or cheating, lowers the wealth of all concerned. The "taker" may be tangibly better off, yet is impoverished by the repercussions of the unfair transaction, such as guilt, shame, and the fear of vengeance. The "taken" is tangibly worse off, as well as burdened with the irritation, shame, and fear of ridicule of the unfair transaction.

Each Interaction with your partner is like a business transaction. Effective Interaction is the mutual, voluntary, and honest exchange of Information. When you and your partner effectively "trade" Information, you are "scratching each other's back" by getting what you want and need to resolve conflict.

Beatrice, Bruno, and BLT Sandwiches

Let's say that Beatrice has oodles of bread and bacon, but no lettuce or tomato. Bruno has lots of lettuce and tomato, but no bread or bacon. The way it is now, Beatrice will have to settle for eating just a bacon sandwich, and Bruno is stuck with a plain garden salad. Now let's say they are *both* craving a BLT sandwich. When they trade with each other, mutually and voluntarily, both are *wealthier* since they both get to have something they wanted, yet didn't have before: a BLT sandwich.

During Interaction, you and your partner each bring something of value that the other one needs – Information. When you exchange Information, you both can have a BLT (Baby, Let's Talk!) sandwich, and resolve issues mutually and voluntarily. A successful Interaction makes each of you *wealthier*.

Ready, Able, and Willing: The RAW Truth

For effective Interaction, both partners need to be **RAW**: (1) **R**eady, by knowing the basics of Interaction, (2) **A**ble, by selecting a mutually appropriate time and place, and (3) **W**illing to participate in the process.

---

1. **READY**: You do not need to be an expert of *The Melfox Method* for effective Interaction to take place. Yet like any other method, the more you understand and embrace the concepts, the easier the execution.

   a. Understanding that resentment is the enemy, not your partner, will help keep the Interaction on track.

   b. Understanding that properly sharing Information is at the heart of conflict resolution will help open up the lines of communication.

   c. Understanding the basic idea of controlling Egoity will help minimize the chance and effect of arguments or other ineffective Interaction results.

2. **ABLE**: As discussed earlier in the *Environment* chapter, the time and place for Interaction have a strong bearing on its success. Whenever either partner is distracted by outside influences, the effectiveness of Interaction suffers. A lack of concentration may result in misunderstandings and frustration, which can only delay or impede effective conflict resolution.

3. **WILLING**: Effective Interaction requires each participant to have the basic desire to resolve conflict, and not go into it begrudgingly just because the other person wants to. There needs to be the willingness to delve into emotionally charged subjects that will periodically upset you and your partner. The more you understand and practice effective Interaction, the more you realize it is worth the effort.

It is this last part that most of us will find challenging when first practicing Interaction. We can learn the basic concepts, and select the proper time and place, yet the willingness to purposely expose our hearts and Egoity to our partner may seem naturally counterintuitive. After all, we have a lot of history and tradition going against us here.

Who's Side Are You On?

In the *Environment* chapter, we briefly discussed the differences between Traditional Relationship Logic and The Melfox Mindset. The following is a simplistic summary:

1. The pervasive approach to conflict resolution when using Traditional Relationship Logic is *fighting with your partner*. You are right and they are wrong.

2. The pervasive approach to conflict resolution when using The Melfox Mindset is you and your partner *fighting resentment*.

As we learned in the previous chapter, whenever your Egoity is evoked, you see your partner on "the other side of the net." So Interaction using Traditional Relationship Logic is like a battle of uncontrolled Egoity. For a review, here is our "tennis courts" diagram:

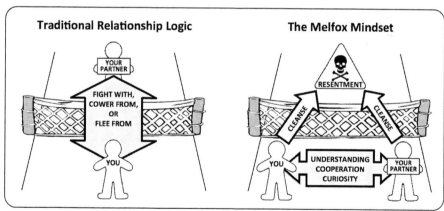

Diagram 24: TRL & TMM with nets

When applying Traditional Relationship Logic, no matter how cooperative the initial intentions, eventually the Interaction erodes into an Egoity battle. Each partner ends up fighting with, cowering from, or fleeing from, the other. In contrast, those applying The Melfox Mindset *use* Egoity to identify resentment and the reasons behind it, which leads to conflict resolution.

What's the Objective?

That is one question you should be asking and answering to yourself during Interaction.

1. Do I want to win an argument... *or resolve conflict?*

2. Do I just want to get along and wait this out... *or resolve conflict?*

3. Would I rather just sneak out the back door... or *resolve conflict?*

Obviously, most of us will intentionally prefer the latter options, yet Egoity will periodically prod us into seeing our partner on the other side. We go into Interaction with the intended objective of resolving conflict, yet when a belief is threatened, we autonomically go into protection mode and our focus on conflict resolution takes a back seat.

Depending on your experience with Traditional Relationship Logic, it may take quite a bit of Interaction practice to consistently remember that the enemy is resentment, not your partner. Most of us have gone our entire lives seeing conflict as a "me versus you" type of experience. The more you understand and practice The Melfox Mindset, the easier it will be to stay on track and be aware that resolving conflict is the primary objective during Interaction.

Placing Blame vs. Conflict Resolution

Even with The Melfox Mindset, there is a constant struggle to stay on the same side with your partner during Interaction. For it to be effective, you have to keep on reminding yourself that your focus should be on resolving the conflict, not fighting with your partner.

When Egoity flares, it may be easy to blame your partner of being wrong or for not understanding you. It's important to regain control *as soon as you know you have lost it*, and reassure each other throughout Interaction that the intent is to resolve the underlying resentment, *not to hurt each other*. Success depends on understanding that effective Interaction is a mutual battle against resentment, not a battle with your partner to be won or lost.

With Traditional Relationship Logic, once conflict arises, you're instantly in blame mode. Even if you just want to "get along" and don't overtly accuse your partner, your nonverbal communication and internal dialog make it clear that you see them as the guilty party. You end up feeling that it's a choice between (1) continuing to battle, or (2) avoiding the causative conflict by not bringing up the subject, and evading it if your partner does. The talks you end up having are cold and lifeless.

That's how Interaction can look with Traditional Relationship Logic: A useless activity that only brings additional resentment since all you do is battle with your partner, and defend yourself against them. With each painful skirmish, your vulnerability gets heavier and heavier, choking the life out of any curiosity you might still have with your partner.

The only alternative seems to be avoiding or evading *the very subjects* that need to be discussed, preventing their toxic effects from being cleansed from the relationship. Resentment steadily builds until there is no communication left between you, and you're only left wondering who's to blame. Does that sound familiar? Not exactly a fairytale ending, huh? It begs the question: Why do we even *use* Traditional Relationship Logic?

Re-examining Traditional Relationship Logic

Like other things in life, much of what we learn about relationships comes from stories and observations, and through trial and error. As a child, you may have heard and sung cheerful songs that warned you that you'd better not cry or pout, "for goodness' sake," as if the only reason for any crying and pouting is that you are being naughty. You may have heard and read stories of the magic that comes with finding that special someone, and living  "happily ever after," as if you will never ever experience conflict again – the trick is finding that "special" someone.

The virtues of "behaving good" and the myth of everlasting maintenance-free bliss are reinforced everywhere. You see them in TV shows, movies, novels, commercials, video games, and magazines. They teach that simply finding that "certain something" will lead to eternal happiness, as well as the perils and drama of (gasp!) attempting conflict resolution. When a celebrity dares to suggest publicly they have to "work" at their marriage or relationship, the rumor mills are filled with stories of their impending doom. But of all the influences that shaped and continue to shape our understanding of relationships, it is the lessons learned through the observation and appeasement of authority figures that probably have had the most impact.

For the most part, Traditional Relationship Logic is a set of lingering rules of suppression that we learned to obey as children, or suffered the consequences if we didn't. As everyone knows, kids can be a handful. For adults, there is a natural desire for children to "be little angels" and to always "behave themselves." To that end, children who suppress their wants and feelings in order to "get along" and "behave" are praised, while those who express their wants and feelings are punished. If we were raised with this Traditional Relationship Logic, we were rarely (if ever) allowed or even *taught how* to effectively resolve conflict.

Beatrice and Hot Coffee

Sometime back when Beatrice first tried coffee, she was simply handed a scalding hot cup of java without being taught how it should be drunk. She lifted the mug and started to take a big drink like it was water. The painful experience on her mouth and tongue left her wanting to only drink it cold, which tasted rather blah, so she gave up drinking coffee altogether.

Later, when Beatrice met Bruno, he reintroduced hot coffee to her and taught her the proper way drink it. Beatrice restored her relationship with coffee, and they lived happily ever after.

Without our knowing, understanding, and applying the basic concepts of effective conflict resolution, any attempts to address issues quickly erode into messy, noisy quarrels that resolve nothing. These unproductive and disruptive events are naturally undesirable.

As children, we learned that when we engaged in such conduct, we were punished twice: once with the painful experience itself, and then again with the wrath of any annoyed authority figure. We were simply told to "get along" with one another, yet seldom taught *how* this should be done.

Suppressing Your Egoity

As children, most of us were taught and learned to suppress our Egoity whenever conflict arose. When Billy stole our pencil during class, we were punished if we got up from our desk and tried to get it back. If our brother called us ugly, we learned to "just take it" instead of risking punishment for expressing our natural desire to "debate." We were ridiculed, sent to bed without supper, made to sit in a corner, put in "timeout" and grounded. We learned that if we dared convey a viewpoint that was contrary to authority, we risked punishment for simply having and expressing that viewpoint.

For the sake of peace and quiet, many of us learned (and still choose) to value the needs and wants of others, *above and at the expense of our own.* "For goodness' sake," we learned to suppress our true feelings, and for that, we were praised for being such good girls and boys. Those who couldn't or chose not to suppress their feelings were ridiculed and punished with the crime of simply behaving in a way that bothered authority.

Suppressing Egoity is like holding your breath – eventually it has to come out. A steam boiler can only take so much pressure before it blows up. And when Egoity blows, it's usually out of desperation and not very pretty. We destructively "let off steam" or "blow up" with temper tantrums, evasion of responsibilities, vindictive passive-aggression, or worse.

It's like getting a no-limit credit card without being taught or knowing that it needs to be paid off. With no sense of consequences, we may see the card as "free money" and freely use it. Everything is fine until the collectors come calling, at which time things usually get pretty ugly. If we were *taught* and learned the responsibility of using credit  cards, we would be more likely to make better shopping choices and stay within a reasonable budget.

Suppressing your Egoity and true feelings for the sake of "getting along" is like irresponsibly using a credit card – you (and those around you) pay for it eventually, and sometimes dearly. Until we learn that purposely suppressing our feelings is irresponsible and destructive, we will continue to think it is the compassionate, "nice," and correct thing to do.

On the flip side, there are some of us who learned (and still choose) to freely express our feelings *with no regard* of the needs and feelings of others. We choose to play the role of "the authority" and take advantage of the compassion of others. Instead of suppressing our Egoity for the sake of peace and appeasement, we choose to become the *receiver* of appeasement. We're still using Traditional Relationship Logic yet at some point we learned we could choose to adopt the role of the oppressing authority, instead of continuing to play the role of the oppressed child.

Interaction Styles Using Traditional Relationship Logic

When a couple uses Traditional Relationship Logic (TRL) in conflict resolution, they usually settle into assuming opposing roles, one partner being the *oppressor,* and the other being the *oppressed.* Just like Egoity manifestations, an individual's role may be different in different relationships, and may change within the same relationship, depending on the subject discussed.

Interaction Style Using TRL #1: **OPPRESS<u>OR</u>**

1. Egoity representation: **The Lion**

2. Childhood role: Caretaker

3. Personality type: Aggressive

4. Methods of getting partner to "play their role":
   - Intimidation
   - Bullying
   - Forced confrontation

5. Confrontation mottos and mantras:
   - "Self before others"
   - "It's a dog-eat-dog world"
   - "Listen to me!"
   - "#1: I'm right. #2: If you think I'm wrong, see #1"

6. What is the "right" thing to do?: Brutal honesty at the *expense* of compassion

7. Typical labels and nicknames: Takers, trouble-makers, meanies, bullies, abusers

8. How partner appears: Wimpy, weak, distrustful, wary, shy

Interaction Style Using TRL #2: **OPPRESSED**

1. Egoity representation: **The Turtle**

2. Childhood role: Child

3. Personality type: Nonassertive (Passive)

4. Methods of getting partner to "play their role":
   - Passive-aggression
   - Manipulation of facts
   - "Baiting a trap"

5. Confrontation mottos and mantras:
   - "Others before self"
   - "Don't make waves"
   - "To get along, go along"
   - "If you don't start nothing, there won't be nothing"

6. What is the "right" thing to do?: Omit or alter Information for the *sake* of compassion

7. Typical labels and nicknames: People-pleasers, doormats, "nice" people, pushovers

8. How partner appears: Rude, crude, and socially unacceptable (J. Heller)

If you're wondering why the Egoity representation of Deer is not in this chart, it is because Deer do not participate in Interaction. They do all they can to avoid, evade, or ignore any confrontation.

"Nice" Has a Price

When many of us were children, we were taught how to think in terms of moralistic judgments at the expense of expressing our wants and needs. Our caretakers may have thought that their only responsibility was to teach us right from wrong, appropriate from inappropriate. Sadly, what this often really taught was how to suppress and disassociate from our true feelings, and only express ourselves in judgmental terms when dealing with other people. It's no wonder we learned to be "nice" and stop expressing ourselves early on in life. We were so wounded by the punishment or ridicule from others when we expressed our wants and needs that we shut down our natural desire to be understood. We learned that if we didn't express our desires, we didn't get in trouble. We would decide to say things that *weren't even true*, just so we wouldn't experience the punishment for being confrontational.

Because of this, many of us have a natural tendency to avoid conflict, especially when it involves our partner. We'll do *anything* to avoid conflict. To a "nice" person, it would be "rude" to say anything that could be considered controversial.

Remember Bruno's "nice" response to his birthday present from Beatrice?

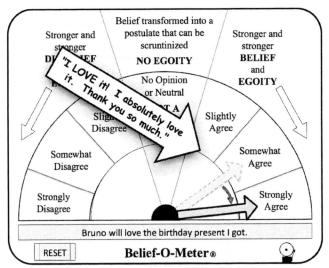

Diagram 25: Belief-O-Meter® "Nice" Response

Bruno decided to *avoid conflict* by being "nice" and acting like he loved the lime-green T-shirt. Of course, this only *transferred* the primary feeling of resentment from Beatrice to Bruno. In essence, Bruno just *deferred* conflict to a later time. Eventually resentment will rear its ugly head when Beatrice notices Bruno never wears the shirt, or if Bruno finally admits he doesn't "absolutely love" it.

Always being "nice" prevents your partner from receiving the proper Information that would resolve conflict. You try to meet the need for compassion and gentleness, at the expense of honesty and trust of your partner. Your partner will never know where you really stand or what you really believe, which only widens the gap of understanding between you. You're always "walking on eggshells" and always thinking of just "nice" things to say to your partner. In addition, you're in a constant state of anger, thinking that your partner should have to be "nice" too.

The Aggression Obsession

This is where the compass points in the opposite direction. If being "nice" is north, this is south. If being "nice" is the good guy wearing a white hat, this is the bad guy wearing a black hat. This is the "might makes right" attitude of *authority*. This is
the flip side of the Traditional Relationship Logic coin. But it is the same coin with being nice.

In a traditional childhood, we learned to be "nice" to avoid confrontation, yet we also learned the ways of our caretaker and how to act like the authority. You're playing the same oppressive game as the "nice" person, just the complementary role. We learned from our oppressive caretakers to voice our feelings, yet ignore the feelings of others. We learned how to dominate, humiliate, and intimidate to get our way, at the expense and alienation of others.

Think back on all the arguments and conflicts you've had. There's a good chance that one of you played the "oppressed Turtle" and the other played the "dominating Lion" just like you learned in your childhood. Once you understand what is going on and where you learned it, it is easier to refuse to play the Traditional Relationship Logic game. We can learn that we don't have to wear a white hat *or* a black hat.

Cultivating The Melfox Mindset

As opposed to Traditional Relationship Logic, where you're either a good guy wearing a white hat or the bad guy wearing a black hat, those adopting The Melfox Mindset *wear no hat*. They are not "nice" in that they do not suppress their feelings, yet they do it in such a way that respects their partner's feelings as well.

When each partner uses The Melfox Mindset, they work together without either feeling oppressed, or feeling the need to dominate the other. With understanding, cooperation, and curiosity, they focus on resolving conflict through Interaction by sharing Information and controlling Egoity.

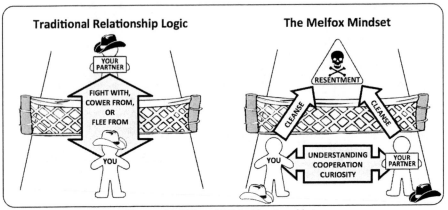

Diagram 26: TRL vs. TMM with nets and hats

With The Melfox Mindset, each partner understands that the goal is to cleanse resentment from the relationship, not battle each other. They play "Canadian doubles" against resentment, not "singles" against their partner with Traditional Relationship Logic.

The Melfox Mindset Is Assertive

When you use The Melfox Mindset during Interaction, you're expressing feelings, needs, wants, and ideas without intentionally trying to oppress or hurt your partner. Your shared Information is honest, expressive, direct, spontaneous, and *real*. Egoity is only used to  identify resentment and the reasons for it, and then turned off like a smoke alarm. The Melfox Mindset creates free, honest, and open communication Environment with your partner as you work out issues, and expose and re-evaluate limiting or presume beliefs.

When we use The Melfox Mindset, we refuse to play to role of the bully or the bullied. We stand up for what is right, take responsibility for our feelings, ensure our beliefs are valid, and defend ourselves when needed. By staying on the same side, we work out issues with our partner cooperatively, fairly, and directly. No desire to find out "who's fault it is" and cast blame.

Beatrice and Bruno and the Relationship Garden – Take 1

Let's say that a beautiful magical flower garden appeared when Beatrice and Bruno first started their relationship, and both were given Egoity hoes. After awhile, a few resentment weeds appear amongst the flowers. The question is: What do Beatrice and Bruno do with their Egoity hoes?

1. If they both use Traditional Relationship Logic, neither takes any responsibility for the garden, and therefore neither can *see* the weeds. They can only *feel* the weeds' *smothering* effect on the relationship garden. As the flower garden slowly gets choked out, Beatrice has only Bruno to blame for its condition, and Bruno can only blame Beatrice. Eventually, one or both may get tired of being hoe-prodded by the other, and move on in search of another garden.

2. Now let's say only one partner, let's say Beatrice, uses The Melfox Mindset, and Bruno stays with Traditional Relationship Logic. Beatrice can *see* the resentment weeds, and how they are choking the life out of their relationship garden. Bruno can only *feel* the weeds, and tries to get Beatrice to take blame by prodding her with his Egoity. Beatrice tries to weed their relationship garden by herself, while defending herself from Bruno. She may be successful in keeping the garden weed-free *in spite of* being attacked by Bruno. Or she may give up trying and move on to another garden.

3. When Beatrice and Bruno *both* use The Melfox Mindset, *each* sees the resentment weeds, just like in a regular garden. Instead of blaming each other. They each take responsibility and, using their Egoity hoes, work together to keep their relationship garden free of weeds. They may occasionally clang their hoes together, yet both accept that this happens sometimes. Their garden remains weed-free, all season.

Another way of understanding the difference between Traditional Relationship Logic and The Melfox Mindset is by knowing who the opponent is, and who the opponent is *not*...

Check the Program Next Time!

Imagine there are two professional wrestlers named Mighty Morgan and Powerful Pat. They have the same manager and are best of friends, yet go in the wrestling ring each week battling each other in the main event.

One day, their manager signed the pair up as a tag team to go up against another opponent. Problem is, their manager didn't tell them. As the bell sounded, and Mighty Morgan and Powerful Pat began their normal routine of tossing each other around, the crowd started laughing. Not knowing that the program called for a tag team match, Morgan and Pat stopped and looked around to see what all the fuss was about.

There, sitting on a stool in another corner was their real opponent, laughing with the crowd watching Mighty Morgan and Powerful Pat wrestle each other, instead of it.

Traditional Relationship Logic has us battling with our partner, instead of our real opponent: resentment. At the end of the Interaction match, regardless if anyone "wins" the battle, resentment remains untouched. It just sits there in the corner, laughing at the two of you, while its devastating impact on your relationship gets stronger and stronger.

The Melfox Mindset has us working together like a tag team to cleanse resentment, instead of battling with each other by defending our beliefs. The objective of Interaction is to suspend our threatened beliefs and figure out the reasons for resentment. It's not to win an argument, or just hide in your shell and "keep the peace" until the match is over.

Traditional Relationship Logic and The Melfox Mindset answer the same question – "What's the objective?" – differently. One has you battling *each other*, and the other has you battling resentment *together*.

Interaction Tools and Strategies

In previous chapters we have discussed the challenge (*Environment*) and the components for the solution (*Information* and *Egoity*). So far in this *Interaction* chapter, we have looked at how these components are used together in resolving conflict, as well as how different mindsets affect the effectiveness of Interaction.

If Interaction was a tag team game of chess, we learned about the game board, the objective, and how the pieces move in the previous chapters. In this chapter, we were taught the significance of consistently remembering that the real opponent is resentment. We explored the fine balance between offensively attacking its king, and properly respecting its defenses. It is time to talk strategy, and build your Melfox resentment-battling arsenal.

Rule #1: There Are No Rules Here

They say all's fair in love and war, and when you think about it, Interaction is both. There is not going to be a list of things to do or not to do. You've had enough rules as a child. If you've read and sufficiently understand the concepts discussed so far, you know how the pieces move and the objective of Interaction – conflict resolution. You and your partner, based on things like skill set, style, relationship type, and preference, will develop how you go about achieving that objective.

Throughout the remainder of this chapter there will be tips, tools, and suggestions at your disposal to help you build your own unique strategy custom-designed for your relationship. They can help increase your chances of success if you're new at Interaction, or help make it an easier and smoother experience if you are more experienced.

You may use or alter any of these ideas, or come up with some on your own that work for you and your partner. The only universal guideline to bear in mind is respect. Try not to suppress your partner's feelings or your own. Otherwise it's all war, and no love.

Props, Mascots, and Cheat Sheets

Here are some ideas for things to use, adopt, or create prior to Interaction. These are the kinds of things that will help you stay on the right conversation track and remain focused on your goal of conflict resolution. Things that can help remind you and your partner not to use the same old destructive conversation patterns, and focus on battling resentment, not each other.

1. **Harry, the Relationship Bear:** A key element of effective conflict resolution is consistently remembering that *resentment* is the opponent. So why not have resentment physically represented during Interaction? Like an awful hat on a teddy bear named Harry who isn't too happy about it. Harry represents your relationship, and the hat is resentment, which is only to be removed when  *resentment* is removed. To help with your visualization, make the hat really silly, really old, or just plain ugly.

   The plan is, when you look at Harry during Interaction, you and your partner will feel sorry for him, and feel a strong desire to remove that bad hat. That should help both of you maintain The Melfox Mindset by focusing more on battling resentment, and less with battling each other. Externalizing resentment to an inanimate object could help break the natural drift toward Traditional Relationship Logic by keeping you and your partner on the same side, battling a common foe.

You could bring out Harry and put the resentment hat on him as a subtle cue to your partner that you need Interaction, or your partner could do the same. After Interaction is complete and resentment has been cleansed, you can celebrate together by taking that bad hat off Harry, and putting him away until next time.

1. **Squeakers, the Resentment Mouse:** Similar to Harry above, with a twist. When it's time for Interaction, bring out a toy mouse named Squeakers that represents resentment. During Interaction, you and your partner could each wear something akin to being a cat like a mask, or simply pretend to be cats. That way, whenever Egoity kicks in and you start clawing at each other, you could look at the mouse and pretend it is laughing at you. That should get you back on track at clawing at *resentment* instead, and focusing on resolving conflict.

2. **Same Team Uniform:** Buy matching hats, shirts, or jerseys of a favorite sports team, and something representing a rival team. If you wear Chicago Bears jerseys, you could get something like a Green Bay Packers doll or a piece of cheese to represent resentment - your bitter nemesis. Before Interaction, put the matching jerseys on to reinforce cooperation and teamwork, and set the resentment object on the table like a poor helpless sacrificial lamb. Cheerleaders, eye black, and grunting are all optional.

3. **Same Team Name:** Since you are to consider you and your partner as being on the same team, name your team and use it when referring to Interaction. Beatrice and Bruno could use "Team Beano," of course, yet any name that represents you and your partner's unique relationship will do. "Team Grumpy Gills" maybe, or "Team Us" comes to mind. Using a team name could help you and your partner emotionally hold hands, and stay committed to trusting each other throughout the turbulent storm of Interaction.

4. **Written Reminders:** There are no rules here, so why not use crib notes? Before Interaction, write out your team slogan, mission statement, or any

other affirmations on 3x5 index cards. To help with developing these declarations, think of the kind of things people say to each other when they make up their own wedding vows. As an example, you're welcome to use our Curiosity Mantra:

> *When I speak, I will always be curious, not judgmental.*
> *The words I use and the way I say them convey a sense of wonder*
> *so that I understand my partner, and my partner understands me.*
> *I have a burning desire to understand my partner,*
> *and for my partner to understand me.*
>
> *When I listen, I will always assume my partner*
> *is being curious, not judgmental.*
> *If there's ever a question of my partner's motive, I will calmly ask*
> *so that I understand my partner, and my partner understands me.*
> *I have a burning desire to understand my partner,*
> *and for my partner to understand me.*

To reduce the threat of going back to Traditional Relationship Logic, refer to these affirmations early and often during Interaction. When Egoity starts to take over, read them to yourself or with your partner to help get back (or stay) on the same side. You could also include portions of the affirmations whenever you text your partner or include it in salutations in letters or emails. For example, use "IBOYSA" (I'll Be On Your Side, Always) when ending correspondences. This can help remind you and your partner to use The Melfox Mindset, stay on the same team, and work together during Interaction.

5. **Ice Breakers:** When beginning Interaction, it's convenient to already know the resentment issue, or something that may *cause* resentment when it is discussed. It's also nice if you know the reasons *why* you hadn't shared that Information until now. If you have a feeling you know these things, before Interaction starts, try this exercise:

For each issue, answer the following questions:

A. What I would like to say to my partner is: _____.

B. What I'm afraid might happen if I say it is: _____.

C. What I'd like to have happen by saying it is: _____.

Put your answers into the script below.

Dear [Partner], there is something I haven't told you. I hadn't said it until now because I'm afraid of the following: *[Answer from B]*

What I would like to have happen by my telling you: *[C]*

What I'm not telling you is: *[A]*

Thank you for listening. What would you like to share?

Memorize it, or read during Interaction. Here's an example:

Dear [Partner], there is something I haven't told you. I hadn't said it until now because I'm afraid of the following:

> *You will lose all respect for me.*

What I would like to have happen by my telling you is:

> *We reach a deeper level of love, trust, and intimacy.*

What I'm not telling you is:

> *I was fired from my job a week ago and too afraid to tell you.*

Thank you for listening. What would you like to share?

Refuting Shared Information and Other Interjections

During Interaction, there will be times when you may want to question or dispute something your partner says. This urge may be slight, or it may make you want to scream. To indicate to your partner that "you wish to add something" and minimize the impact, you could use a unique nonverbal indicator. This indicator and its intended use should be discussed and agreed upon with your partner prior to Interaction.

Here are some suggestions you could use to gently help your partner know you don't agree or "wish to add" something" to the conversation:

1. Your reaction to refutable Information may be a simple gesture like pointing a finger or raising your hand. One downside this type of indicator is that it may be easily ignored. If you and your partner understand that it is part of solving the resentment mystery, it should work just fine. It's better than loudly clearing your throat or shouting "Oh, huh!"

2. As you and your partner have more experience at Interaction, you may want to create a sign or write on ping-pong paddles the more common interjections you and your partner run across. One side of the paddle may indicate a question ("Why?"), and the other may indicate a dispute ("Refutable"). Here are some examples that you're welcome to use:

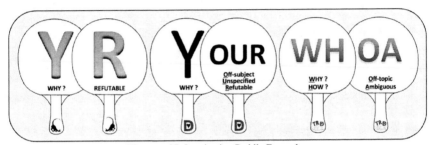

Diagram 27: Interjection Paddle Examples

These YR, YOUR, or WHOA paddles could be part of your Melfox arsenal as you battle resentment through effective Interaction. They can help keep the conversation on track, and allow you and your partner to question or dispute shared Information, while respecting each other by not verbally or overtly interrupting.

Preparing for Interaction

In this section, we will be discussing the prerequisites to effective Interaction. These things are necessary for Interaction to take place and greatly impact its probability of success.

Remember that Interaction is proactive, objective-oriented, and purposeful. It is not "a new way" of talking with your partner in your normal everyday style. This is not going to be a *casual* conversation. There is resentment in your relationship that needs to be cleansed. Interaction is a structured mechanism to help you and your partner open your communication doors, discover the reasons for resentment, and eliminate its effect on your relationship.

Hello, Mr. Lion

When first learning and practicing Interaction, deciding to initiate the process may be a daunting task. It may feel like you are *voluntarily* exposing you and your partner to the same pain and frustration of uncontrolled Egoity and arguments you had in the past. It may feel as though you are *choosing* to walk into a cage with a wild animal, or stick your hand into a hive of angry bees.

Hopefully, you are beginning to understand your partner as not a hungry lion wanting to eat you, or a swarm of stinging insects. It is resentment caused by *threatened beliefs* that you are battling, not your partner. It's like the Aesop fable *Androcles and the Lion*. Androcles overcame the fear of a roaring lion to address the real issue – a thorn in the lion's paw. It is *threatened beliefs* that make us "roar" or evoke our Egoity, not a desire to threaten our partner.

Think of you and your partner's relationship like the one with Androcles and the lion. Just like you, your partner has the thorn of resentment in their paw. We may interpret their moaning and groaning as a warning, and stay away. Or we may see it as a cry for help. The more we understand what is *causing* the moaning and groaning, the more we can focus our attention on "pulling the thorn out" and healing our relationship.

Making Interaction a Priority

The critical step in initiating the Interaction process is deciding to do it. Setting aside the time and effort for Interaction may seem like a big investment, especially when you are unfamiliar with all the beneficial results. Here are some indicators that you probably have resentment that is ripe for the cleansing efforts of Interaction:

1. You can't stop thinking about an issue you have with your partner.

2. You have a sense of being wronged by your partner, whether or not it is true.

3. You feel your Egoity evoke every time the issue comes up in conversation.

4. When you get upset about some unrelated topic, your thoughts go back to the issue.

5. You find yourself feeling irritated at your partner "for no reason at all."

If you answer yes to any or all of these, you should consider having an Interaction session with your partner. You may have a leg up by already knowing the issue or issues, or have Interaction help uncover the reason why you are irritated or feel any negativity toward your partner.

When There Is Only One

As discussed earlier, engaging in Interaction when you're the only one who understands *The Melfox Method* is like trying to battle resentment with one arm, while holding off your partner's Egoity with the other. It may take longer and be more cumbersome, yet it can be done. It reminds me of a story from my youth.

The Square Knot Challenge

Back in Boy Scouts, when I had my final Eagle badge panel review, one of the interviewers showed me a rope and asked me to do something very familiar: Tie a square knot. Yet when I tried to take the rope, I found that he was holding fast to one end and smiling. I smiled back and got to work. It took longer and was more cumbersome to do than if I had *both* ends, yet I was able to figure it out, make the square knot, and pass the test. The challenge was made easier by my understanding of square knots, and my desire to pass the test and be an Eagle Scout.

When you are familiar with the basic concepts of *The Melfox Method* and have a strong enough desire to restore your relationship, you too can resolve conflict with "only one end of the rope." Finding the reasons for resentment and getting  both of you to accept them may just take more time and effort.

Of course, there's the possibility that your partner will reject even *trying* Interaction. That would be like my interviewer tugging on his end of the rope, preventing me from tying the knot. There needs to be enough trust and desire on the part of your partner to at least go through the Interaction process without refusing or purposely sabotaging it.

Flying Solo

It is sometimes tough to attempt Interaction when your partner is still using Traditional Relationship Logic or otherwise wary of confronting conflict. Here are some suggestions to help persuade your partner to attempt Interaction, and ideas for doing it with when you are the only one familiar with the concepts of *The Melfox Method:*

1. **Be Prepared:** Obtain or create all the props, cheat sheets, and Interaction techniques you would like to try with your partner. Show your partner how serious you are about attempting this way of resolving conflict, by having it all ready before even asking them to participate.

2. **Smell That Grease Paint:** Have an imaginary "dress rehearsal" of how a possible Interaction would unfold with your partner. Again, *take your time* and run through a real Interaction scenario line-by-line like an improvisational and esoteric off-Broadway play. Envision the exchange of Information and Egoity, as you protect and expose hidden beliefs.

    Practice using what you know of The Melfox Mindset and imagine how that would intermingle with your partner's typical Interaction style. Were you able to handle their Egoity? Do an appraisal of your Interaction strengths and weaknesses. If need be, go back to your dressing room and study the script some more. Rinse and repeat, as needed.

    So... how did it go? Did your partner follow the script? Did *you* follow the script? Oh, that's right; *there is no script.* Try to remain curious of the "adlib" conversation, and not judge the "performance" with what you feel should have happened.

3. **Make it a Game:** Instead of a scripted play, envision your Interaction as a skit at an improvisation comedy club or a parlor game with some friends. Pretend the emcee picked you and your partner from the crowd for a little contest.

    Here's an example: You are told that each will be given a unique mission to accomplish. The winner will be the first one to fulfill the objective as stated in the instructions. You are given the following directive:

Your mission is to figure out the *secret* hidden belief that has just been given to your partner. Your partner's mission is to keep you from knowing this secret, until *you* give up trying. Think of it like the combination of the game show *Twenty Questions* and seeing who can hold their breath longer. The challenge is your partner may lie, omit, resist, provoke, and do a lot of moaning and groaning. Good luck.

SPOILER ALERT: Your partner was given the exact same instructions.

4. **Write it Out:** Take your time and think of all the reasons to do Interaction to counterbalance you and your partner's fear of Egoity. Write it out, review it, edit it, and then *share* it with your partner. Express your desire and commitment to restoring your relationship in your own words. Let your partner know you are serious about training your Egoity and cleansing resentment.

5. **Quid Pro Quo:** Cut a deal with your partner. Tell them you will fix their favorite meal or take them to their favorite restaurant, in exchange for their cooperation in trying this new approach to conflict resolution. Make it a deal that they can't refuse. Once they try it, they just may like it.

And perhaps most important…

6. **Don't Assume:** Don't assume your partner will instantly be on board this new Interaction train when it starts to pull out of the station. Prepare yourself for the possibility that your partner (and even you) will fight, withdraw, or evade throughout initial attempts of Interaction. When Egoity flares and one of you runs like a Deer, try to be empathic toward your partner, learn from the experience, and try again later.

Also, don't assume your partner will *not* be on board with this conflict resolution approach. Try to forget all the frustrating arguments and failed conflict resolution attempts from the past. You may very well be surprised at the effectiveness of Interaction and how well your partner "behaved" when facing issues with conflict. Remember, they are on the same train as you, and want to restore the relationship too. *That* you should assume.

Indicating Desire for Interaction

When the time is ripe for Interaction, you or your partner could just coldly stare and announce, "We need to talk" with crossed arms. Another way would be to have some kind of unique, non-confrontational method of asking for Interaction. It should be unique in that both you and your partner realize this is a request for *Interaction*, not just another casual conversation. The following are a few ideas that you and your partner could use to peacefully signify it is time to cleanse resentment:

1. Place the "bad hat" on "Harry, the Relationship Bear" and put it on the living room table.

2. Bring out "Squeakers, the Resentment Mouse" and put it where your partner will see it.

3. Put on your special matching Interaction jersey or shirt.

4. Include your team name in conversations with your partner ("Go Team BEANO!").

5. Handwrite a special request and place it on the kitchen table with a red rose.

There are countless other ways of indicating it's time for Interaction, like turning a special refrigerator magnet upside down, or a simple text or email. Make it fun. Play with your partner and find a special loving way that is uniquely yours.

Proper Environment

When scheduling Interaction, make sure it is when and where there will be a minimum of outside distractions and interruptions. Details of this can be found in the *Environment* chapter.

Ready? Grab your YR, YOUR, or WHOA paddles, put Bad Hat Harry on the table next to you and your partner, and let's go!

Curiosity State of Mind

OK. You're sitting down next to your partner, set to start Interaction. Are you ready, able, and willing? Are you sure you *want* to do this? What's the objective again? Here is some more imagery that may help you get and stay in The Melfox Mindset, and firmly focus on rooting out resentment with your partner. Let's start out with reviewing Traditional Relationship Logic and how it can discourage our desire for Interaction.

What's Going On?

There's always something new and wonderful you can learn about anything or anyone, especially your partner. Wouldn't it be awfully boring if you thought you knew and understood everything about a person, and there was nothing left to explore? Yet with Traditional Relationship Logic, that's how it seems. For some reason, over time, we lose interest in, and curiosity of, our partner. And our partner does the same.

Think about it. Think back when you first started an intimate relationship that blossomed into one you wanted to last forever. Remember how it felt to be with that person. Recall the ever-rising level of curiosity, attraction, and excitement you each shared. Anyone would want this extraordinary experience to last until the day they die, so you and your partner ponder, discuss, and agree to "go all in" and marry your lives and fortunes together forever.

Traditionally, *that* is thought of as the ultimate goal in relationships. Marriage or a similar type of commitment is generally considered a celebratory melding of two people into one entity. It's as if you and your partner are traversing raindrops, willfully blending on a windshield. You no longer just feel "connected" *to* your partner as separate entities, you actually feel "as one" *with* your partner.

For many of us, it is at this point that things change. For the first time with this person, we get a strange sense of relaxation. The relationship at some level suddenly has an eerie sense of calm to it. We feel settled, "locked in," and rigid. We can feel the warm tingly whirring motor of excitement slowly grinding to a halt.

We begin to look at our partner differently. The cute, funny, idiosyncratic things they have *always* done now have a tendency to be irritating and even obnoxious. Before, we were totally accepting and even *curious* about our differences in beliefs and choices. Now, when our partner chooses to go *left*, when we would have gone *right*, it fills us with a great deal of stress. Interest and curiosity somehow gets replaced with criticism and judgment. Why does that sometimes happen?

It may be that when we traditionally "tie the knot" with someone, an unspoken agreement is made for neither to *ever change*, thus how you feel about each other *will never change*. "I vow to always love *you*... that is, the *you* I believe you are, *right now*." Reasonable enough logic, it would seem. Like locking in a price on a stock, or signing off on that final edit, or capturing a songbird. You did the work; now it's time to cash in your chips, and live off the interest.

Beatrice and Bruno and the Relationship Garden – Take 2

Let's say this time, when Beatrice and Bruno first got to know each other they created a beautiful rose garden, complete with terraces and a wooden swing for two. When it was just the way they wanted it, Beatrice and Bruno admired it arm-in-arm, took a bunch of pictures, and showed them to their family and friends. Later, they looked at those pictures and sadly reminisced how beautiful their garden used to be before the weeds took over, and the weathered terraces collapsed and the swing rotted away. Separately, of course. The End.

Notice there wasn't any mention of garden hoes, paint, toolboxes, or maintenance of any kind in this story? With Traditional Relationship Logic, that is how we tend to look at relationships. We feel that making a *mutual commitment* to always want to be with and accept each other will somehow magically remove the need to *ever* maintain it.

Traditionally, we may think of a commitment with a partner like a chance to collapse after a long exciting day at an amusement park. Wild rollercoasters are fun, but at a certain point, everyone gets tired and wants to  go back home, back to their nice warm bed, and go to sleep. A commitment may be seen as a *mutual promise and wish* of fulfilling such a similar desire after years of dating and courting.

We feel a chance to escape from the chaotic and turbulent world of uncertainty, a chance to relax back into the peacefully blissful womb of predictability and *mutual dependency*. We click the heels of our ruby slippers together three times, and we're back *home* where there is no place like. Back to a place where we always feel safe and taken care of, so we can snuggle back in and take it easy. We go back to a familiar place we learned as a child – assuming the roles of dependency.

Effect of Traditional Relationship Logic on Interaction

Of course, this game plan, as it turns out, has a bit of a snag. We are totally *dependent* on our partner's holding their end of the unspoken, yet we feel still binding, vow of *never changing*. Or at least not changing to the point we don't like it. That's what we expect and signed up for: an eternally weed-free, maintenance-free, *ever-perfect* relationship garden.

The thing to remember is this: Our partner is not a share of stock, manuscript, and especially not a caged animal. Neither are we. Regardless of *any* vow or assumptions we may make, or how much we wish it not to happen, *things will change* and resentment *will* form.

New Information or other Interaction tools *could* be shared to "weed, clean up, and repair" resentment in our relationship garden. Yet as long as we use Traditional Relationship Logic, these tools are instead used *against* our partner, since *they* broke their promise to never change and preserve our perfect relationship. Of course, our partner may feel exactly the same way *about us*.

When Interaction begins and Egoity gets evoked, you may be tempted to revert back to Traditional Relationship Logic and feel you need to battle with your partner. It may help to think of how we learned about relationships and how this still may be influencing how we react when under stress of Egoity.

Isn't it possible that unless we learn otherwise, our relationship mindset is the same type we grew up with? Those of us raised by caretakers with smothering, controlling rules of proper behavior and suppressed feelings will tend to apply those same rules in other interpersonal relationships. If you were raised and still accept this Traditional Relationship Logic, you would naturally feel the need to suppress your partner's feelings in moments of conflict, *and* expect your feelings to be suppressed by your partner. We learned to handle conflict by *oppressing* our partners, and allowing our partners to *oppress* us.

The Melfox Mindset strips all of that away:

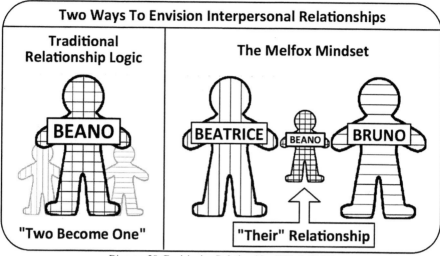

Diagram 28: Envisioning Relationships TRL & TMM

Traditional Relationship Logic	The Melfox Mindset
We are *in* a relationship.	We *have* a relationship.
My partner broke OUR vow.	Let's clean up OUR relationship!
Rigid, smothering, suffocating, controlling	Room to breathe, flexible to adapt to changes.
You complete me.	Let's co-create something special!
I *deserve* respect from my partner, and *my partner* deserves *my* respect.	I *earn* respect from my partner, just as they earn *my* respect – on a *continuous* basis.
It's time to *settle* down.	I never want to have to *settle* for anyone.
My partner *adds* something special to my life, as I *add* something special to their life.	My partner and I *have* something special.

If we were raised by caretakers who respected our feelings and allowed us to debate conflict, we naturally learned something different about interpersonal relationships. We saw that conflict could be peacefully resolved with understanding, patience, and trust. When we adopt this mindset, we naturally seek an intimate relationship with the same type of mutual respect. We would also naturally reject any potential partner if they ever desired and were willing to be *oppressed* by us, or if they insisted on *oppressing* us. That would indicate they were seeking a traditional relationship with mutual dependency and rigid rules of behavior.

The Melfox Mindset gives partners *enough space* between each other, so that they can *see* each other as individuals. We can get as *close* as possible, but we still need to *see* each other as individuals if we are to accept and understand any changes in the relationship. If we didn't learn this mindset as children, it's never too late.

In reality, our partner's perceived value of us will bounce up and down, we will forever be writing our life stories, and you can cage the songbird but you can't make it sing. In our pursuit of a healthy relationship, we need to able to honestly accept the actions and beliefs of our partner, *and* respectfully let them know whenever we don't. We need to willfully release them to write their own life's manuscript, *and* compassionately let them know whenever we don't like it.

Pep Talk Time…

As a final push to keep you and your partner on the same side as much as possible, it may help to have certain personally inspiring sayings and mantras etched in your mind. Here are some examples and suggestions you are more than welcome to use:

- [My partner] is on my side, always

- I want to cultivate a sense of curiosity about [my partner]'s world.

- I am comfortable with the idea that resentment is going happen in any relationship, just like weeds in a garden.

- I am not going plow under our relationship garden just because a few weeds come up.

- Remember – *it will be worth it.*

Let's take a break from Interaction preparation and mindset exercises for now. It is time to review and further clarify the objectives and reasons why we are engaged in Interaction. Let's explore the tasks at hand for a while.

Transforming Beliefs Into Postulates

In the *Egoity* chapter, we developed our Resentment Cause Analysis to determine the dependent subsequent tasks required to strengthen a relationship:

RESENTMENT CAUSE ANALYSIS

1. In order to strengthen your relationship,
   you need to be able to resolve conflicts.

2. In order to resolve conflicts,
   you need to be able to discover the reason(s) for resentment.

3. In order to discover the reason(s) for resentment,
   you need to be able to identify resentment.

4. In order to identify resentment,
   you need to be able to effectively share Information.

5. In order to effectively share Information,
   you need to be able to control Egoity.

6. In order to control Egoity,
   you need to be able to stop feeling a belief needs protection.

7. In order to stop feeling a belief needs protection,
   you need to be able to **transform the belief into a postulate**.

During effective Interaction, changing a belief into a postulate is your first course of action. It enables the other tasks to take place. Now that we know the steps to get rid of resentment and strengthen your relationship, it's just a matter of following the instructions, like a game.

"Save Your RelationShip!" - Part One

Imagine for a moment that this book is just an instruction manual for the game called *"Save Your RelationShip!"* In this "Interactive" game, you and your partner play co-captains of a vessel called the *Curiosity* that you custom build together. You each bring on board your own loyal crew of experiences, knowledge, interests, and beliefs.

The objective of the game is to navigate through a variety of exciting and challenging passages, while keeping your vessel afloat for as long as possible and having fun! Of course, with this game, there are no cheat codes. Along the way, you deal with things like Information officials, Egoity shipmates, stowaways, saboteurs, pirates, rough waters, and regular ship maintenance. It would be a delightful game for boys and girls of all ages.

So far in our instruction manual and game, we have covered the basics. With each page, we have described the Melfox tools and techniques you need to guide your relation*ship* safely to the bonus level and beyond. It is time now to set sail and put those tools to use. Here is your first challenge in the game *"Save Your RelationShip!"*

"Save Your RelationShip!" Challenge #1

Randomly throughout the game, an Information official boards the *Curiosity* uninvited, claiming one of two beliefs working below deck is a saboteur. Without knowing the lessons in our manual, your first impulse might be to defend the entire belief crew and throw the Information official overboard. After all, *all* beliefs below deck are loyal, right?

Your first challenge is to grant permission to the Information official to determine whether or not your belief is the saboteur, by allowing it to stand trial on its own merits.

As you can see, the first step to *save your relationship* is to change a threatened belief into a postulate that can be scrutinized. This is the initial objective of Interaction. By reversing the order of our Resentment Cause Analysis, let's make a step-by-step Interaction to-do list. The following are the challenges you face to maintain your *RelationShip* and keep it seaworthy:

Interaction To-Do List	Check
1. Transform a threatened belief into a postulate	
2. Control Egoity protecting the belief	
3. Share effective Information	
4. Identify the reason(s) for the underlying resentment	
5. Resolve the conflict (which strengthens the relationship)	

So the first thing on your list is to identify and challenge the threatened belief. It's pushing the reset button on our Belief-O-Meter® and daring to ponder the validity of something we currently believe to be true. That's the first challenge on our conflict resolution obstacle course, with a restored and healthy relationship waiting at the finish line. Here are some more thoughts and ideas on this concept, and on making it happen.

Something's Gonna Have to Give

One of the major roadblocks to conflict resolution is holding on tight to a belief or to what someone else says or believes, and not allowing anything to be revised with new Information. There is a natural tendency to defend our beliefs, or think what someone says or believes will *always* be true to them. We feel that changing our minds on what we believe to be true is somehow a sign of weakness. We are encouraged to defend what we believe as if it is set in concrete and discount contrary Information.

In order to resolve conflict, we need to be strong enough to swallow our pride and be ready, willing, and able to uproot even our deepest beliefs if new Information shows them to be false. By removing the concrete and putting little question marks on everything, we can set the stage for finding the reasons for resentment and cleansing the relationship Environment.

Remember our four major reasons for resentment:

1. Lack of Sufficient, Pertinent Information
2. Misunderstanding
3. False Assumption
4. Jumping to False Conclusion

All of these reasons require either you or your partner to change what is believed to be true. Odds are that half the time, *you* will be the one who needs to change a belief or opinion (unless you consider yourself infallible and omniscient). We believe something is true based *solely* on our current *limited* perceptive of knowledge. Allowing new Information to challenge our beliefs opens a pivotal door toward restoring your relationship.

It is the act of transforming beliefs into postulates, by you or your partner or both, which allows differences to be *reconciled*. To help explain this, let's take a look at a job that has *reconciliation* as part of its duties.

Reconcilable Differences

Let's say Beatrice is a full-charge bookkeeper at a small company. One day she received a monthly statement from a vendor for $40,000. After looking up the vendor in the company's accounting system, Beatrice found that the records showed the company only owed the vendor $35,000. First, let's look at this situation using Traditional Relationship Logic.

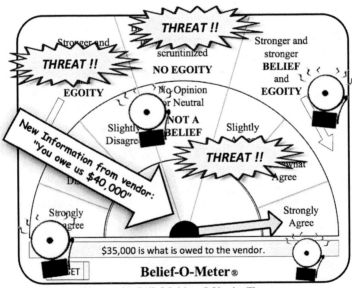

Diagram 29: Belief-O-Meter® Vendor Threat

The alarm will sound loudly from Beatrice's Belief-O-Meter® as she defends her believe that $35,000 is what is owed to the vendor. All of her attention is on defending that belief, and none on reconciling with the vendor.

Beatrice would just slouch at her desk, frown, and cross her arms thinking that the vendor was wrong. She would hold fast to her original belief of what was owed and think that the vendor was wrong. Beatrice would believe the $35,000 figure was correct as long as she believed the accounting books were correct – and they *must* be, because they are her responsibility.

If anything different were owed, it would mean that *she was wrong*, and that would not be acceptable. Of course with this logic, the vendor will believe they are right without a doubt as well. This creates a stalemate of sorts, since Beatrice and the vendor both think they right, and see the other one as wrong. The inability to reconcile means that Beatrice is not doing the job she has been assigned, which is also not acceptable.

With The Melfox Mindset, Beatrice would hit the reset button on her Belief-O-Meter® and change the belief into a challengeable postulate by simply putting "*I'm curious if...*" in front of the belief. This frees her up to compare the individual invoices in the accounting system with the listing provided on the vendor's statement.

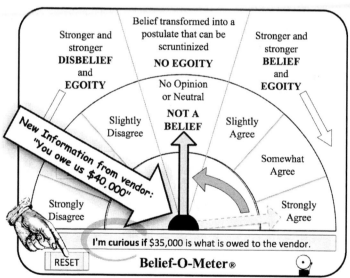

Diagram 30: Belief-O-Meter® Vendor Threat Reset

If the vendor is still using Traditional Relationship Logic, it may take more time and effort to reconcile, since Beatrice would have to deal with the vendor's defensive Egoity. Remember, you can still tie a square knot with only one end of the rope.

When Beatrice is able to accept that she *may be* wrong about her original belief, the action of reconciliation can take place. It may be that Beatrice was missing an invoice of $5,000, or a $5,000 invoice was mistakenly duplicated on the vendor's statement. Accepting that her belief may be wrong allows her to dig into the reason or reasons for the difference, and reconciliation is achieved.

Tools for Changing Beliefs Into Postulates

One of the more challenging aspects of effective Interaction is being able to swallow you pride and admit that a belief (gasp) may be wrong. Here are a few suggestions to help you and your partner put beliefs "on trial" so their validity can be confirmed or nullified. As we have learned, this is critical for effectively resolving conflict.

1. **Exposing Your Beliefs:** After identifying a threatened belief, change it to a conditional statement by including a dependent clause like "*I may be wrong but I believe...*" or the like. This should help you see your belief more like something that can be scrutinized. Ending them with "*...but that's not written in stone*" may also help you push that Belief-O-Meter® reset button.

2. **Exposing Your Partner's Beliefs:** To help your partner push their reset button on a belief, try this suggestion: Confirm the belief that is threatened, then add: "*It is possible your belief may not be true. Can you accept that?*" This forces your partner to see if they can let go of the belief, which sets the stage for conflict resolution.

3. **Game Theory:** Think of Interaction like a game in which the object is to find that *one thing* that someone believes that simply isn't true. Someone is assuming something that isn't correct, and both players work together to discover what that is. The real trick is staying on the same side. When that happens, both players win, and resentment loses.

4. **Solving a Mystery:** Think of you and your partner as a crime-solving team, like Sherlock Holmes and Dr. Watson, or Hong Kong Phooey and Spot. Or you may pretend to be the amateur sleuth team in *Hart to Hart* with each Interaction being its own TV episode. Working together, clues are uncovered, buried beliefs are exhumed, and the mystery of resentment is solved.

INTERACTION

Bumping Up Against Limiting and Presuming Beliefs

As you have no doubt experienced or surmised, some beliefs are harder to let go of than others. A conflict may be resolved with a belief so weak that it is easily challenged and discarded with a single statement of new Information. Other beliefs are held on to for dear life. If an issue is a simple case of conflicting preferences, Interaction is just sharing Information and deciding on which direction to take. For an example, let's eavesdrop on Beatrice and Bruno:

Beatrice's Belief: We should go to Chicago during spring break.

Bruno's Belief: We should go to Cincinnati during spring break.

= CONFLICT

Interaction:

BRUNO: I believe we should go to Cincinnati during spring break.

BEATRICE: I believe we should go to Chicago for some real deep-dished pizza!

BRUNO: Remember those ribs you had the last time we were in Cincinnati?

BEATRICE: Oh yeah… Yes. Now that I think about it, I would rather go to Cincinnati!

Beatrice's **NEW** Belief: We should go to *Cincinnati.*

Bruno's Belief: We should go to Cincinnati.

= NO CONFLICT

Oh, if every Interaction were that easy. Beatrice's original belief of going to Chicago was easily challenged with the new Information of reminding her of a preferred experience anticipated in Cincinnati. With a single statement, she was able to push her Chicago belief "reset button" and put it "on trial" *based on its merits* against the new Information Bruno shared. This spring break Montgomery Inn won out; next year, maybe Gino's East.

As we learned in the Egoity chapter, factors that determine the *strength* of a belief include how much you *identify* with it, and how much you are *invested* in it.

Let's spy on Beatrice and Bruno a little more:

Bruno's Belief: Beatrice does not think I am a good cook.

Beatrice's Belief: I think Bruno is a good cook.

= CONFLICT

Interaction:

BEATRICE: I resent that you don't cook anymore!

BRUNO: Remember the last time I cooked? You didn't say a word the entire meal.

BEATRICE: That's because I was too busy stuffing my face! I loved it!

BRUNO: Why didn't you say you loved my cooking after you were done stuffing your face?

BEATRICE: I'm sorry. I should have said something earlier. I really love your meals!

BRUNO: Ohhh… kaaay. I believe you now.

Bruno's **NEW** Belief: Beatrice *does* think I am a good cook.

Beatrice's Belief: I think Bruno is a good cook.

= NO CONFLICT

The above is an obviously simplistic example of what we will call a *limiting belief*. These beliefs "hold you back" and keep you from fulfilling your true potential in life. They keep you from doing things that *in reality* you *are* capable of doing. We have been taught or experienced painful lessons that reinforced these beliefs. As long as we have a limiting belief about something, we will feel we are not worthy of it, or even trying it. You also can have limiting beliefs concerning the "worthiness" of your partner.

On the other side, there are *presuming* beliefs. These have you believing in things that you are, *in reality*, not capable of, or ready for. If you *presume* you can fly, you could step off a ten-story building to demonstrate your belief. It may be only then that your belief will come crashing down, along with you. You also can have presuming beliefs concerning your partner. These beliefs, like all beliefs, create conflict in a relationship when they do not agree with your partner's.

An example of a presuming belief's causing an issue is Beatrice's belief that Bruno will love the birthday present she got him, when *in reality*, he doesn't. As long she protects the presuming belief, the issue and its resentment will persist in their relationship.

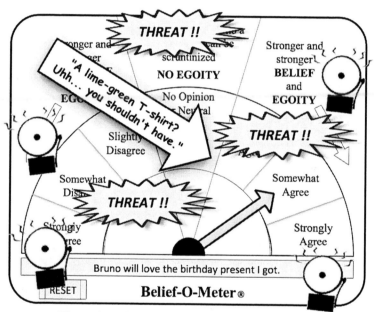

Diagram 31: Belief-O-Meter® Birthday Present Belief Threat

Limiting and presuming beliefs are burdens. They not only cause resentment in your relationship, they also blindly prevent us from experiencing our true potential, or blindly expose us to potentially dangerous situations and major setbacks. When you engage in effective Interaction, one of the side benefits is challenging such beliefs and possibly replacing them with ones that are more *realistic* with the help of your partner. Your partner is a mirror reflecting back these buried beliefs, and helping you remove the blinders that keep you from seeing them. And of course, you help your partner do the same. We will be getting more into these types of benefits in the *Outcome* chapter.

> *Progress is impossible without change, and those who*
> *cannot change their minds cannot change anything.*
>
> - George Bernard Shaw

Containing the Buildup of Egoity

If I were a betting man, I would put money on *this* being your biggest challenge during Interaction. Up until now, you've probably had to endure a lot of arguments and other painful experiences when attempting to resolve conflict. It may take a lot to convince yourself to overcome your natural hesitation of subjecting yourself to the possibility of such pain again. Let's begin.

The Missing Piece

The ability to control Egoity during those tense moments determines whether or not Interaction will be successful in resolving conflict or erode into an all too familiar argument. It is the inability to hold Egoity in check that deters us from wanting to have Interaction in the first place.

Save Your RelationShip! - Part Two

Imagine again that this book is just an instruction manual for the game called *"Save Your RelationShip!"* You and your partner play co-captains of a vessel called *Curiosity* that you custom build together, and each brings on board their own crew of experiences, knowledge, interests, Egoity, and beliefs. The objective of the game is to navigate through a variety of ex-  citing and challenging passages, while keeping your vessel afloat for as long as possible and having fun!

You have completed the first challenge by granting permission to the Information official to determine whether or not your belief is the saboteur. You did this by allowing your belief to stand trial on its own merits. Let's see what's next on the agenda:

"Save Your RelationShip!" Challenge #2

The Information official has determined that one of two beliefs working below deck on the *Curiosity* is a saboteur: One accused belief is from your crew, and one is from your partner's crew. With the help of the Egoity crews, the two beliefs have been identified and summoned to the deck to face trial. Egoity crews are very loyal and protective of their fellow crewmates. Unless contained, your Egoity crew will defend *your* belief, while your partner's Egoity crew will defend *their* belief. As co-captain, you are responsible for the conduct of your crew. Until you take control and order your crew to stand down, the Egoity battle will escalate. Tensions will run high, and little spats will break out between the different Egoity crews with a lot of trash talk. Voices will get louder and tempers hotter as the divided crews fight, cower, and flee.

Your second challenge is to control your Egoity crew before there is destruction and mass mutiny on the *Curiosity*.

The second step to save your *RelationShip* is to contain the buildup of Egoity as you try to determine which belief is trying to sabotage it. The following is your progress report on learning how to keep your *RelationShip* afloat:

Interaction To-Do List	**Check**
1. Transform a threatened belief into a postulate	✔
2. Control Egoity protecting the belief	
3. Share effective Information	
4. Identify the reason(s) for the underlying resentment	
5. Resolve the conflict (which strengthens the relationship)	

So the second thing on your list is to control Egoity as it protects a threatened belief. It may seem as simple as soothing a slightly upset child, or like trying to single-handedly stop an angry lathered-up mob from massive destruction. Success is easier when you stop Egoity escalation as soon as possible. This is the second challenge on our conflict resolution obstacle course. Here are some more thoughts and ideas on this concept, and on making it happen.

"Your Biggest Challenge"

You may understand all the concepts of Interaction and have done all the preparations. You sit down with your partner and begin to hash through what is bothering you. You may think positively, look determinedly at your partner, and silently whisper an affirmation like …

> *I commit to seeing you as an ally.*

Yet isn't *this* what we sometimes mean? …

> *I commit to seeing you as an ally…. unless you do or say something that shows me that you are obviously NOT an ally, and in fact, intentionally trying to HURT me.*

Isn't *that* how it *really* is sometimes? We say we will be on our partner's side, yet once our partner's Egoity flares, we tend to suddenly freak out and see them as the enemy since they are *acting like one*. When this is the case, what we are not fully appreciating is that Egoity actions *we use* to defend against our partner's Egoity make *us* the enemy in *their* eyes as well. Each *defensive* response to an Egoity attack is seen as an *offensive* attack that needs defending. We justify our Egoity since we feel "they started it" and we're just *defending ourselves*. What we may also be failing to realize through all this is that our partner is feeling *exactly* the same thing.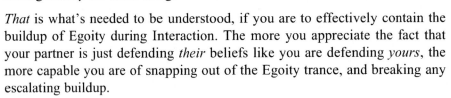

That is what's needed to be understood, if you are to effectively contain the buildup of Egoity during Interaction. The more you appreciate the fact that your partner is just defending *their* beliefs like you are defending *yours*, the more capable you are of snapping out of the Egoity trance, and breaking any escalating buildup.

Bracing for Impact

Egoity. It's gonna happen. Brace yourself. Cringe if you must, but remember this: *You want it to happen.* Well, only if you want to be able to identify threatened beliefs, resolve your conflicts, cleanse out resentment, and restore your relationship.

We may go into Interaction totally focused and committed on working with our partner to resolve the conflict. Yet as much as we want to keep our partner on our side, something will happen during Interaction that, at least temporarily, throws them on the other side.

If it makes you feel any better, even the super-strong Mr. Incredible has to cringe and brace himself for an impact of a speedy locomotive. It has to be done; he knows he can handle it, yet he still feels the need to emotionally and  physically prepare himself. You can tell by his self-control and instant decision-making that this is all in a day's work for a superhero. It may sting a bit, and he may even be unsuccessful and bounce off the train, yet he *knows* it will all be worth the effort.

So does it take super powers to stand in the path of Egoity? Nope. Just the understanding of what it is, what's going on, and the confidence that comes with practicing effective Interaction. Theorically of course, I'm almost certain that Mr. Incredible didn't know how to stop a bullet train as an infant. He had to learn for himself the power he inherently possessed. So can you.

> *Listen to people when they are angry, because*
> *that is when the real truth comes out.*
> - Unknown

Recognizing and Containing Your Egoity Animal

As discussed in the last chapter, Egoity is expressed in three forms: We (1) fight with, (2) cower from, or (3) flee from belief-threatening Information. The following are some techniques you may find helpful to trim the buildup of Egoity during Interaction. Use them when you catch yourself (or your partner) roaring like a Lion, cowering like a Turtle, or running like a Deer.

Taming the Egoity Lion

When your inner Lion comes out roaring, its primary objective is to attack the threatening Information *or* the messenger. It does this by aggressively refuting or counterpointing the Information, or aggressively attacking the character of the Information source. With loud, offensive words and intimidating body language, the Egoity Lion mimics authority by threatening *physical punishment*. It attacks the threat by *being a bigger threat.*

1. **Ask Yourself:** The moment you feel, hear, or see yourself getting loud and intimidating, ask something like, *"Why am I acting so harshly?"* or *"What just caused me to react like that?"*

   These or similar self-directing inquiries break the hypnotic hold the Lion has on you. It shifts your attention away from *defending* the threatened belief, by getting you to *identify* and *externalize* the belief. Once you realize that it is a *belief* that is threatened and not *you*, your Egoity Lion will calm down, until next time. Again, rinse and repeat as needed.

2. **Empathize With Your Partner:** Each time you hear or see your partner getting loud and intimidating, try to remember that they are just defending a *belief.* They are exhibiting threatening Lion behavior toward *you* since *you* are threatening a belief they still feel the need to defend. When you realize this, you will be better able to empathize with your partner, and ask them what is the matter. This will get them to focus their attention away from defending the belief, thus calming their Egoity Lion.

Encouraging the Egoity Turtle

When your inner Turtle hides inside its protective shell, its primary objective is to defend itself by blotting out, deflecting, and deforming Information, assuming it is *all* threatening. Like an adaptive child who's learned to cope with oppressive authority, the Turtle closes down the possibility for effective Interaction, yet stays for the battle. Because of one or two offensive words, it "covers its ears" for the rest of the Interaction concert.

1. **Ask Yourself:** Whenever you catch yourself *constantly* defending yourself with everything said, ask yourself things like, *"Do I really feel my*

partner is intentionally trying to hurt me?" or *"If I don't trust my partner to not hurt me, why am I even here?"*

Self-inquiring about your partner's true intentions instills a degree of empathy that weakens the need for the protective shield and helps to remove the battle line between you and your partner. It helps you see them as the caring, devoted partner *you choose to be with*, and not as an enemy with whom you have *no choice* but to battle.

2. **Empathize With Your Partner:** As you see your partner put on their rigid Information-protecting armor and look at you with wary eyes, try to remember that they are just feeling the need to defend a *belief*. Impatiently tapping on the shell, trying to get the Turtle to "come out and play," only makes it want to protect itself more. Understanding this concept helps you to share only calm, encouraging, empathetic statements, or to patiently leave the Turtle alone until it peeks its head out on its own.

Inviting the Egoity Deer

When your inner Deer feels like running away, its primary objective is to defend itself by simply not participating in Interaction. It doesn't feel it has the offensive *or* defensive capabilities needed to counter the threatening Information, so discussing it any further is simply forbidden. You may evoke a little Lion and roar, "I don't want to talk about it!" or do a
little Turtle by threatening to leave if your partner insists on talking about it. Yet the objective is the same: *Don't talk about it.* At that moment, the need for self-preservation prevents conflict resolution from even being a possibility. It will evade, ignore, leave: anything to avoid discussing the conflict.

1. **Ask Yourself:** When you feel yourself doing *anything* to avoid talking about a certain subject or seeing your curious partner as "verbally abusive," ask yourself: *"What is so forbidden that I can't even talk about it with my partner?"* or *"Why am I running away and disrespecting the feelings of my partner?"*

Thinking about the possible answers to these kinds of questions will help you focus on the reality of the subject and the real intentions of your partner. Instead of defensively assuming your partner is intentionally being cruel by asking hurtful questions, you are better able to relax and re-direct your attention to resolving the conflict.

2. **Empathize With Your Partner:** Each time your partner turns away or says they don't want to talk about something, try to understand that there is something there that is really scaring your partner. It scares them so much that they are unable (at this time) to talk to you about it. Imagine something so scary that you can't even share it with your cherished partner. Accept the fact that for whatever reason, the trust level is just not strong enough yet. The more you accept that, the better you empathize with your partner, and patiently wait for their trust to be strong enough to discuss the subject.

More Egoity Control Concepts and Strategy

Remember, when you are in Egoity mode, you don't know that you are. At that time, you feel you are doing absolutely the right thing to resolve conflict; it's just that your partner is preventing that from happening. "I want to resolve conflict... but defending *myself* takes priority." Once you "snap out of it" and realize you are defending *a belief*, you take back control from Egoity. Once you realize you are not in control, you regain control. The instant you perceive that you're fighting with your partner, stop, regroup, and notice what *scared* you.

To avoid getting emotionally hurt, we all use defensive techniques cultivated throughout life. Up until now, you may have never really thought about your Egoity, or its impact on the quality of your relationship. You may have never contemplated the need to control (or at least contain) Egoity, if conflict resolution is the goal. Up until now, you may have always played the victim and blamed your partner whenever things went bad in your relationship.

Here's a chance to change all that. With knowledge of *The Melfox Method* and willingness to practice effective Interaction, you can manage your Egoity. Here are some more ideas and suggestions you're welcome to try to help make that happen:

1. **Lights! Camera! Interaction!** One technique to understand the effect of Egoity is to record an Interaction session and see your own Egoity in action. Seeing your own Lion, Turtle, or Deer emerge can be a very enlightening experience. You have the opportunity to see the Egoity exchange *objectively* and *critically*, just as your partner and others see it. My golf game dramatically improved after seeing a video recording of

my swing. I had *no idea!* My swing was so bad; it looked like I was chopping wood. Seeing your Interaction "swing" *for yourself* may open your eyes to its strengths and weaknesses, and help show you ways to contain your Egoity.

2. **What Are You Afraid Of?** When you see your partner get too comfortable in their Lion, Turtle, or Deer suit, simply ask them what they are afraid of. Calmly ask them: "What Information was shared that is making you so defensive?" This not only helps get your partner to settle down, it also gets them to focus on identifying the threatened belief, moving the Interaction process forward toward conflict resolution.

3. **Special Password:** Use a special predetermined affirmation or phrase that changes the state of the conversation like "Fried Yellow Posies!" or similar nonsense. Make it you and your partner's own secret password. This phrase should be so unique, it only has one meaning: "Please stop fighting." It is to be uttered whenever either partner realizes that Egoity is running the con-  versation. When heard, the partners "promise" to do their best to purposely pull back the Egoity reins and stop defending the threatened belief. This "resets" the conversation with the level of Egoity brought down, at least temporarily.

4. **I'm On Your Side:** Constantly use words of reassurance and reminders of being on the same side and team. These should be something to trigger you and your partner into remembering the objective is conflict resolution. Remember also that in order for you and your partner to move forward past the Interaction and enjoy the "good part of life," Egoity must be contained and conflict resolved.

There are, of course, countless other imaginative ways to help get your or your partner's Egoity to settle down during Interaction. The more you learn and practice containing Egoity, the easier it is to handle the next challenge that will resolve the conflict.

So far we have discussed changing threatened beliefs into challengeable postulates, and how doing that helps control Egoity. When Egoity is under control, the lines of communication are opened and the sharing of resentment-cleansing Information becomes possible.

Sharing Effective Information

As long as Egoity is contained, we are able to pursue this next challenge. This is what real communication feels like without the impact of Egoity. This is how we envision talking with our partner about anything in an ideal world. Now that we've opened the door that Egoity has been guarding, we are able to share Information that will eventually resolve the conflict.

Save Your RelationShip! - Part 3

This is part three of imagining this book as just an instruction manual for playing an "Interactive" videogame called *"Save Your RelationShip!"* You and your partner play co-captains of a custom-built vessel called the Curiosity, and each brings on board their own loyal crew of experiences, knowledge, interests,  and beliefs. The objective of the game is to navigate through a variety of exciting and challenging passages, while keeping your vessel afloat for as long as possible and having fun!

So far we have completed the first two challenges:

1) Granting permission to the Information official to determine if your belief is the saboteur, by allowing it to stand trial on its own merits

2) Containing your Egoity crew.

Let's see what's next:

"Save Your RelationShip!" Challenge #3

Now that you and your partner have contained your Egoity crews after they identified the accused beliefs, the Information official can commence determining which belief is the saboteur. The Egoity crews from both sides will still act up occasionally, yet as long as they are not "out of control," the trial of the two beliefs can continue.

Your third challenge is to begin the process of assisting the Information official in determining which of the two beliefs is the saboteur aboard the *Curiosity*.

The third step to *save your relationship* is to share Information with our partner that will expose the relative strengths of the threatened beliefs and eventually resolve the conflict. Successful belief exposure occurs when you share effective Information with your partner.

The following is your progress report on effective Interaction:

Interaction To-Do List	Check
1. Transform a threatened belief into a postulate	✔
2. Control Egoity protecting the belief	✔
3. Share effective Information	
4. Identify the reason(s) for the underlying resentment	
5. Resolve the conflict (which strengthens the relationship)	

So the next thing on our list is to begin sharing Information that will lead to effectively resolving conflict. For this to happen, we need to contain Egoity, which requires us to continuously scrutinize the threatened belief by seeing it as postulate. As long as this is done, the lines of effective communication are open, and you and your partner will move closer to resolving the conflict.

The third challenge on our conflict resolution obstacle course is to direct the conversation toward conflict resolution by effectively sharing Information that will expose the resentment. Here are some thoughts and ideas on this concept, and on making it happen.

Cutting to the Chase

There once was a mother, father, and their 6-year-old son who just yesterday got a bad haircut. The mother wanted to take the boy to a different barber and pay again for something that was just done the day before. The father stated they shouldn't have to spend more money on another haircut, so we have the classic setup for resentment caused by conflicting beliefs.

Mother: We should spend more money on another haircut.

Father: We should not spend more money on another haircut.

At this point, it may seem that resentment is inevitable. Either the mother will go ahead and spend money on another haircut, which will be resented by the father; or the mother will not seek another haircut, which will cause resentment in her. Given the current "set in stone" level of understanding by both the mother and father, the conflict cannot be resolved. Regardless of who gets their way, and unless and until they talk it out, they will have to live with resentment caused by their differing beliefs.

Yet what if the parents didn't see their beliefs as permanent and knew that it was a simple case of *lack of Information* on somebody's part that was the cause for the issue? By adopting this type of mindset, each parent would be open to hearing more Information from the other regarding the issue, and be open to changing their belief.

1. For instance, after hearing the father's point of view in more detail, the mother may change her mind and agree that spending more money on another haircut is not something she really wants to do. No compromise; no "agreeing to disagree." With the additional Information and willingness to scrutinize her original belief, the mother decided to drop the idea of spending more money on a haircut, and the conflict disappeared.

2. Or after hearing in more detail how important it is to the mother that their son has a nice haircut, the father may change his mind and agree that spending more money on another haircut is the right thing to do. Again, no compromise; no "agreeing to disagree." With the additional Information and willingness to scrutinize his original belief, he decided to change it to agree with the mother's belief, and the conflict disappeared.

In either case, effective sharing of Information naturally resolved the conflict. With additional Information, each partner gains a better sense of empathy for the other. They have a clearer idea of their partner's motivations and strength of conviction, compared with their own.

Keeping the Lines of Communication Open

When dealing with Egoity while sharing Information, there's always the tendency to lash at your partner, recede even further into your shell, or look for the nearest exit. When you start to share conflicting Information and sense that warm feeling of Egoity's ire on the back of your neck, here are some suggestions to help you keep your cool, and your eye on the prize:

1. **Hear, Listen, and Then Talk:** For Interaction to be effective, you need to make sure you are truly hearing what your partner is saying and what their needs are. During the stress of Egoity, words may be misspoken, misheard or misunderstood. Taking the time to truly hear, focus on, and listen to your partner before talking helps reduce the chance of bogus Information creeping into the Interaction.

2. **Remember "SIR" Statements:** When Egoity starts to creep up, make an intended effort to make statements Specific, Irrefutable, and Relevant. This will help keep the conversation on track and minimize disruptive Egoity responses from your partner.

3. **Echoing Back:** If there is *any* doubt of the Information shared by your partner, take the time to echo back to them, in your own words, what they shared, to minimize misunderstanding. Egoity has the habit of occasionally causing words to be left out or misspoke. Repeating back what was said will help ensure that you and your partner are on the same page. It should keep the conversation on the clear path toward resolving conflict, as well as show you are serious about cleansing your relationship.

4. **"Feeling" Statements:** To avoid sounding accusatory, change declarative or exclamatory statements concerning your partner into conditional statements. An easy way to do this is to begin with "*I feel like.*" For example, "*I feel like... you're a jerk!*" It still may evoke Egoity, but at least it's not refutable.

Isolating Resentment

With Traditional Relationship Logic, we are not taught to think sharing Information that purposely exposes resentment is a wise thing to do. Anything that exposes imperfectness in our "perfect" relationship is usually met with distain, resistance, and Egoity. It is seen as only adding to the resentment inflammation, like intentionally punching an already bruised arm muscle.

With The Melfox Mindset, things are seen differently. Sharing Information that purposely exposes resentment is encouraged, not avoided. It is through the sharing of such Information that threatened beliefs are identified. Providing that Egoity containment is maintained, those beliefs can then be scrutinized, leading the Interaction toward conflict resolution.

Traditional Relationship Logic views your partner's sharing Information that purposely exposes resentment as akin to a bully intentionally hurting you by poking at your already bruised arm.

The Melfox Mindset sees the same actions from your partner as a doctor purposely trying to isolate the exact muscle bruised. "Tell me where it hurts," the doctor says while feeling around the area until the patient says, "There!"

Egoity shows you "where" the resentment is, which helps identify a threatened belief. Instead of feeling that your partner is purposely hurting you, you accept the temporary discomfort as serving a purposeful means to an end. This understanding helps keep Interaction on track and moving closer to the resolution of the conflict.

The Egoity Faucet

One way to control Egoity while sharing effective Information is to visualize regulating the flow of Egoity like a faucet. Better yet, think of it like something to be processed. Close the faucet after letting a little Egoity squeeze out, then you and your partner "process" it by talking about what belief was threatened. Continue regular conversation until Information is shared that evokes Egoity.

At that point the talk shifts to investigating what was threatened to cause the defense response. The shift may be the non-Egoitized partner saying, "OK, let's stop and go over what just scared you" or another previously agreed-upon phrase. Focusing on exposing and identifying the threatened belief, along with the willingness to challenge it, reduces the need for Egoity to protect the belief.

The conversation continues normally until a little more Egoity dribbles out. Again, "shut off the faucet" and process what was threatened. Rinse and repeat until there is no more Egoity left to process on the resentment subject. By purposely looking for and reacting to the presence of Egoity, we help reduce the chance of it escalating and possibly drowning Interaction.

Resentment Bucket Dumping

Especially when you are first learning and practicing Interaction, the idea of sharing Information that exposes resentment may seem daunting. One way of getting the show on the road is to imagine "dumping" resentment on your partner. Care needs to be taken in the delivery of such information to minimize sounding critical and accusatory, which could quickly escalate your partner's Egoity and end the Interaction.

Phrasing what you say as conditional "I feel" statements should help minimize the Egoity response. For example, "*I feel* rejected when you don't stay with me at parties."

Think of resentment as something that fills a bucket over time. Every time your partner does something that you don't like, it adds resentment to the bucket. We need to be able to empty or "dump" our resentment bucket as needed to keep it from totally choking off our relationship.

Many times, the mere act of "dumping" resentment resolves conflict by bringing to your attention something unknown or not considered prior. Safely letting your partner know what is really bothering you gives Interaction a great head start in determining the cause for the resentment. Remember, your partner has a resentment bucket too. At times you will be the "dumper," and at other times you will be the "dumpee."

Discovering the Reasons for Resentment

This is why we have Interaction. This is conflict resolution's promised land. There may be other doors that needed to open first, but this is the ultimate destination and where the journey ends. This is your goal. This is the "aha moment" of Interaction.

Your ability to (1) acknowledge that a belief may not be *true, (2)* control its Egoity, and (3) share needed Information has set the stage for this moment. You are now primed to solve the resentment mystery and figure out the reasons why you and your partner are at odds.

To illustrate this, let's return to and finish up our videogame analogy:

Save Your RelationShip! - Part Four

This is the fourth and final part of imagining this book is just an instruction manual for playing an "Interactive" videogame called "*Save Your RelationShip!*" You and your partner play co-captains of a vessel called the *Curiosity* that you custom build together, and each brings on board their own loyal crew of experiences, knowledge, interests, and beliefs. The objective of the game is to navigate through a variety of exciting and challenging passages, while keeping your vessel afloat for as long as possible and having fun!

We have completed the first three challenges by (1) granting permission to the Information official to determine if your belief is the saboteur, by allowing it to stand trial on its own merits, (2) containing your Egoity crew, and (3) beginning the process of assisting the Information official in determining which of the two beliefs is the saboteur. Here is the last challenge:

"*Save Your RelationShip!*" Challenge #4

Once you and your partner begin the process of assisting the Information official in determining which belief is the saboteur, your Egoity crews will resist in earnest. With each new clue, damaging evidence, or deduction, the Egoity crew for the accused will roar and hiss. This, of course, will prompt a retaliatory response from the opposing Egoity crew. In Challenge #2, you learned how to control your Egoity crews. Part of this challenge is for you and your partner to *continue* containing the antics of your Egoity crews, so the trial of the beliefs can continue. As long as this is done, you and your partner can continue assisting the Information official in determining which of the two beliefs is a saboteur.

Your fourth and final challenge is to continue the process of controlling your Egoity crews and assisting the Information official until the true belief saboteur is revealed. When this challenge is complete, the Information official will escort the belief from the *Curiosity*. It will live the rest of its days with its pals on Broken Belief Island.

The fourth step to *save your relationship* is to continue to control Egoity and share Information with your partner until you determine the reason why a belief is wrong - the reason for resentment. This is the "aha" moment, when it all becomes so clear why you were battling with your partner about the issue. After this moment, the issue is not an issue anymore. You can sense a piece of paper (or a whole ream!) float away that was between the magnet and steel. The following is your progress report on effective Interaction:

Interaction To-Do List	Check
1. Transform a threatened belief into a postulate	✔
2. Control Egoity protecting the belief	✔
3. Share effective Information	✔
4. Identify the reason(s) for the underlying resentment	
5. Resolve the conflict (which strengthens the relationship)	

The next thing on our list is to continue sharing Information until the reason for the resentment is discovered. For this to happen, we need to continue to contain Egoity, which requires us to continuously scrutinize threatened beliefs by seeing them as postulates. As long as this is done, the lines of effective communication are open, and the shared Information has a chance to reveal the reason for the resentment. The fourth challenge on our conflict resolution obstacle course is to stay on task and get to the reason. Here are some thoughts and ideas on making this happen.

Fundamental Reasons for Resentment

Let's review in more detail the four major reasons for resentment from the *Environment* chapter. The cause of most all resentment can be boiled down to one or more of these.

1. Lack of Sufficient, Pertinent Information

Information that is omitted from conversation can easily be converted into resentment. Decisions made by yourself or your partner without adequate Information can lead to conflict, and if not adequately exposed, resentment can easily set in. This is often the case when the relationship is new. Care needs to be taken early in the relationship to learn essential things about your partner's preferences, values, and idiosyncrasies.

2. Misunderstanding

There are 2 major areas of misunderstanding when comes to resentment:

1. Not hearing your partner correctly (thinking they said X when they said Y)

2. Not understanding your partner (not knowing or having different definitions of a word or phrase)

In either case, you or your partner innocently bases decisions on inaccurate Information. It is easily seen how this can cause resentment. Just like in the case of lack of sufficient Information, identification and sharing of misunderstandings squelch any chance of resentment occurring.

3. False Assumption

One of the more common causes for resentment is the use of false assumptions. Causes for this include expected patterns, social norms, past experiences, and simple laziness.

4. Jumping to False Conclusion

The basis for the conclusion in this case is protection. An event or series of events triggers you into Egoity mode. Out of fear or habit, you skip over the idea of gathering additional Information in favor of protection for the worst possible scenario. Once bitten, twice shy.

Effective conflict resolution does not mean you talk about something *just enough* so you can tolerate each other's presence. That would be something like conflict *appeasement* or conflict *reduction,* not conflict *resolution.* The "resolution" part means the reason(s) why whatever caused the conflict has officially been discovered and *accepted* by both partners.

Achieving Full Conflict Resolution

As shared earlier, this is the endgame of Interaction. It is figuring out and both *accepting* "what happened" ultimately to cause conflict. You can tell you've reached this point when someone says something like:

- *I thought I told you that it was a masquerade party.* (Lack of Information)

- *If I'd had known you didn't like coconut, I wouldn't have made that German chocolate cake.* (Lack of Information)

- *Fifteen? I thought you said fifty!* (Misunderstanding)

- *I thought you knew how to drive a car.* (False Assumption)

- *I automatically thought you were cheating when I saw that credit card receipt. I should have asked you about it.* (Jumping to False Conclusion)

Each one of these is an "aha moment." It is that *moment* when either you or your partner *learns* something that was previously *unknown*. It was that *lack of knowledge* that was causing the conflict. When both partners are aware and *accept* it, the conflict is resolved.

OK, that's simple enough. Just get to the point where you and your partner discover what was unsaid, misunderstood, assumed, or erroneously concluded. Once you figure out what caused the resentment, it vanishes like dust in the wind. The trick, of course, is to be able to control your Egoity long enough to figure out the reason for resentment.

Settling for Less Than Full Conflict Resolution

Of course, you can just take the Interaction process to whatever depths you want. When you feel that the Interaction has been "good enough" or if controlling Egoity is becoming a bit too much, you and your partner can agree to end it, and enjoy whatever increase in understanding is gained from it.

Understand this: Until and unless the conflict is *resolved*, it will continue to have an adverse affect on your relationship, albeit lessened by whatever understanding was gained from Interaction. The impact of sharing Information that exposes the resentment may be less after a truncated Interaction, yet the impact is still there. Until fully cleansed, resentment lurks in your relationship like a hidden landmine waiting to be stepped on again and again.

Remember what the boy did in the storybook *A Fly Went By*? He kept asking questions. After understanding that the frog was running away from a cat, *not* running to chase the fly, the boy could have stopped asking questions. Maybe all that the boy was interested in was the safety of the fly. Once he learned that the frog wasn't after the fly, he could have stopped the investigation and returned to the boat happy. Even though the fly may feel safe now knowing that the frog is not *intentionally* trying to hurt it, nothing has been done to address *why* the frog is running in the first place.

Stopping Interaction without fully resolving conflict is like just cutting out the top of a weed. It is only a temporary reduction in resentment, since its roots remain to regenerate. It is only through finding and accepting the reason for resentment that we eliminate the entire weed, roots and all.

Beatrice and Bruno – LIVE!

Imagine your Interaction as a reality TV program with a studio audience being privy to all the assorted details of the conflict you have with your partner. After the Interaction, the audience is asked for their rating of the conflict resolution. What do you think would be their overall consensus? Would they see the conflict resolution as totally complete, or would they still feel there's still some conflict there?

Whenever there is any lingering doubt as to the resolution of a conflict, the conflict is not totally resolved. Would they say that the Egoity was well contained throughout Interaction, or would they say that one of you had a tough time with it? Looking back on an Interaction through third-party eyes reveals strengths and shortcomings that can't be seen during Interaction. In this way, you could see the Interaction from outside both you and your partner. It will give you the most objective understanding of the conflict.

Interaction Disruptions

In this section we will explore the different ways that the sharing of effective Information may be delayed, terminated, or interrupted in anyway. Whether overt or subtle, these disruptions are always an expression of Egoity defending a threatened belief.

Why Disrupt?

We have just gone over how to open the four doors to get to the reason for the conflict. You know that it's a matter of sharing enough Information, asking enough questions, and answering enough questions until you eventually get to that reason. You know that getting to that reason will cleanse resentment and strengthen the relationship between you and your cherished partner. Waiting on the other side is restored trust and closeness and attraction with the one person you chose to be with of all the people in the world.

For whatever reason would you <u>ever</u> want to disrupt that process?

The only reason would be if the need to defend some belief, at least temporarily, was greater than your desire to resolve conflict, and even overrides your common courtesy. For at least that moment, your Egoity is evoked, causing you to defend yourself and disrupt the Interaction process. *Any* disruption by either partner during the Interaction process is a sign that a belief has been threatened.

Egoity is a faithful servant, and will vigilantly defend a belief as long as you hold on to it. The sooner we are able to stop defending a belief, the sooner Egoity is controlled and Interaction can resume. Remember our LABOUR chart describing the different types of hyperarousal?

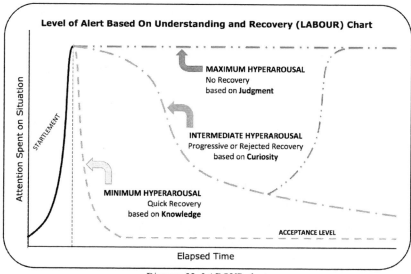

Diagram 32: LABOUR chart

Sometimes a threatened belief only produces a little more than startlement as an Egoity response before we take control and challenge the belief. Recovery time is swift and has a minimal effect on the Interaction process. Other beliefs may take longer to stop defending, yet as long as there is *curiosity*, the process is working toward taking back control.

Exploiting Disruptions

When either partner disrupts the Interaction process, it is in defense of a belief. The traditional response to disruptions is to shame, scold, and accuse the disrupter of behaving badly. This sets up the typical defense buildup on both sides and Interaction shuts down even more.

A different approach would be if you and your partner *use* this disruption as a *clue* to the identity of the threatened belief. Once the belief is identified, it can be scrutinized, freeing the protective Egoity and recommencing the Interaction process toward resolution.

The real trick to understanding effective Interaction is seeing it as a belief validation and modification machine. Interaction gives you the *opportunity* to expose and rectify conflicting beliefs, which is the basis of resentment. It is just a matter of being ready, able, and *willing* to expose each belief that gets threatened to scrutiny. If you come across a belief you are not ready, able, and willing to challenge, the Interaction process will be disrupted until you are ready, able, and willing.

Repairing Your Relationship Road

Interaction is the process of validating and modifying conflicting beliefs like a road crew repairs potholes in a road. Sometimes, you may get momentarily "stuck" defending a belief, like a steamroller may get stuck in the hole it's trying to repair. For the Interaction to move forward, the focus  needs to shift to "repairing" the conflicting beliefs by being ready, able, and willing to validate and modify. Until then, the Interaction is stuck, spinning its wheels and making the conflict pothole even bigger.

Since Interaction is a crucial part of the conflict resolution process, it is important to recognize the different ways that you or your partner may disrupt it. The sooner you see you have found another pothole, the sooner and easier it is to repair it.

Here are some common ways that Interaction is disrupted:

1. **Interrupting Your Partner:** Interruptions are obvious, direct expressions of Egoity. The Lion will verbally interject, the Turtle will dramatically turn away and sigh, and the Deer will simply threaten to leave. Whatever was just said has threatened a belief. It is just a matter of seizing that opportunity to identify what belief was threatened. After such an interruption, the other partner may simply ask, "What belief of yours did I just threaten?"

2. **"I Don't Know" and Other Stall Tactics:** Responding with "I don't know" or some other non-answer to a direct question puts the Interaction "on hold" since curiosity has stopped. Answering that question may threaten a hidden belief or move the conversation dangerously close to threatening one. The line of questioning is left in limbo, until the belief is identified and made challengeable. The partner may help this process by remaining patient and curious, and ask, "OK, I realize you don't know. But if you *did* know, what would be the answer?" This may move the conversation closer to revealing the threatened belief.

3. **Judging the Questioner:** Instead of answering a question that would threaten a belief, you or your partner may question that validity of the question. "Why do you need to know that?" is the typical response using this tactic. Forcing the questioner to defend the question at least temporarily delays the Interaction process. Again, with patience and curiosity, the questioning partner can break though the defenses and get their partner to reveal the threatened belief.

With conflict comes opportunity. Disruptions give us the opportunity to correct our sense of reality about a subject or event. It is at *the moment* of disruption that we can identify a threatened belief. Focusing on what Information that was just shared to evoke an interruption, keep asking: "What belief was just threatened?"

259

Disappointment and Empathy

One of the ways that we can describe our feelings of resentment with our partner is with disappointment. When our partner says, does, or believes something that we don't like, we naturally feel disappointed. We expected and would have preferred they had said, did, or believed *something else*. When we cannot accept this reality from our partner, it's because we do not fully understand *why* they said, did, or believes it. If we *did* understand *why*, then we wouldn't have a problem with it and there wouldn't be conflict or disappointment. That's where Interaction comes in.

Interaction gives you the *opportunity* to understand *why* your partner said, did, or believes something that is disappointing to you and causing resentment. Interaction provides the Information you and your partner need to understand and *empathize* with each other's world. After a conflict is resolved, any disappointment you have with your partner associated with that conflict disappears. When your beliefs line up with your partner's beliefs, there is no disappointment.

We feel disappointment when we realize we need to change or abandon a belief. There is a natural resistance to altering beliefs, due to the effort required to do so.

Permitting Belief Examination

Let's say Bruno is a front desk security officer. His job is to screen visitors and do all the things necessary to grant them access to the building. There are IDs to check, forms to go over, IDs to double-check, confirmations to make, and badges to issue. He has a comfy swivel chair and plenty to entertain him just sitting at the desk. Each time Bruno has to get out of his chair and go through all the procedural steps to grant access to a visitor, it takes effort.

Bruno likes his job except for actually doing it. He frequently resists even acknowledging a visitor's presence, because it would mean having to get out of his comfy chair. He questions, stalls, and tries his best to discourage a visitor at every stage of the access process. There's always that chance the visitor will give up trying to gain access, allowing Bruno to go back to idly sitting at his desk, playing Minesweeper.

If Bruno had gone through new employee orientation (like he was supposed to) he may have learned the importance of granting access to *all* qualified visitors. He may have come to realize that each visitor has the potential of providing the means for increased profits. Understanding this, Bruno would happily whisk though all qualified visitors, knowing each one may be the source of a bigger bonus.

Think of our natural reluctance to examining beliefs, like the reluctance Bruno has for granting access to visitors. The reason we have beliefs is to maximize our efficiency of effort. They allow us to do normal, everyday things without thinking about them. The price we pay for that convenience is the risk of being wrong. The more vigilant and the sooner we are able to examine a threatened belief, the sooner we can resolve any conflict caused by the belief.

> *One's best success comes after their greatest disappointments.*
>
> - Henry Ward Beecher

Cruising for a Bruising

Beliefs are time and energy savers, like autopilots on an *Airplane!* We have enough confidence in a belief's validity to hand over the responsibility of the cockpit, and party with the other passengers. Yet, what if our belief *is wrong?* What do we do if winds of change from our partner cause things to fly off course? Do we ignore a sudden drop in altitude and remain confident that our autopilot belief still has things under control? What if the belief is just a bunch of hot air and starts deflating?

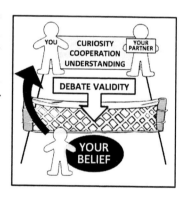

As *disappointing* as it will be to have to leave the fun of partying with the other passengers, at a certain point you need to stop and check the status of things. Otherwise, you may be still dancing the limbo in the aisle as the Interaction (and even the relationship) makes an expected and sudden stop, permanently ending your dance.

It is this natural reluctance to examine and take back control from a belief that you experience as *conflict* with your partner. You experience disappointment throughout the period of adjustment between A) realizing you and your partner have conflicting beliefs, and B) the reconciliation of that conflict. The sooner you resolve the conflict to the point of acceptance, the sooner you can stop feeling *any* disappointment around it.

Your personal belief system is primarily built on opinions. You may have a very, *very* strong opinion about something, or an opinion so weak it waffles back and front with the slightest breeze. Yet *all* opinions substitute for reality. When you take an opinion and defend it as the truth, it becomes part of your loyal team of belief autopilots. Regardless if the belief is right or wrong, the trust you have in the belief stops you from seeking and even seeing other possibilities. When you defend your beliefs without question, you close your mind to anything else.

When we defend a belief without examining it, we place more value on trying to *win* than seeking the *truth*. This is the classic difference between Traditional Relationship Logic and The Melfox Mindset. You may successfully defend your beliefs by winning an argument, yet the resentment with your partner continues to grow. Seeking, finding, and accepting the true cause of resentment by debating the validity of conflicting beliefs eliminates its toxic effects from your relationship.

Expect nothing and accept everything and you will never be disappointed.

- Laurence Overmire

Empathy – the Remedy for Disappointment

You feel disappointment when your partner's belief does not match your expectations and acceptance. There's an internal struggle that occurs so long as there's a difference between how your partner feels about something, and your acceptance of it. The disappointment wanes whenever you accept that reality, or your partner adjusts their perception of reality to match yours, or a combination of the two.

The way we accept another person's reality is seeing it through their eyes, and understanding why they have their belief. This understanding is achieved through effective sharing of Information. Interaction is the intended sharing of such Information. "Understanding Your Partner's World" could be the subtitle for Interaction, since it is only through empathy that we can justly reconcile conflicting beliefs.

Peeling the Empathy Onion

Back in the *Environment* chapter, we discussed how empathy is achieved one layer at a time through patient dialog while remaining open to whatever your partner has to share. Here are some more suggestions and techniques you are welcome to use to help you understand your partner's world, and help them understand yours:

1. **Holding Space:** Our partner deserves our full respect as we work together to resolve conflict and restore our relationship. Holding space means being able to accept whatever Egoity your partner throws your way, and not giving up on the Interaction. It's opening ourselves up to the reality that *this* person is the one we chose to be with. We could choose to understand them, and stop feeling they are intentionally trying to hurt us.

2. **Making a Pact:** Another way to help focus on understanding your partner is to make a special "pact" that allows both of you to share your feelings *out loud* without the threat of the other person leaving, or going into full-tilt Lion or Turtle mode. Notice this is a pact, not a rule. It gives you the chance to ask empathic, belief-threatening questions, with the assurance from your partner that they will contain their Egoity.

3. **Using Humor:** If you think something is funny and your partner thinks it's offensive, you have just been offered a glimpse into their world. Being offended or outraged by someone else's attempt at humor signifies some unresolved conflict or belief concerning the subject matter. Trying to understanding why your partner was offended helps you see into their world and appreciate your differences in viewpoint.

4. **Remaining Curious:** Anything that can be done to keep both partners on the same side throughout Interaction helps peel the empathy onion, eliminate disappointment, and drive the couple closer to conflict resolution. The moment you start looking for blame or defending yourself, the Interaction process shuts down. Staying curious about your partner and their world keeps you from ever seeing them on the other side. Let's see our Curiosity Mantra, one more time:

> *When I speak, I will always be curious, not judgmental.*
> *The words I use and the way I say them convey a sense of wonder*
> *so that I understand my partner, and my partner understands me.*
> *I have a burning desire to understand my partner,*
> *and for my partner to understand me.*
>
> *When I listen, I will always assume my partner*
> *is being curious, not judgmental.*
> *If there's ever a question of my partner's motive, I will calmly ask*
> *so that I understand my partner, and my partner understands me.*
> *I have a burning desire to understand my partner,*
> *and for my partner to understand me.*

Interaction Is Like a Three-Legged Race

Interaction is like you and your partner teaming up in a three-legged race. You can 1) run as fast as you can and hope your partner keeps up, or 2) run as fast as you can while working together and making adjustments to each other's actions. Winning teams work on ways to run together to maximize the quality of the relationship. If you fail to reach sufficient cooperation with your partner, you will fall, or drag your fallen partner for a while before quitting or falling yourself.

Teams that strictly use Traditional Relationship Logic have no empathy for their partner. They try to "win" individually by running as fast as they can, *ignoring* the fact that one leg is tied to their partner. During the Interaction race, when they fall down, get tripped up, or have to slow down, they are disappointed, with all the blame going to their partner. After all, if it weren't for their partner, they wouldn't have fallen, tripped, or slowed down, right? By not recognizing the need for cooperation and empathy, they fail to take responsibility for their share of the relationship, and it eventually falls down.

Teams that use The Melfox Mindset understand the importance of empathy for their partner. They know that it is through cooperation and understanding of their partner that they remain "in sync" and easily sail through the entire Interaction race.

Sacrifices, Compromises, and Forgiveness

As talked about earlier in this chapter, you may use Interaction to get to the point where you can tolerate your partner and then stop. You may say that that's good enough. After all, that is probably as far as you have ever gotten with traditional conversation. Yet stopping Interaction at that point is like having a fancy sports car and only driving it across the street for groceries. It is there for so much more.

Effective Interaction is designed to *cleanse* resentment, not just to dab at it a couple times with a damp cloth. When we intentionally "agree" to abridge the Interaction process, the remaining resentment surrounding the issue is swept under the rug or otherwise covered up. Any sacrifice, compromise, or forgiveness involving an issue does *not* make its associated resentment go away. That bears repeating:

> *Any sacrifice, compromise, or forgiveness involving an issue* ***does not*** *make its associated resentment go away.*

It will still affect your relationship like paper between a magnet and steel. About the only thing that changes is that you and your partner agree to *not talk about it again*. Think about it.

For the "sake of peace" between you and your partner, you may "sacrifice your feelings" and agree not to nag at your partner anymore about a certain subject. You may "agree to disagree" and allow the conflict to persist by substituting understanding with compromises. You may wave your magic "forgiveness wand" and declare that the resentment is gone. Yet all that means is that you won't mention it again. When you say you "forgive" someone for something, you are "pretending" the issue is resolved, when in reality it is still there, affecting your relationship.

Only You Can Prevent Resentment Fires

In Boy Scouts, one of the things you learn early on is respect for campfires. When putting one out, we learned to sprinkle the coals with water and stir them around until the fire was *completely* out. We were even taught to touch the soggy ashes to make sure they were cold. A single smoldering ember and breath of wind could be the start of a devastating forest fire.

The same can be said for resentment. If we sacrifice, compromise, or forgive prior to acceptance, resentment lies waiting to flare up from the smoldering ashes. All it takes is a similar event or reminder of the suppressed feelings to break through the artificial treaty and fan the flames of resentment. When we make sure the resentment "fire" is completely out by getting to the point of acceptance, we prevent any flare-ups when similar events or reminders of the resentment issue arises.

Again, It's Not Over Until It's Over

Back in the *Information* chapter, we discussed the need to keep asking "why?" to get to the root cause of resentment and effective conflict resolution. When you reach that "aha moment" of acceptance in conflict resolution, any lingering feelings of doubt about the malicious intent of your partner vanish into thin air. You have gathered enough Information to determine that the issue is dead, at least in your eyes. In fact, you may consider the issue *so* over; you don't want to talk about it anymore. Your partner may have other ideas.

This is not unlike the feeling you have when you like things they way they are, and are not open to discussing anything that threatens that. In your mind, everything is fine the way it is, so why rock the boat? Again, your partner may have a different understanding of the situation.

Compromises, Compromises

It's not until *both* partners get to the acceptance point that an issue is *truly* over. Denying discussion of a conflict subject just because *you* feel it's not an issue keeps the conflict alive. By withholding the exchange of Information, you are preventing your partner from getting to *their* point of acceptance. To your partner,  you are playing the elusive Egoity Deer, which only feeds the resentment fire over time. You are helping create a situation in which your partner has to compromise their feelings, since you are not open to hearing them.

Of course, your partner has their share of responsibility in this situation. Your partner needs to make sure that Information sharing in this conflict is done out of respect for *your* feelings of Egoity surrounding the issue. Trying to force-feed a scared Deer will only make it run faster and farther away from you.

Compromising, whether forced or voluntary, short-circuits the conflict resolution process and the relationship. As long as a couple feels it's fine to have compromises in their relationship, resentment will continue to fester. Compromising partners would not pass a campfire safety test. By shutting down or preventing Interaction by "agreeing to disagree," they leave the resentment embers warm and ready for the next breeze of conflicting Information.

The Need for Forgiveness

Anytime we feel we need to forgive someone, it shows we have not yet resolved the conflict to the point of acceptance. Like compromising, forgiving someone ends the Interaction process before it was able to solve the mystery. Resentment is automatically cleansed *without the need for forgiveness* when you understand that your partner is sorry for what they did and learned from it. By the same token, your partner bypasses the need to forgive when they understand you are sorry for what you did and learned from it.

Settling for forgiveness is like saying, "I don't know why they did it, but I will be the better person and not nag them about it anymore." We fool ourselves into thinking that suppressing our feelings about a subject will eliminate its effect on the relationship. It is the "don't know why" part that is the resentment indicator. As long as you don't know why, there is resentment.

Remember, for effective conflict resolution, the whole resentment weed needs to be pulled, roots and all. One more time:

Any sacrifice, compromise, or forgiveness involving an issue does not make its associated resentment go away.

Concluding the Interaction Process

As you gain experience through practice, you will notice that Interaction has its own place and routine in your relationship. At times it will be brutal, other times refreshingly quick and easy. To avoid the confusion of cross-purposes, it is important to make the distinction between the structured, goal-oriented Environment of Interaction, and regular carefree conversation. It is important to have an agreed-upon understanding between you and your partner of when you are in Interaction mode, and when you are not.

Ending an Interaction Session

Whether or not an issue has been resolved, both partners should agree upon the end of an Interaction session. This is not always a simple switch to turn off that is clearly known to both. A predetermined and agreed-upon signal to mark the end of the Interaction session will help avoid confusion and additional resentment. Here are few ideas that you and your partner are welcome to use to clearly signify that Interaction is over:

- If the conflict was resolved with both accepting the reason for resentment, take the "bad hat" off "Harry, the Relationship Bear" and put them both back in the closet.

- If the conflict was *not* resolved, leave the "bad hat" on "Harry, the Relationship Bear" and put them back in the closet.

- Put "Squeakers, the Resentment Mouse" away until next time.

- Change out of your special matching Interaction jersey or shirt.

- Gather up all the crib notes, cheat sheets, paddles and any other Interaction aids and store them away in that special place.

There are countless other ways of indicating that Interaction is complete, like simply stating a unique agreed-upon phrase. Standing up and saying something like, *"Thus endeth the Interaction"* may be all that is needed, providing your partner is in agreement.

Non-mutual Interaction Shutdowns

There may be times when one partner may want to shut down the Interaction session but the other one doesn't. After signaling the end of the Interaction session, persistence from a partner to continue may appear as badgering and cause resentment. On the other hand, cutting off the Interaction before you are ready may be frustrating and cause resentment as well.

Empathy for your partner can help minimize any resentment caused by non-mutual Interaction shutdowns:

1. Understanding your partner's desire to continue the Interaction process may help you reconsider closing down the process and continue it to the point of their satisfaction.

2. Understanding your partner's desire to close down the Interaction process may help you consider they have reached their limit, for now. No sense chasing after a Deer.

There is a difference between shutting down the Interaction due to overload of Information, and shutting it down to avoid talking about an issue. If you find yourself or your partner consistently evading conversations and Interaction when dealing with a particular subject, Deer-mode Egoity is engaged. Becoming aware of the impact this avoidance is having on the relationship can help relax the Deer enough to allow Interaction to commence.

Taking an Interaction Break

An effective way to deal with non-mutual shutdowns is to agree to take a break. A break is a timeout from Interaction for a specified time. This gives the partner wishing to terminate the Interaction a chance to catch their breath and possibly a second wind. It also gives the partner wishing to continue the process the assurance that it will continue.

Enjoying the Interaction Process

Throughout the Interaction process, there may be times that you will be tempted to walk away. The inability to change a belief into a challengeable postulate will greatly lower your desire to continue listening to conflicting Information. The inability to control your Egoity can make effective Interaction impossible. Not directing the flow of Information toward the reason for the resentment renders Interaction meaningless.

Understanding the enormous benefits that effective Interaction will have on your relationship could help you overcome the temptation to end it prematurely. Until you practice effective Interaction and see for yourself, you may have a difficult time realizing its true potential in transforming and restoring your relationship.

Remember, effective gardeners enjoy the process of weeding because their actions have readily apparent benefits. They *know* that without sufficient weeding, their garden will suffer. It is the responsibility of every gardener to ensure weeds are not having an adverse affect on their garden.

With patience and practice of effective Interaction, you can enjoy its cleansing impact on your relationship, and enjoy the process itself. In time, resolving conflict will be a pleasure. You may not believe "it will all be worth it" now. Eventually you will not just be told; you will know it.

In Conclusion

Think of Interaction as like solving a mystery. Let's say you find your dog Sam scarfing down doggie treats that were scattered all over your kitchen floor. You recall leaving the bag of treats out on the counter instead of putting it away safely in the cupboard. You quickly deduce that Sam knocked the bag off the counter. Sam is not to blame if he has not been properly trained to  ignore any goodies on the counter. If you just clean up the floor and put the bag of remaining snacks back on the counter, Sam will probably just knock it off again. You have identified the issue, yet haven't take the time and effort to effectively resolve it.

Think of the combination of Sam's not being properly trained and leaving the treats within his reach as *resentment*, and Sam's knocking the treats off the counter as *Egoity*. Like Egoity, Sam is just doing what comes naturally. Even after you identify resentment, if you don't resolve it, Egoity will expose it again and again.

Effective Interaction is not just identifying resentment; it's identifying the reasons behind it. When we don't take the time and effort to sufficiently understand *why* resentment was formed, we are just leaving the doggy treats on the counter for Egoity to knock off again and again.

The condition of resentment and the possibility of Egoity will remain until you properly store the doggy treats, or properly train Sam to not knock things off the counter.

In solving a mystery, we discover "who dunnit." Yet imagine if after figuring out that the butler did it, the detective-in-charge simply left without changing the situation. The butler would be free to do "it" again and again until he was removed from the mansion. It would be like discovering that the horrible smell coming from the kitchen was from smelly cheese left out of the refrigerator for a few days. You may have figured out that the odor came from the cheese, yet until you remove the cheese, the odor will continue.

Effective Interaction is identifying resentment *and* removing it. We need to do more than discover "what dunnit." As discussed in the *Environment* chapter, Interaction is effective only when we identify resentment and discover the reasons for it. We need to know "what dunnit" *and* "why diddit."

Interaction - Recap and Review

In this chapter, we have discussed the following:

Interaction - The Solution

Interaction is the integrating of Information and Egoity. We need to see that resentment is the enemy, and have the common goal of getting to its root cause.

Effective Interaction

Properly shared Information, along with controlled Egoity, creates the opportunity for effective Interaction. This is impossible if shared Information is not proper *or* Egoity is not controlled.

The Power of Mutual and Voluntary Exchange

When a business transaction is mutual, voluntary, and honest, both participants are *wealthier,* since they are better off than they were before. Each Interaction with your partner is like a business transaction. Effective Interaction is the mutual, voluntary, and honest exchange of Information.

For effective Interaction, both partners need to be RAW:

1. Ready, by knowing the basics of Interaction,
2. Able, by selecting a mutually appropriate time and place, and
3. Willing, to participate in the process.

Re-examining Traditional Relationship Logic

The virtues of "behaving good" and the myth of everlasting maintenance-free bliss are reinforced everywhere. For the most part, Traditional Relationship

Logic is a set of lingering rules of suppression that we learned to obey as children, or suffered the consequences if we didn't.

For the sake of peace and quiet, many of us learned (and still choose) to value the needs and wants of others, *above and at the expense of our own*. On the flip side, there are some of us who learned (and still choose) to freely express our feelings *with no regard* for the needs and feelings of others.

Cultivating The Melfox Mindset

Those adopting The Melfox Mindset do not suppress their feelings, yet they share them in a way that respects their partner's feelings as well. They work together without either feeling oppressed or feeling the need to dominate the other. With The Melfox Mindset, each partner understands that the goal is to cleanse resentment from the relationship, not battle each other.

Interaction Tools and Strategies

Props, Mascots, and Cheat Sheets:

- Use *Harry, the Relationship Bear* wearing a "bad hat" representing resentment.
- Use *Squeakers, The Resentment Mouse.*
- Wear the same team hat, shirt, or jersey.
- Select and use your relationship "team name."
- Write out and refer to your team slogan, mission statement, or other affirmations.
- Create and refer to "ice breaker" dialog assistance.

Refuting Shared Information and Other Interjections:

- Use a simple gesture like pointing a finger up, or raising your hand.
- Make and use indicators like YR, YOUR, or WHOA paddles with common interjections.

Preparing for Interaction

This is not going to be a *casual* conversation. There is resentment in your relationship that needs to be cleansed. Interaction is a structured mechanism to help you and your partner open your communication doors, discover the reasons for resentment, and eliminate its effect on your relationship.

We also discussed when to initiate the Interaction process and suggestions when only one partner is familiar with its concepts.

Curiosity State of Mind

You're sitting down next to your partner, set to start Interaction. Are you ready, able, and willing? Are you sure you *want* to do this? What's the objective again?

Traditionally, we may think of a commitment with a partner like a chance to collapse after a long exciting day at an amusement park. We are totally *dependent* on our partner's holding their end of the unspoken, yet we feel still binding, vow of *never changing*.

With The Melfox Mindset, we naturally reject any potential partner if they ever desired and were willing to be *oppressed* by us, or if they insisted on *oppressing* us. We can get as *close* as possible, but we still need to *see* each other as individuals, if we are to accept and understand any changes in the relationship.

Transforming Beliefs Into Postulates

The first step to save your relationship is to change a threatened belief into a postulate that can be scrutinized. By removing the concrete and putting little question marks on everything, we can set the stage for finding the reasons for resentment and cleansing the relationship Environment.

Tools for Changing Beliefs Into Postulates:

1. Change a threatened belief to a conditional statement by including a dependent clause.

2. Confirm your partner's threatened belief, and then ask if they can accept that it may not be true.

3. Think of Interaction as a game in which the object is to find that *one thing* someone believes that simply isn't true.

4. Think of you and your partner as a crime-solving team solving the mystery of resentment.

Limiting beliefs "hold you back" and keep you from fulfilling your true potential in life. Presuming beliefs have you believing in things that you are, *in reality*, not capable of, or ready for.

Containing the Buildup of Egoity

The second step to save your relationship is to contain the buildup of Egoity as you try to determine which belief is trying to sabotage it. Suggestions were given for taming your Lion, encouraging your Turtle, and inviting your Deer. They focused on asking yourself Egoity-busting questions and empathizing with your partner.

More Egoity Control Concepts and Strategy:

1. Record an Interaction session and see your own Egoity in action.

2. When your partner gets too comfortable in their Egoity, ask them what they are afraid of.

3. Use a special predetermined phrase that changes the state of the conversation.

4. Constantly use words of reassurance and reminders of being on the same side and team.

Effectively Sharing Information

The third step to save your relationship is to share Information with your partner that will expose the relative strengths of the threatened beliefs and eventually resolve the conflict.

Keeping the Lines of Communication Open:

1. Take the time to truly hear, focus on, and listen to your partner before talking.

2. Make an intended effort to make statements Specific, Irrefutable, and Relevant (SIR).

3. Take the time to echo back what your partner shared to minimize misunderstanding.

4. Change declarative or exclamatory statements into conditional statements.

Discovering the Reasons for Resentment

The fourth and final step to save your relationship is to continue to control Egoity and share Information with your partner until you determine the reason why a belief is wrong - the reason for resentment.

After a review of the four major reasons for resentment, the benefits and need for achieving full conflict resolution were discussed.

Interaction Disruptions

Whether overt or subtle, Interaction disruptions are always an expression of Egoity defending a threatened belief. The traditional response to disruptions is to shame, scold, and accuse the disrupter of behaving badly. A different approach would be if you and your partner *use* this disruption as a *clue*.

How Interaction Is Disrupted:

1. Interrupting your partner
2. "I don't know" and other stall tactics
3. Judging the questioner

Disappointments and Empathy

When our partner says, does, or believes something that we don't like, we naturally feel disappointed. When we cannot accept this reality from our partner, it's because we do not fully understand *why* they said, did, or believe it. Interaction provides the Information you and your partner need to understand and *empathize* with each other's world. The way we accept another person's reality is seeing it through their eyes, and understanding why they have their belief.

This understanding is achieved through effective sharing of Information.

Peeling the Empathy Onion:

1. Our partner deserves our full respect as we work together to resolve conflict.

2. Make a pact to allow feelings to be shared *out loud* without the threat of leaving.

3. Being offended or outraged by someone else's attempt at humor signifies some unresolved conflict or belief concerning the subject matter.

4. Staying curious keeps you from ever seeing your partner on the other side.

Settling With Sacrifices, Compromises, and Forgiveness

Any sacrifice, compromise, or forgiveness involving an issue *does not* make its associated resentment go away. About the only thing that changes is that you and your partner agree to *not talk about it again*.

Concluding the Interaction Process

Ending an Interaction Session:

1. Put *Harry, the Relationship Bear* back into the closet with the "bad hat" on or off.

2. Put *Squeakers, the Resentment Mouse* away until next time.

3. Change out of your special matching Interaction jersey or shirt.

4. Put away all the crib notes, cheat sheets, paddles, and any other Interaction aids.

Empathy for your partner can help minimize any resentment caused by non-mutual Interaction shutdowns. An effective way to deal with non-mutual shutdowns is to agree to take a break.

With patience and practice of effective Interaction, you can enjoy its cleansing impact on your relationship, and thus enjoy the process itself.

****

Now that we have established that a relationship's only enemy is resentment and have discussed its causes... and that properly shared Information is the key to revealing those causes... and that controlling Egoity enables Information to be shared properly... and that effective Interaction reveals the causes of resentment and resolves conflict...

Use and Enjoy!!

CHAPTER FIVE - OUTCOME

Beatrice and Bruno were taught the basics of Interaction by "Beano." They acted out possible scenarios and developed their own strategies for controlling Egoity. They felt the thrill of proactively and effectively resolving conflict. After a while, Beano got up from the kitchen table.

"My time is done here," he said. After thanking Beatrice and Bruno for the water and their time, he smiled. He knew they were both open to thinking about what he had come to teach them.

"Now I want you kids to promise me you'll practice and learn what we have talked about," Beano said with a mock scolding and finger wag. "Don't make me come back here!" He then relaxed and beamed a warm smile full of gratitude and appreciation.

"Thank you both, so much, for your interest and desire to learn how to maintain your relationship. If you ever need a refresher, I'll always be around. One last word of advice: Try to control your Egoity, not each other."

Beatrice and Bruno looked at each other and smiled. "We will," said Beatrice as she opened the front door. "You take care of that cough!" she added, suddenly realizing that Beano couldn't do that by himself.

"Oh, I'm feeling much better already," he said, smiling at Beatrice and Bruno at the threshold. "You take care of yourselves, and for MY sake...," Beano broadly grinned, pointing at their hearts, "take care of each other." He then turned and walked away into the misty night.

Beatrice and Bruno gave each other a big hug and then looked back out the door. "We will!" Bruno shouted with a big smile. He then turned to Beatrice and noticed she was tearful again. He wiped her cheeks with his handkerchief, gazed into her eyes, and smiled. "Now, where were we?"

Beano left with his head held high, a hopeful heart, a chuckle to himself, and a curious thought: "If they only knew."

****

Outcome - The Reasons

Outcome is the result of Interaction. Each Interaction has its own unique outcome. An issue may be resolved, unresolved, or deemed irresolvable. In this chapter we will be discussing each of these results, as well as what to expect with effective Interaction. We will be discussing its effect on the relationship with your partner, yourself, your family, and your world.

Interaction Results

Think of your Interaction like a tennis match. Did you and your partner *win*? Did resentment *win*? Did you resolve some or all of your conflicts? Rain-delayed? Injury timeout? How well did you stay on the same side of the net?

The Outcome may not be fully realized directly after Interaction. Sometimes it's not until after the Interaction dust settles, and partners have a chance to think about and self-reflect, that the true Outcome emerges. Acceptance of the reason for resentment may not come until later, after a partner reviews the Information shared in private and works it all out. This contemplation may result in additional questions and Information exchange before the issue is put to rest.

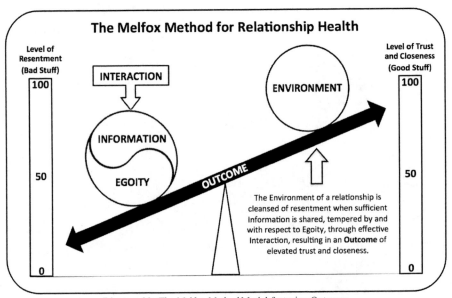

Diagram 33: *The Melfox Method* Model featuring Outcome

Depending on how well the Environment was cleansed of resentment determines the extent that trust and closeness are elevated. Even if an issue is not completely resolved, any progress made toward that end cleanses the relationship. The issue may still exist, yet any Information shared that brings the partners closer to understanding and acceptance helps bolsters trust and resolve to continue the resentment cleansing process.

Your Backstage Pass to the Solution

Practicing Interaction with your partner is like learning *together* a new language that is all your own. This chapter gives you a sneak peak into what learning that skill can and will do for your relationship moving forward.

Accepting Relationship Struggles

Toward the end of the 2012 baseball season and into the playoffs, Alex Rodriguez was in one of the biggest slumps of his career. This decision to removed him from the starting lineup obviously put stress on A-Rod's relationship with the team. In response to the slugger's struggles and how the decision would affect their on-going relationship, Yankee manager Joe Girardi had this to say:

> *I ain't worried about years ahead. Just let me worry about today. The best relationships, the strongest relationships, are always relationships that go through some struggles.*
>
> *Relationships just aren't perfect. I mean you put a husband and wife together where the relationship was just perfect without any struggles, and you're probably not living on this planet. So relationships go through that.*
>
> *So, I mean if things have to be, you know, built back up, we can do that. I have had to do that before. So I don't worry about that.*

Mr. Girardi demonstrates the natural need for maintenance in a relationship. Like we discussed earlier, healthy relationships need to be regularly cleansed of resentment like a healthy garden needs to be regularly cleansed of weeds.

Just for fun, let's look at some of the concepts in the above quote replacing the word "relationship" with "garden," and "struggles" with "weeding":

> - *The best **gardens**, the strongest **gardens**, are always **gardens** that go through some **weeding**.*
>
> - *A **garden** that is just perfect without any **weeding** is probably not living on this planet.*
>
> - ***Gardens** go through that. If things have to be built back up, we can do that.*

Makes sense, doesn't it? Effective Interaction is a way of providing the means to keep your relationship weed-free and growing strong. Traditionally, we sit back and watch the resentment weeds grow strong, thinking there is nothing to do but blame someone and abandon the garden.

With each cleansing Interaction and continuing practice, we learn an effective way to face our significant relationship problems. By learning effective Interaction skills and adopting The Melfox Mindset, we bring conflict resolution up to a whole new level. As Albert Einstein is cited to have said:

> *The significant problems we face cannot be solved*
> *at the same level of thinking that created them.*

It's All Good and "All" Means Everything

Let's say that you and your partner are traveling down your relationship "road" and come across a fallen tree blocking your way. You may perceive removing it as a natural part of the relationship process, or needing to remove it as a disappointment and a bother. The first mindset makes the experience positive, and second one, not so much.

Accepting the fact that resentment will occasionally hinder your relationship path will help you engage in the process to remove it. When we refuse or are unable to accept the conflicts that naturally arise, we resort to blaming our partner or ourselves, and prevent effective Interaction from clearing out the resentment debris.

Reviewing the Interaction

Since Interaction is a type of conversation that may be new to you and your partner, discussing it afterward can help relieve any anxiety you may have concerning the Interaction. It will give you and your partner a chance to adjust to your new level of thinking about your relationship and its maintenance. First, let's do some self-evaluation:

Interaction Debriefing

Remember our Interactive *"Save Your RelationShip!"* video game? You and your co-captain (partner) are asked to perform four challenges to expose and remove saboteur beliefs from your "RelationShip." Players are able to sail on to exciting bonus levels, providing they are always able to answer the challenge of rooting out threatening beliefs.

How well did you do with each challenge during your Interaction?

1. How often did you allow your beliefs to be tried on their own merits? How often did you defend your beliefs by preventing the trial from taking place? How well did your partner do?

2. How well did you contain your Egoity? How often did your Lion, Turtle, or Deer control your actions? How quickly were you able to regain control? How well did your partner do?

3. How well were you able to share Information during the Interaction? How often were your statements specific, irrefutable, and relevant? How effective was the Information exchange in resolving the conflict? How well did your partner do?

4. Were you able to find the reason for the resentment to the point of acceptance?

   - If so, do you know if your partner accepts the resolution?
   - If not, are you hopeful future Interaction will resolve the conflict, or are you thinking resolution is hopeless?

Asking these types of questions after Interaction helps you to see your strengths and weaknesses in effective conflict resolution. Improving your Interaction shortcomings starts with knowing what they are. Asking yourself these challenge questions and honestly answering them will give you the clues you need to make your next Interaction even more effective.

Tell Her (or Him) About It

Either directly after Interaction or following some self-debriefing, you may want to have a follow-up discussion with your partner regarding your Interaction experience. Think of it like a critical review of a Broadway play or movie. Remember, this is not the play or movie itself.

It may be easy to slide back into Interaction mode when discussing it with your partner, but now is not the time. This is simply a discussion of lessons learned, helpful suggestions, interesting observations, and the mutual celebration of any conflicts resolved.

This gives you and your partner the chance to talk about how the Interaction has affected the relationship. Sharing revealing "I didn't know that..." or "If I only knew..." moments can be motivating memories heading into the next Interaction. Even if the conflict isn't totally resolved, sharing the feelings of progress and improvement may very well entice you for more.

Discussing lessons learned and suggestions are extremely helpful in adjusting your and your partner's mindset and style for future Interactions. Of course, you have to be open to hear them.

Open to Suggestions

Just like in effective Interaction itself, it is important to be open to your partner's feelings and opinions about the Interaction. Defending the decisions you made during Interaction is like defending threatened beliefs. You can either 1) defend them by preventing them to be scrutinized using Traditional Relationship Logic or 2) allow them to be cross-examined and criticized utilizing The Melfox Mindset.

Accepting the Past

When the smoke clears after Interaction, we are able to look at the new Information and do some self-reflection, or "Self-Interaction," if you will. We are left with the sometimes-unsettling task of evaluating our responsibility for the conflict. The reason for resentment may have been a simple misunderstanding. No harm, no foul. We are easily able to accept the reason and take responsibility for our part. Other Interactions may reveal a reason for resentment that is harder to swallow. We may find it difficult to look back at the conflict we caused by the Information we omitted, the conclusion we jumped to, or the assumption we made.

Lamenting

Sometimes, the last piece of a conflict resolution puzzle is getting to the point of acceptance for *your role* in causing and sustaining the conflict. We may discover something that we did or believed caused a lot of conflict and declare:

"I can't BELIEVE I did that!"

This expression and the feeling behind it are revealing your *inability* to accept your part in the cause of the conflict. The feelings of guilt and shame are preventing you from clearly understanding what happened. This lamenting is keeping you from accepting the reason for the resentment and resolving the conflict.

Lamenting is essentially resentment with *yourself.* You are unable to accept and let go of something you did in the past. For a conflict to be totally resolved, you need to accept what *you* did, as well as what *your partner* did.

Lamenting is like entering a magic portal and experiencing past events again. Only this time, we relive those events with the Information *of the present.* We are not remembering the events as an outside observer. We replay the role as if it were happening *now.* As they play out the past experience, lamenters *can't accept* the actions they took, given the Information they have *now.* They are forced to relive their previous actions yet are powerless to change anything. They feel the stress of being a puppet of the present, totally controlled by the strings of the past.

> *Wasn't it a wonderful moment, when you first realized that you could not change the past and viewed it inert as fossils and libraries, rather than sad, disappointed ghosts with wagging fingers?*

Should I Have Known Better?

In reality, there are no magical time machines to travel back in and relive the past. The past is written in stone and there is nothing you can do about it. Lamenting is *reliving* the past, instead of *remembering* it like an observer. Ask yourself the following questions if you start to lament:

- Are you a controlled puppet, or are you watching a puppet show?

- Are you the victim, or are you reading about a victim in a newspaper?

- Are you acting in a play, or watching one?

Lamenters think that they *should've* known better, instead of accepting the fact that they simply *didn't* know better.

The fact is, you are doing the very best you can *at your present level of awareness*. Notice this says *present*, not future. You can only judge your past actions based on the *limited* Information you had *at the time of the actions*.

The more you are able to see the past as simply a library of lessons learned, the better your chances of accepting it. Once we accept the past, we are able to learn from it. We have to be willing to open and read from the book of regrets, to learn what to change and do better next time.

Interaction Outcomes

Whether immediate or after some self-reflection, each conflict settles in to a particular Outcome. It is left unresolved, deemed irresolvable, or successfully resolved. The conflict is resolved when both partners agree with the reason for the resentment and accept their share of the responsibility for it. When conflict resolution is not complete, it can be seen as either "in progress" or hopeless.

Clearing Our Relationship Road

Interaction is an attempt at cleansing resentment from our relationship. On our relationship road, resentment naturally builds up like potholes or debris, blocking or hindering the closeness we feel with our partner. The ability to resolve an issue depends on a number of factors, including:

1. The relative strength of the beliefs threatened
2. The desire of the partners to understand each other and resolve the conflict
3. The understanding and working knowledge of effective Interaction

Resentment may seem like a few fallen branches or an entire redwood tree. Curiosity and knowing effective Interaction skills can go a long way in removing even the most daunting obstacles. They give you the tools you need, like chainsaws and bulldozers, for clearing out the big resentment logs.

Without curiosity and effective Interaction skills, resentment cleansing can be like trying to clear a road of debris without so much as a garden rake. Maybe we don't even think about getting out of the car, and blindly drive through the resentment until the damage to the relationship is beyond repair.

Our passion and confidence level help determine the extent we are willing to go to clear our relationship road. Is the debris a piece of cake to remove? Will it take multiple Interactions to resolve? Is the debris too much for us to handle? Is it simply not worth it?

Did you clear the road? If not, do you feel like continuing to try to clear this relationship road, or do you feel more like seeking an alternate route?

Conflict Status Outcomes

After Interaction, the resulting status of a conflict will be determined. It will fall into one of three possibilities:

> 1. *Unresolved:* The issue was not resolved, yet resolution is regarded as in progress.
>
> 2. *Irresolvable:* The issue was not resolved, and resolution is regarded as not possible.
>
> 3. *Resolved:* The issue was resolved, with both partners accepting the reason for resentment.

Let's examine these types of Interaction Outcome in a little more detail.

Unresolved Issues

As much as we would like, conflicts are not always resolved in one Interaction session. Some types of bread dough need several kneading and rising sessions before they're ready to be put in the oven. The more complicated types of conflict need time between Interaction sessions so that new Information has a chance to soak in. Seeds sown can take root and bear fruit weeks or even months later.

Keep in mind that progress is made with an Interaction even if all that is accomplished is clarifying, or even just informing or being informed of the conflict. It's like the old adage of peeling back the layers of an onion. An Interaction session may only remove one or two layers, yet you are one or two layers *closer* to your resolution goal.

The Twang of Resentment

Along with our natural appreciation for beauty and seeking perfection, we have a natural aversion to anything out-of-kilter. Things like misused grammar, clothes that clash, out-of-tune singers and guitars, and too much pepper on your paprikash.

The resentment caused by unresolved issues is like an out-of-tune string on your relationship guitar. The song you play with your partner should be harmonious and beautiful. An unresolved issue puts an out-of-tune "twang" in the music of your relationship. Whenever casual conversation brings up that issue, the notes are not pleasant to hear and Egoity is evoked. The Lion will verbally complain, the Turtle will cover its ears, and the Deer will leave the room.

Interaction is taking time out from playing your relationship guitar to "tune" it with your partner. Sometimes it takes a few Interaction sessions before the issue is acceptably tuned to the satisfaction of both. An issue is totally resolved only when you and your partner can talk freely and openly about it, and not have *any* Egoity response. Until then, the resentment "twang" will persist in your relationship.

Don't Touch the Sides!

In the classic board game *Operation,* players use their dexterity skills to remove a variety of objects from a cartoon surgical patient without touching the metal sides with the metal tweezers. When the sides are touched, an electrical circuit is closed, the patient's nose lights up, and a "buzz" is felt, indicating that the player has failed.

Conflict resolution using Traditional Relationship Logic is like playing *Operation*. We guide our conversations around an issue to avoid touching the sides of Egoity. Effective Interaction is not about avoiding Egoity; it is about *removing the batteries*.

Without the fear of Egoity, the "wrenched ankle" issue can then be taken out and talked about, without feeling the need to carefully tiptoe around it. Until an issue is "discharged" with effective Interaction, the Egoity alarm is always armed and ready to protect any threatened beliefs.

Unresolved issues affect your relationship like an electrical charge. Effective Interaction weakens this energy with each session. With sufficient desire, curiosity, knowledge, patience, and practice, you can be neutralize and discharge resentment surrounding any issue.

Thought of Everything?

Before dumping an unresolved issue into the irresolvable bin, seek every avenue for answers. Chances are, someone else had a very similar issue and found a way to resolve it.

For instance, let's say you have a seemingly irresolvable issue of seeing "too much" of your partner. You have a place together because that is traditionally what you do when you're in an intimate relationship. Resentment from the lack or invasion of personal privacy may build up significantly at any time. This type of resentment is almost automatic and "built-in" when you share personal space. But what can you do? Isn't sharing space just a necessary compromise in an intimate relationship?

When you seek answers and open yourself to any and all possibilities, you may find solutions that are surprising. For example, in March 2012, *Elle* magazine ran an article titled "Divide and Conquer: Married But Separate" by Kate Bolick. Here is an excerpt:

Hard numbers are impossible to come by, given that the Census Bureau doesn't count this demographic, but it has become increasingly common for two people in a loving, committed union, married or otherwise, to maintain separate living quarters. One survey indicates that in the United States some 6 percent of women and 7 percent of men live separately from their partners; throughout northern Europe, it's about 10 percent—a quarter of all the people there who live alone.

With enough desire, imagination, open-mindedness, and patience, you can resolve *any* issue without feeling the need to sacrifice or compromise. But what if you or your partner (or both) simply *doesn't have* the desire or patience? What if you come to a definitive decision that attempting to resolve an issue *is not worth* the time and effort?

Irresolvable Issues

No matter how great your desire to resolve conflict, there may be an issue that is so overwhelmingly dug-in and painful that you feel additional Interaction sessions would be useless.

Bruno's First Car

Bruno bought his first car in the late fall and happily drove it around. As summer approached and temperatures started to rise, Bruno was hit with a grim reality: *His car didn't have air conditioning.* Rolled-down windows are not much help in bumper-to-bumper traffic in the heat of the day, and the noise was sometimes so loud he couldn't think. Bruno would look around at the other drivers all cool and content in their quiet bubbles, as beads of sweat would ski down his face.

Bruno knew he needed to make a decision, since discomfort was quickly turning to intolerance. Installing a custom AC system in his car was not worth it. Bruno wanted and needed to drive around, yet his present vehicle was not filling the bill. Later that day, Bruno started looking for a trade-in. His next car will have air conditioning.

Decision Time

Sometimes an irresolvable issue doesn't reveal itself until the change of the seasons, like the lack of air conditioning in Bruno's car. After looking at the price he would have to pay, Bruno may decide to stay with his old car and live with the discomfort throughout the summer. Yet like toxicity in a relationship, when discomfort reaches a certain level, the decision will need to be made to get another car.

Sometimes an irresolvable issue develops from a change in situation. Let's say you and your partner love zooming around in your two-seat roadster. When baby is going to make three, it's time to trade in for a sedan. When you get to the breaking point of intolerance and have exhausted all possibilities,  ending a relationship with something that is not capable of fulfilling your needs is the correct and healthy thing to do.

We all go through natural changes in preferences, needs, goals, and desires in life. New experiences and Information may awaken previously dormant interests and talents that require a major shift in lifestyle if they are to be pursued. Sometimes these shifts are too great and unacceptable for the partner, or directly threaten the relationship itself. A decision needs to be made to either give up your new dreams, or give up on the restrictive relationship preventing them from happening.

Pauline Friedman Phillips for decades wrote the popular "Dear Abby" newspaper advice column under the name Abigail Van Buren. Here is what she had this to say about marriage:

> *I always thought that marriage should be forever. I found out through my readers that sometimes the best thing they can do is part. If a man or woman is a constant cheater, the situation can be intolerable. Especially if they have children. When kids see parents fighting, or even sniping at each other, I think it is terribly damaging.*

Although she mentions only cheating, *any* issue with enough resentment can be intolerable. If it is deemed irresolvable, parting sometimes is the best thing to do.

"Deal Breakers"

Let's say that you and your partner are driving down your relationship road and find that it closed with flashing lights and
barricades. Or maybe you come across a huge redwood tree
blocking the road. In either case, the conditions are such that
continuing to attempt to drive down this road any time soon is
hopeless. Of course you may decide, as many couples do, to park and idle on
the side of the road, waiting and hoping for your relationship road to clear
up. As others live joyful happy lives, you may choose to remain committed
to your partner *for years* and live with the choking toxicity from the resentment you can't get rid of. For whatever reason, you choose to stay in a stag-
nant noxious relationship and hope, rather than changing course.

Eventually, you get tired of waiting and become intolerant of the poisonous
effects of the resentment. When things get bad enough, it's time to double
back and take another route. This is the point of relationship "irresolvablity,"
as you decide to abandon it and start preparing for a possible alternative. The
time and effort required to resolve the conflict is simply *not worth it*, and it
becomes a "deal breaker" or "last straw" in your relationship. Any commitment or affirmations like our Curiosity Mantra no longer apply. We no
longer can say: *"I have a burning desire to understand my partner, and for
my partner to understand me."* The fire has burned out.

Opportunity for Closure

With effective Interaction, at least you have the chance to know what caused
the breakup. Instead of going around singing "Baby Come Back" and feeling
blue, which is traditionally the case, you can use Interaction to pinpoint the
irresolvable issue and even the threatened beliefs causing the resentment. It
may not be resolvable, yet with sufficient Interaction, at least you can know
more about the cause of the breakup.

The more you empathize and understand the nature of the conflict, the more
likely you will be able to part ways without bitter feelings. Interaction can
help both in seeing the issue clearly and agree that it is irresolvable. After
surrendering your relationship to the victorious resentment on the other side
of the net, you will be able to "shake hands" on the same side and amicably
walk away. Without sufficient empathy and understanding as in traditional
breakups, the ex-partners are less likely to be as cordial, and more likely to
storm off the court blaming each other.

Lessons Learned

The decision to end a "deal breaker" relationship is not unlike the decision to trade in a vehicle. If you didn't properly maintain it and the repair costs are prohibitive, it's time to end your relationship with it. After reaching the "not worth it" point, any repair attempts with Interaction become futile and even viewed as abusive. All you can do is try to end the relationship with as much understanding and empathy as possible, and learn from it for next time.

Resolved Issues

This, of course, is the preferred and expected Outcome from Interaction. When an issue is acceptably resolved, any resentment associated with it vanishes. Like the removal of an electrical charge, it no longer has any toxic impact on the relationship. Seeking issue resolution is the *reason* for Interaction. An issue may be temporarily unresolved or eventually deemed irresolvable, yet the goal of effective Interaction is always *resolution* of issues.

Keep in mind that an issue is not totally resolved until both partners agree and accept the reason for the resentment. As a review, this reason is usually one or more of the following:

1. Lack of Sufficient, Pertinent Information
2. Misunderstanding
3. False Assumption
4. Jumping to False Conclusion

An issue may be unresolved directly after Interaction, yet resolved after one or both partners have a chance to think about it and let the new Information soak in. Overcoming the need to lament or similar resistance is sometimes required before full acceptance of the reason(s) for resentment is achieved.

You Know an Issue Is Resolved When You Can...

1. Talk and laugh about the subject of the issue, with <u>no</u> Egoity.
2. Sing and dance on the issue's grave.
3. Bump the Egoity sides of the issue with your *Operation* tweezers, with <u>no</u> reaction.
4. Touch the coals of the issue fire, and find them <u>cold</u>.

One Less Stress

With each successful issue resolution, there is a natural feeling of relief, joy, and celebration you share with your partner. You get the distinct feeling of stronger attraction, like when paper blocking a magnet from steel is removed. Each resolved issue is like pulling a weed from your garden or performing some necessary maintenance on your car. Each resolved issue also means *one less thing* to think about, worry about, and fret over in your life. You are freed from its toxic resentment forever, and so is your partner.

Getting Better All the Time

Resolving an issue does much more than cleanse its associated resentment. Especially when you are new at effective Interaction, resolving an issue gives you the confidence to tackle more and bigger issues in future Interaction sessions. Each resolution is one more piece of evidence that you and your partner *can* restore your relationship and keep it that way. As we talked about in the *Introduction*, "success begets success," with each resolution strengthening your belief in more and greater successes in future Interaction sessions.

Beyond the Outcome

So far in this chapter, we have discussed…

- *Debriefing:* The important role of critical evaluation of Interaction sessions, with or without your partner, in improving the effectiveness of future Interactions.

- *Lamenting:* How accepting the past and responsibility for your share of a conflict is just as vital to its resolution as accepting your partner's share, and the reason for resentment.

- *Results:* The description and effect on the relationship of the three possible resulting Interaction Outcomes on an issue: a) Unresolved, b) Irresolvable, and c) Resolved.

In the next few sections, we will be discussing how the *type* of relationship you have with your partner plays an underlying role in the frequency and intensity of conflict. This includes the circumstances and responsibilities agreed (or "forced") upon, as well as your expectations and vision you have for the relationship.

Interaction Mindset Review

As discussed earlier, how you view your partner during Interaction has a critical impact on its Outcome. How often did you see them as an *individual*; respect their unique interests, beliefs, and awareness; and work *together* to resolve conflict? How often did you allow that respect to fade away, and choose to *battle* when your partner's interests, beliefs, and awareness didn't agree with yours?

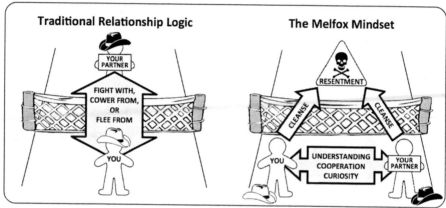

Diagram 34: TRL and TMM with net and hats

The more we see the relationship we have with our partner as a *blended* entanglement, the less tolerance we have when they do something we don't like. Their beliefs and awareness level somehow have a direct reflection on *us* when they don't agree. Curiosity and empathy naturally give way to judgment and criticism.

Beyond Interaction

The same type of thing goes on when we decide to blend relationship *responsibilities*. Throughout the stages of the relationship, you agree to blend certain areas of your lives together. Each one of these areas of responsibility has its own set of circumstances that determine its volatility and vulnerability to conflict. Blended responsibilities are breeding grounds for resentment.

In addition, the way we envision the relationship plays a pivotal role in the accumulation of resentment and our ability to remove it:

- Do we see the relationship as the voluntary co-creation of two individuals?

- Do we have a natural desire or sense of duty to control certain aspects of our partner's life *without* their approval? Would we want our partner to do the same?

Blended Responsibilities and Control

When we choose to be in an intimate relationship with someone, we are simply agreeing to be with that person and forsake all others. Period. That is the only requirement and our sole responsibility. Regardless of what we've been taught or choose to believe, there is no need for the responsibilities in an intimate relationship to be any more than that.

When we choose to entangle additional areas of our life together with our partner, we are relinquishing full control of those areas. Blending your worlds together may seem like the normal and natural thing to do, and as long as you totally agree on all blended aspects, there is no problem. Yet what do you do when you don't agree?

Extenuating circumstances like children and financial dependency do not exempt you from the resentment that can form from issues that arise from them. These types of situations require special care, understanding, and empathy to ensure that the resentment is continuously removed.

Color My World

Visualize blending red paint and yellow paint together. When you first start stirring, you see a delightful dance. The red and yellow streaks beautifully swirl around each other like Fred Astaire and Ginger Rogers. But alas, they soon blend together into a solid shade of orange, and the dance is over. What was once a striking display of contrast and movement is now just a homogenous lifeless blob. It may be a great shade of orange, but the dancing partners have disappeared.

In contrast, one of the interesting things about lava lamps is that the dance never ends. The colored glob flows up and down, yet never *blends in* with the clear liquid. If it ever did, it would just be a colored lamp and the dance would be over. And what's interesting about that?

Intimate relationships can be viewed like the swirling and blending of two colors. In certain areas of responsibility, we allow the boundary protecting our personal identities to be breached, and we see *no difference* between our partner and us. We allow what was once *only* in our control to be lumped in with our partner where it can be judged and controlled by them. Things that were once "yours" and "mine" - are now "ours." The more our red or yellow turns to orange, the more we lose our personal identity, and the more we lose our ability to see and appreciate our partner as a separate person.

Blended Responsibility Examples

Here are a couple of areas of our personal lives we can choose to *blend* with our partner, and examples of the seeds of resentment they invariably sow:

- **Personal Property**
    - *Finances*: What was once empathy for and *curiosity* about how our partner spends *their* money becomes *judgment* and criticism of how they spend *our* money.
    - *Preferences:* If you really want your new boat to be red, and your partner really wants it to be blue, what can you do? You can only afford one boat, and purple is out of the question.

- **Place of Residence**
    - *Personal Space:* The inability to adequately express our personal identity and freedom at times may be bone of contention and a source of resentment.
    - *Preferences:* What was once empathy for and *curiosity* about how our partner decorates *their* place becomes *judgment* and criticism of how they decorate *our* place.
    - *Chores:* What once was empathy for and *curiosity* of how our partner maintains *their* place becomes criticism and *judgment* of how they maintain *our* place.
    - *Manners:* What once was cute and tolerable can become a constant source of irritation and resentment when you live together.

When we allow or feel we must *blend* residence, property, finances, and other personal matters, we set a volatile stage ripe for judgment, criticism, and resentment. The more we blend in an area of responsibility, the more attention is needed to keep the constant growth of resentment weeds under control.

The Breakdown of Boundaries

For each area of your life that is blended with your partner's, a boundary protecting both of your individualities is breached. While choosing to blend may seem normal, natural, and overall beneficial for the relationship at the time, things may not stay that way.

Living together or sharing finances may be correct things to do for a given circumstance, yet what about when it's not? And what about the conflict that naturally arises if you or your partner ever (gasp!) has differing opinions about how *your* lives are to be spent?

Imagine if we were able and chose to remove our skin boundary and blend physically with our partner, just like we can choose to blend other areas of our lives. If you're joined at the shoulder, you can't go upstairs to the tower and get a runway diagram while your partner checks down the field for emergency equipment at the same time. Blending responsibilities at first may feel like the thing to do; yet if you and your partner ever desire *autonomy* in that area, resentment awaits and abounds.

Taking Back Full Control

There may come a time when the stress and resentment caused by a blended responsibility become so great that something has to change. Traditionally, that is a sign that something is wrong with your relationship, and it is doomed to failure. It is traditionally thought that when someone moves out or gets their own checking account, the relationship is *over*.

But does it have to be over?

It may just be that circumstances have evolved to a point that necessitates a change of responsibility in an area of your relationship. Reversing the blend and taking back full responsibility for an area in your life may not be as easy as the blending; yet it may be what is needed to keep your relationship from dying from suffocation.

Orbiting Relationships

The way we envision "our ideal relationship" helps determine the areas of responsibilities we are willing to blend with our partner, and to what extent. The more you imagine the perfect relationship to be one in which you and live "as one" with your partner, the more willing you are to blend responsibilities with them.

Another way of visualizing relationships is as the co-creation of something *separate* from the individuals. This mindset sees blended responsibilities as a *breach of separateness,* which deadens the relationship by neutralizing the attractive, dancing energy between the two partners. This attractive energy is like the pull between our magnet and steel. The *closer* you get to touching, the *stronger* the pulling force.

Feel the Force

As with any attractive force, the farther apart two items are, the weaker the pull of the force. The *closer* they get, the *stronger* the pull of the force. Yet if and once they *collide,* the attractive force gives way to attachment and the loss of the exciting dancing energy.

If we look at relationships in this way, the strength of attraction you have depends on how *close* you are, without "colliding" and blending control with each other. In essence, the more you collide and allow responsibilities and control to blend, the less "exciting" the relationship. Think of the similarity of these exciting moments:

- The best tennis shots are the ones *closest* to the line, *without* being out.

- The one who can go the *lowest, without* touching the limbo stick, is the winner.

- The one who can clear the *highest* pole vault bar, *without* knocking it down, is the winner.

- The less a bobsled *touches* the walls of the track during a run, the *faster* it goes.

- The *closer* our hero is to peril, *without* being hurt, the more exciting the movie scene.

These moments are exciting because they push the limits of an activity, while respecting the inherent *boundaries* of the activity. When relationships are looked at in the same way, we can say the following:

- The *closer* you get to your partner *without blending,* the *more exciting* the relationship.

It may seem that it requires constant discipline to resist the constant pull of attraction and prevent "colliding" into your partner's world. Colliding may seem to be the natural endgame for an intimate relationship. It makes sense to think that two items that are attracted to each other will eventually touch. There is, however, another way of looking at relationships that doesn't require discipline to keep from colliding. It requires *trust.*

The **Closer** I Get to You

If we were to visualize ourselves in relationships as a free-floating planet, how we would *relate* with other planets? When you come across someone you would like to be in a relationship with, what is your goal?

- *Traditional Relationship Logic:* To mutually collide and blend with them and become "one planet" in as many ways as possible.

- *The Melfox Mindset:* To mutually engage in an orbiting spiral around each other, without ever getting so close that you fall out of orbit and collide.

With The Melfox Mindset, partners start out an intimate relationship by dancing or "orbiting" at a respectful distance. This distance is shortened as they get to know and *trust* each other. As the couple gets closer, it could be said that they are *falling* for each other. But instead of colliding, they maintain a stable orbit while getting closer by naturally increasing their rate of speed, or as we feel it, the rate of *excitement.*

This concept is like the seemingly magical way a figure skater spinning around increases the speed of the "orbit" by bringing their arms closer to their body. In the science world, this is known as the law of conservation of angular momentum. A spinning figure skater or someone spinning on a lazy Susan reduces their "moment of inertia" by pulling in their arms, causing rate of rotation rate to increase. If you see yourself as one hand of a spinning skater and your partner as the other, the closer you get to each other, the faster and more exciting the experience.

Satellite of Love

This same concept and law applies to orbiting satellites. The distance away from Earth and the speed of the satellite must be complementary if the satellite is to remain in a stable orbit. Without enough speed, the satellite *collides* with the Earth and the dance is over. With too much speed, it spins away aimlessly, endangering it and whatever it may run into out in space. In a stable orbit, the satellite is simultaneously falling toward Earth and moving away from it at the same time.

Couples using The Melfox Mindset see their relationship like two satellites going around each other in an exchange orbit. In outer space, an exchange orbit occurs when two co-orbital objects are of similar masses and thus exert a non-negligible influence on each other. Any exchange of two people causes a "non-negligible influence" on each other. When the trust and closeness level increases, the rate of excitement increases. If the trust and closeness level ever goes down, putting distance between the partners, the rate of excitement naturally decreases.

With this mindset, you can literally be *falling* for each other continuously, while still maintaining a stable respectful orbit. A *closer,* ever-tightening orbit requires a *faster* and thus more *exciting* orbit. This is similar to our game of Tug-Of-Trust described the *Environment* chapter. The more trust you have with your partner to not let go of the relationship rope, the further you can lean back, and the greater the excitement.

Curiosity State of Mind (Part II) Broken Down

This book has stated the problem and offered a solution. Resentment is the problem, and Interaction is the solution. Along with the components and techniques of effective conflict resolution, we have discussed our relationship state-of-mind, and how it determines the effectiveness and efficiency of the Interaction process. This perspective also determines the extent responsibilities and control are allowed to blend, and how much respect separateness and boundaries are given.

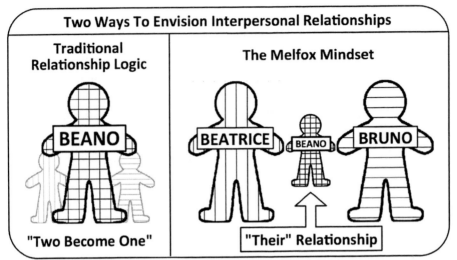

Diagram 35: Envisioning Relationships TRL & TMM

Throughout this book, we have been contrasting and comparing Traditional Relationship Logic with The Melfox Mindset. In this section we will continue our exploration of these two points of view, and how they shape our relationship world.

As discussed earlier…

- Those using Traditional Relationship Logic see the relationship as one *blended* entity.

- Those utilizing The Melfox Mindset respect individuality and see the relationship as an *orbiting* dance.

Suffocating the Fires of Passion

When sharing an intimate commitment with 100% Traditional Relationship Logic, we blend responsibilities and control in as many areas as possible. We blend into *one* like two raindrops on a windshield. We feel a deadening sense of relaxation around our partner, like having a cushy job at a company our parent owns. We feel we can play around and be as rude as we'd like, since we *know* we will never be fired.

Initially, we feel emotionally safe since our partner took a vow to always hold onto our relationship rope and be there for us. We slumber in the warm, comfortable bed of arrogance, since we feel there is nothing left to prove, and nothing left to win. One day, we wake up and realize that the music has stopped and we've stopped dancing. For many of us, it is only then that we see that the emotional shackles we put on our partners, we put on ourselves as well. Of course, right around then, your partner is probably realizing the very same thing.

In many ways and in a very real sense, each partner feels they *blend* into the other, like a *Ghost* possessing Oda Mae Brown, or one entering the secret door to *Being John Malkovich*. These films do a great job of portraying the consequences of feeling you possess the power to directly *control* someone else, when they don't *want* to be controlled. Remember that elevated level of curiosity, attraction, and excitement you once shared with your partner? The more you blend, the less the attraction.

In our attempt to preserve the relationship like a beautiful flame or butterfly, we sometimes capture it, put it in an airtight jar, and consequently snuff the very life out of it. The more we try to blend with and control something, the less alive it feels to us. We may be attracted to and want to be with someone, yet if we don't respect their needs and our differences, the resulting blending neutralizes the relationship's energy, sexual and otherwise.

Keeping the Fire Alive and Kicking

With The Melfox Mindset, partners in a committed relationship are respectful of each other's needs, wants, and differences. It is the healthy feeling of *separateness* that allows the fire of passion and attraction to breathe and grow.

In the 1981 movie *Stripes*, Sean Young's character invites Harold Ramis' character to play a friendly "force field" game. The object is to get as close as possible to each other *without actually touching*. "If someone breaks your force field, you win." (She won. He didn't care.) You wouldn't expect this "not touching" game to be very popular in the physical world, yet it serves as a good metaphor for The Melfox Mindset view of relationships.

There is a natural desire to be as *close* as possible to our partner. Yet when we "cross the line" and *blend* our identities in a certain area of our lives, we are no longer *close*. Instead of individual preferences and responsibility, that area is now "shared community property" between the partners. We could get really close to and feel the warmth of a candle flame, yet the instant we try to *hold* it, it is snuffed out between our fingers. A child learns that touching a spinning top can make it topple and stop dancing. By respecting and embracing their separateness, partners can enjoy their warm and dancing relationship without causing it to go out or lose its balance.

Khalil Gibran, the Lebanese-American poet and author of the book *The Prophet*, described the need for separation and balance this way:

> *Let there be spaces in your togetherness, and let the winds of the heavens dance between you. Love one another but make not a bond of love: Let it rather be a moving sea between the shores of your souls. Fill each other's cup but drink not from one cup. Give one another of your bread but eat not from the same loaf. Sing and dance together and be joyous, but let each one of you be alone, even as the strings of a lute are alone though they quiver with the same music.*

It is the difference between dancing with your partner, and feeling like one clumsy body with two heads – each wanting to dance a different way.

Controlling the Urge to Merge

Think of the excitement you feel in a blossoming intimate relationship. If you have never been in such a relationship, imagine how it would be like. The intensity increases as you chase and get closer to your new partner. You want to always be with them, and experience the vibrant thrill that the relationship provides. You feel yourself falling closer and closer to your partner.

Traditionally, the ideal intimate relationship endgame is collision. The merging of two people into one. The unity of souls. The blending of responsibilities and control by blurring the lines between our identity and our partner's. That is the objective. With this perspective, the explicit desire is to *end* the chase, *end* the falling, and *end* the dance. To relax from the excitement of dating and courting, and live forever in bliss with your true soulmate. Yet the feeling of bliss you seek was in the chase, the falling, and the dance. When you *merge*, all that goes away. No more chasing, no more dancing…

> *But who says the chase and dance have to be over*
> *after you enter a committed relationship??*

With The Melfox Mindset, intimate relationships are seen as a continuous dance. The excitement in a relationship is the sensation of *continuously* chasing and falling for each other, like two planets in a mutual stable orbit. We see our partners as individuals rather than one-half of ourselves, in order to remain curious and attracted to them. The feeling of attraction is greater the closer the magnet gets to the steel, but once they touch, the dance of attraction is over. When you become so blended that you lose sense of where you finish and your partner begins, you not only lose your identity, you also lose interest in your partner.

The Relationship With Your Partner

Here are some closing thoughts on what to expect as you and your partner learn and practice effective Interaction and use The Melfox Mindset. Dealing with blended areas of responsibility and control will also be discussed.

Afterglow: "Unexplained" Enhanced Attraction

With each conflict resolved through effective Interaction, you and your partner will feel an increase in attraction that is really quite amazing. When you reach that "aha" moment and accept the reason for resentment, it's like a figure skater spinning faster by bringing their arms closer to their body. The shift in the intensity of the relationship is palatable, especially after resolving the bigger issues. You will feel the attraction and trust return to the relationship, which was lost when the issue was formed.

With each resolved issue, the Environment of your relationship gets cleansed and closer to the intensity you felt when you and your partner were the closest. In fact, some conflict resolutions may result in your feeling closer and more attracted to your partner than ever before. As you gain more experience with effective Interaction and adopt The Melfox Mindset, conflicts are seen more like opportunities and less like battles. You may even get to the point where you look forward to conflicts, since they give you the opportunity to further understand your partner's world.

Partnership With The Melfox Mindset

The more you adopt The Melfox Mindset and respect each other's individuality and boundaries, the less likely you will allow responsibilities and control to be blended. In the areas that need to blend, constant vigilance is required to keep the built-in resentment at bay. Whenever responsibility and control is spread to more than one person, there is always the question of where the responsibility and control ultimately resides.

In the business world, there is a desire to have a single point of contact on a project. Responsibility and control rests with one person. When these are shared with multiple people, constant communication is needed to prevent duplicate, conflicting, or omitted actions. Too many cooks spoil the broth.

As long as you and your partner are on the same page regarding a blended area, and satisfied with each other's contribution, there isn't an issue. This requires being in total agreement in every action that affects that blended area of responsibility. As we discussed earlier, any compromises and sacrifices in this area build resentment. If you live together for instance, the décor needs to be acceptable to both. If Beatrice wants to paint the kitchen pink and Bruno wants to keep it white, someone is not going to get their way. Understanding that these types of conflicts naturally occur in blended areas of responsibility may not resolve conflict, but should help reduce the resentment associated with it.

Cultivating an Attitude for Gratitude

The combination of being resentment-free and managing your blended areas creates a honeymoon-like state in a relationship that has no expiration date. The traditional idea of a honeymoon period ends when resentment and colliding take place, causing the relationship to get stale, boring, and toxic. The more we respect our partner's individuality and separateness, the more we can appreciate and care for the relationship we co-create.

When we see our relationship like a creature with two heads, it's a battle for control. We don't see our partner as separate from ourselves, so we ignore personal boundaries both coming and going. Instead of being grateful to be with our partner, we take them for granted.

The more we see our relationship as a co-created entity separate from ourselves, the more we can respect, appreciate, and therefore care for it, as well as our partner. Caring for the relationship, of course, means conflict resolution as needed through effective Interaction. As long as we see it as separate mutual co-creation, appreciation for the relationship will naturally lead to gratitude for our partner, and vice versa. The Outcome is a relationship that is respected, well maintained, and "perma-fresh." And the honeymoon beat goes on…

The Relationship With Yourself

Most of the focus of this book is on how to restore the relationship with your partner. We have covered the components and concept of effective Interaction in revealing the reason for resentment, which resolves conflict. Having a healthy, well-maintained relationship with your partner does more than bring the trust and closeness back. It helps us regain and maintain our own identity while in an intimate relationship. It also provides us the opportunity to improve ourselves. A trustworthy connection with our partner allows us to overcome our vulnerabilities and expose limiting and presuming beliefs.

Respecting Yourself

With Traditional Relationship Logic, there is a constant struggle for control with our partner, just as we learned as children with our caretakers. We feel justified to disrespect and disregard our partner's feelings, beliefs, and individuality in order to "do what's best" for the relationship. There is nary a thought that what we believe is "the best thing" - may *not* be. Regardless of who's right and who's wrong, the disrespect for our partner tears at the very fabric of the relationship.

Traditional Relationship Logic doesn't stop there. Right along with the disrespect for your partner is the disrespect you feel for *yourself*. You have allowed your personal boundaries to be disregarded and someone else to be responsible and control *your* life, which has morphed into *you and your partner's* life. This loss of identity and respect for individual responsibility can play havoc on your feeling of self-worth and self-determination. Being in a relationship that is based mainly on controlling and being controlled naturally suffocates the respect you have for yourself, as well as your partner.

Seeing our relationship as separate from our partner via *The Melfox Method*, we are able to restore our personal boundaries and respect for our individuality. We are able to orbit and dance with our partner separately, instead of being one big blob with each partner struggling for control. We feed off the energy from our respected and maintained relationship, instead of trying to steal energy from each other as done in colliding relationships.

Happiness is having someone to help solve your problems.
- Unknown

Opening and Thinning Out Belief Closets

As discussed in the *Interaction* chapter, during the course of effectively resolving conflict with your partner, beliefs are changed into postulates and challenged on their own merits. When beliefs are determined and accepted to be false, they are discarded and replaced. The exposure and disposal of some beliefs have little influence on our daily lives, the decisions we make, and the way we understand our world. Other beliefs have a tremendous impact on what we see as achievable and realistic in life. Limiting beliefs "hold you back" and keep you from fulfilling your true potential in life. Presuming beliefs have you believing in things that you are, *in reality*, not capable of, or ready for.

Besides conflict resolution, effective Interaction may be used to intentionally expose limiting or presuming beliefs. A cleansed and healthy relationship provides a safe place where we can overcome our vulnerability and freely discuss volatile subjects with someone we really trust.

Think of it like an afternoon with a friend thinning out your closet of clothes that are not in style or don't fit anymore. You try on something, and then model it in front of your friend like you're in a fashion show. Together you decide whether it's a keeper or going to charity. Some clothes may be harder to let go of than others, yet an outside observer can help us see flaws we couldn't on our own. If we trust  our friend and their opinion, we can clean out outdated items from our closet.

In much the same way, we can help clean out outdated beliefs through the "fashion show" of Interaction. The more we identify with or have invested in a belief, the harder it may be to discard it. A trusting partner and effective Interaction can reveal flaws in a belief that we couldn't see on our own. As discussed earlier, our partner can be like a mirror, showing us things within us we weren't seeing otherwise, like we need mirrors to see the back of our head. With effective Interaction, our partner can help us decide which beliefs to throw out for being old-fashioned, or from your outgrowing them.

Everyone comes with baggage. Find someone
who loves you enough to help you unpack.

- Unknown

Relieving the Stress

Perhaps the greatest benefit to yourself in being able to resolve conflict with your partner is the impact it has on your physical health. We all have felt (or can at least imagine) the tremendous stress of conflict from being in a relationship with resentment. It affects the way we live and the way we think. This stress can lead to physical disease itself, or have us want to relieve it with harmful actions to others or ourselves. Overeating, under-eating, ulcers, backaches, rudeness, bad habits, and worse can result from a stressful, resentment-ridden relationship.

Resolving conflicts through effective Interaction and adopting The Melfox Mindset provides relief by eliminating its cause of the stress. A cleansing, dancing relationship reverses the stressful effects of resentment, and provides a safe, nurturing Environment for you and your partner. You are, once again, co-creating the mutually supporting world you have always envisioned intimate relationships can provide. And that's a great relief.

The Relationship With Your Family

The presence of resentment, and the ability to cleanse it from you and your partner's relationship, affects more than just the two of you. Remember, resentment is like a poison that saturates the surrounding Environment like a toxic cloud. There is a natural impact on anyone else living with you or spending a lot of time with you.

And, of course, our knowledge of effective conflict resolution and The Melfox Mindset can be used directly to enhance the relationship with other members of your family. The same principles of Interaction and respect for individuality you learned with your partner can be used to restore and maintain the relationship you have with a child, parent, cousin, live-in in-law, or anyone else.

Take a Look Around

Think what it feels like if you're having dinner at a restaurant with another couple and they begin arguing. It's uncomfortable, and sometimes you feel you may even be in danger from the crossfire. You want to leave, and if it gets any worse, you probably will. You have that choice.

Children and others under your care usually don't have that choice. If you and your partner deal with conflicts by battling each other in the traditional sense, those around you have that same type of uncomfortable and insecure feeling felt at the restaurant. Arguments, moodiness, depression, aloofness, slamming doors, and worse - all affect the trust level and quality of the relationships you have with children and others close to you.

Learning and practicing effective conflict resolution and utilizing The Melfox Mindset clears the air and provides a safety zone in the household. The emphasis is on empathy and curiosity, not blaming and judgment. It's on proper respect and *resolution*, not winning an argument.

For Those in Your Authority

As discussed in the *Introduction*, infants are totally dependent creatures. 100% of the responsibility for infants goes to their caretakers. As children grow, they take on more responsibilities and enjoy the privileges that those provide. The timing of the transfer of responsibility and manner in which it occurs influence the child in how they understand interpersonal relationships.

If responsibility for something is *granted* without adequate explanation or understanding, the child may fail and endanger themselves or others. Giving your car keys to your 12-year-old boy with inadequate knowledge of automobiles will probably have disastrous results. In the meantime, the child may learn and adopt the idea that relationships do not require explanations or understanding.

If responsibility for something is *denied* without adequate explanation or understanding, the child learns that feelings in relationships can be suppressed. Refusing to allow your 12-year-old girl to cross the street alone, without adequate explanation, teaches her to suppress her feelings. In the meantime, the child may learn and adopt the idea that relationships do not require explanations or understanding.

Traditional Relationship Logic sees conflict resolution as authority having its way without the need for explanation or understanding. Conflict resolution is seen as a battle with your partner for *being* the authority, suppressing any opposition, and dictating "what is right" for the relationship.

When we adopt The Melfox Mindset, the status of responsibility on things in a child's world is discussed, explained, and continuously negotiated. Instead of just being told "no" and suppressing their feelings, a child will know *why* they can't go across town on their tricycle to visit Grandma.

The more we respect the feelings and awareness of a child or anyone in our authority, the more they will have respect for us and the decisions we make on their behalf. This will teach them the power of empathy and effective conflict resolution that they can apply to other and future relationships.

> *We don't yet know, above all, what the world might be like if children were to grow up without being subjected to humiliation, if parents would respect them and take them seriously as people.*
>
> - Alice Miller

Teaching Your Children

We have the responsibility to teach children in our care the skills and mindset for effective conflict resolution, curiosity, and respectful relationships. Perhaps more important to them is how we demonstrate it around them in our daily lives. The kind of relationship that parents have, or caretakers have, with their intimate partner, fundamentally teaches children how adult relationships work or don't work.

Traditional Relationship Logic teaches children that adults resolve conflict by fighting with, cowering from, or fleeing from one another. They are not only subjected to the toxic cloud of resentment when growing up, they also are susceptible to allowing the same thing as adults.

As discussed earlier, many movies and entertainment programs reinforce this mindset with dramatic scenes of couples battling with each other when faced with a conflict.

When parents or caretakers use The Melfox Mindset, children are taught that even the most volatile situation can be resolved peacefully and with respect. They learn that conflict resolution means fighting with resentment on the *same* side, not with each other on *different* sides.

The Relationship With Your World

When you think about it, you have a unique "relationship" with everyone and everything that exists in your life. All relationships need to be maintained, like the one with your partner, to prevent the ill effects of resentment. When you have unresolved conflict with *everything*, its appeal is dulled and frustrations grow.

The core concepts of effective conflict resolution taught in this book can help restore the trust and bond with anything in your world. Adopting The Melfox Mindset when addressing any relationship issue sets the stage for empathy, proper respect, and curiosity. This helps us focus on resolving the conflict, not blaming and resenting.

Your Extended Family

We all have issues and unresolved resentment of various degrees scattered across town and across the globe. As discussed earlier, the closer and more valuable a relationship is to us, the more critical the degree of its cleanliness.

Lessons and concepts contained in this book can be applied to relationships of all kinds. Instead of holding grudges or constant bickering, we can use The Melfox Mindset to step into another person's shoes. The key to a healthy, nurturing relationship with anyone is the sufficient *understanding* of each other's world. In addition, many of the same concepts and techniques we have learned regarding effective conflict resolution can be applied to all other relationships as well.

Goodwill To and From Others

Understanding and practicing *The Melfox Method* train us to be more cooperative and respectful with all things in our life. When there is conflict and resentment, the tendency will be more to empathize and resolve, rather than feud, blame, and vilify. When relating with someone, we will be more apt to appreciate and respect our differences in beliefs, awareness, and preferences. The more we adopt The Melfox Mindset, the more likely that appreciation and respect will be reflected back to us.

Our understanding of Egoity and the ability to control it help maintain order in times of conflict. This understanding also helps us accept the Lion, Turtle, or Deer that occasionally emerges from others. The power to maintain or quickly regain control of emotions during volatile exchanges is universally admired and respected. It allows for effective Interaction, sharing of critical Information, and peaceful resolution.

Earning and Appreciating It Everyday

I'd like to end this chapter and book with one more contrast and compare moment with Traditional Relationship Logic and The Melfox Mindset, and the amazing energy and opportunity that well-maintained relationships provide.

Traditionally, we experience relationships in three stages: 1) exciting, 2) a certain leveling off period, and 3) eventually boring. There are exceptions to this, of course, and we always hope to be one of them. You can be filled with devotion and loving care, yet that doesn't alleviate the need to maintain your relationship. Unfortunately, the usual path of a relationship is like the flight of an unmaintained solar-powered airplane:

1. A relationship is full of energy and takes off toward the heavens.

2. Resentment blinds the "attraction grid," energy runs out, and the relationship coasts for a while.

3. Eventually the relationship glides or crashes to the ground.

This book has provided concepts, step-by-step analysis, and detailed instruction on cleaning resentment from your relationship and keeping it "perma-fresh." Those who effectively resolve conflict, and accept and respect each other's individuality, have a different flight plan:

1. A relationship is full of energy and takes off toward the heavens.

2. Resentment is routinely cleansed from the "attraction grid," allowing energy to recharge fully.

3. Rinse and repeat.

The relationship stays afloat and soaring as long as it is worth maintaining and we feel like flying in it. The concepts and methods described in this book are designed for those of us who wish to benefit from the awesome power of a healthy, vibrant intimate relationship. Those who truly appreciate it embrace the responsibility of maintaining this precious gift.

You hold in your hands the tools and techniques to help restore and maintain your relationship. Starting today, you can weed out resentment and feel the closeness, trust, and attraction return. Remember, it's never too late to put curiosity at the heart of conflict resolution.

When I speak, I will always be curious, not judgmental.
The words I use and the way I say them convey a sense of wonder
so that I understand my partner, and my partner understands me.
I have a burning desire to understand my partner,
and for my partner to understand me.

When I listen, I will always assume my partner
is being curious, not judgmental.
If there's ever a question of my partner's motive, I will calmly ask
so that I understand my partner, and my partner understands me.
I have a burning desire to understand my partner,
and for my partner to understand me.

Outcome - Recap and Review

The following summarizes the chapter:

Outcome - The Reasons

Outcome is the result of Interaction. Each Interaction has its own unique outcome. An issue may be resolved, unresolved, or deemed irresolvable.

Reviewing the Interaction

Since Interaction is a type of conversation that may be new to you and your partner, discussing it afterward can help relieve any anxiety. Self-evaluation and debriefing give you and your partner a chance to adjust to your new level of thinking about your relationship and its maintenance.

Accepting the Past

Sometimes, the last piece of a conflict resolution puzzle is getting to the point of acceptance for *your role* in causing and sustaining the conflict. Lamenters think that they *should've* known better, instead of accepting the fact that they simply *didn't* know better.

Interaction Outcomes

Whether immediate or after some self-reflection, each conflict settles into a particular Outcome. It is left unresolved, deemed irresolvable, or resolved.

Unresolved Issues

As much as we would like, conflicts are not always resolved in one Interaction session. The more complicated types of conflict need time between Interaction sessions so that new Information has a chance to soak in. Seeds sown can take root and bear fruit weeks or even months later.

Irresolvable Issues

No matter how great your desire to resolve conflict, there may be an issue that is so overwhelmingly dug-in and painful that you feel additional Interaction sessions would be useless. You simply do not have the proper tools to resolve the issue and cleanse the resentment.

Resolved Issues

This, of course, is the preferred and expected Outcome from Interaction. When an issue is acceptably resolved, any resentment associated with it vanishes. Seeking issue resolution is the *reason* for Interaction. An issue may be temporarily unresolved or eventually deemed irresolvable, yet the goal of effective Interaction is always *resolution* of issues.

Beyond the Outcome

How you view your partner during Interaction has a critical impact on its Outcome. How often did you see them as an *individual*; respect their unique interests, beliefs, and awareness; and work *together* to resolve conflict? How often did you allow that respect to fade away, and *battle* when your partner's interests, beliefs, and awareness didn't agree with yours?

Blended Responsibilities and Control

When we choose to entangle additional areas of our life together with our partner, we are relinquishing full control of those areas. These types of situations require special care, understanding, and empathy to ensure that the resentment is continuously removed.

Orbiting Relationships

One way of visualizing relationships is as the co-creation of something *separate* from the individuals. This mindset sees blended responsibilities as a *breach of separateness,* which deadens the relationship by neutralizing the attractive dancing energy between the two partners. The *closer* you get to your partner *without blending,* the *more exciting* the relationship.

Curiosity State of Mind (Part II) Broken Down

When sharing an intimate commitment with Traditional Relationship Logic, we blend responsibilities and control in as many areas as possible. With The Melfox Mindset, partners in a committed relationship are respectful of each other's needs, wants, and differences. It is the healthy feeling of *separateness* that allows the fire of passion and attraction to breathe and grow.

The Relationship With Your Partner

With each conflict resolved through effective Interaction, you and your partner will feel an increase in attraction that is really quite amazing. The more we see our relationship as a co-created entity, the more we can respect, appreciate, and therefore care for it, as well as our partner.

The Relationship With Yourself

Having a healthy, well-maintained relationship with your partner and adopting The Melfox Mindset help you regain and maintain your own identity while in an intimate relationship. It also provides us the opportunity to improve ourselves. A trustworthy connection with our partner allows us to overcome our vulnerabilities and expose limiting and presuming beliefs.

The Relationship With Your Family

Resentment has a natural impact on children and anyone else living with or spending a lot of time with you. The relationship with them is affected by the resentment toxicity level you have with your partner. And, of course, our knowledge of effective conflict resolution and The Melfox Mindset can be used directly to enhance the relationship with other members of your family.

The Relationship With Your World

When you think about it, you have a unique "relationship" with everyone and everything that exists in your life. The core concepts of effective conflict resolution taught in this book can help restore the trust and bond with anything in your world. Adopting The Melfox Mindset when addressing any relationship issue sets the stage for empathy, proper respect, and curiosity.

****

EPILOGUE

And it came to pass that Beatrice and Bruno <u>did</u> practice and learn how to effectively resolve their conflicts. In time, they became quite good at focusing their attention on resentment when sharing Information and controlling their Egoity during Interaction. With curiosity and each conflict resolved, they felt closer and closer. Soon, the tenderness was back in Bruno's touch, and the sweet smile was back on Beatrice's face.

And since Beatrice and Bruno learned the tools for effective conflict resolution and how to use them, they <u>did</u> live happily ever after.

****

Brief Recap of Chapters

In the *Introduction* chapter, we discussed the various areas of your life that will be benefitted by using and practicing the concepts in this book. Traditional Relationship Logic and the concept of conflict were also covered.

Environment

The playing field and the players were set up and the overall concept and objective were established. The Melfox Mindset was explained and served as the foundation for the rest of the book.

Information

Information is the process of establishing common ground and the reality of the other individual, by challenging and clarifying what each one says. This, in and of itself, serves as the cornerstone for effective conflict resolution.

Egoity

Egoity is our normal, natural autonomic defenses to vulnerability – potential roadblocks in healthy, effective communication. With the understanding of the cause and purpose of this protective mechanism, you will grant proper respect, and proper conflict resolution can commence.

Interaction

Interaction is the combining of Information and Egoity in a structured, purposeful conversation. Subjects such as disappointment, interruptions, and forgiveness were addressed. Techniques and props were suggested to facilitate proper and efficient exchange.

Outcome

In this chapter, we listed the "rewards." If the other chapters were preparations for, and the process of childbirth, this would be the child. It explained the possible results of Interaction, and listed beneficial "side effects."

Diagrams

Additional Information

To learn more about *The Melfox Method* and effective conflict resolution, visit our website TheResentmentDumpers.com or contact us at info@theresentmentdumpers.com. Your comments, ideas, and suggestions are always welcomed. Thank you for taking the time and effort to seek solutions to situations that  affect us all. Hopefully this book has helped you gain some insight into getting your relationships resentment-free and healthy, and getting them to stay that way.

Grumpy Gills Publishing
Atlanta, Georgia USA
www.grumpygillspublishing.com

GLOSSARY

The following are definitions of special terms used in the book:

belief:
confidence in the truth or existence of something that is neither susceptible to, nor constantly scrutinized by, rigorous proof.

conflict:
incompatibility or interference of one idea, desire, event, or activity with another individual.

Egoity:
startlement and possible hyperarousal response (fight, fright, or flight) caused by interpreting Information as a threat to a belief.

Environment:
pertaining to and measurement of relationship health. It serves as the holder of resentment and the "arena" for conflict resolution.

hyperarousal:
sustained "fight or fright or flight" defensive response to a perceived threat.

Information:
shared verbal or nonverbal communication that is specific and organized for a purpose, has been verified to be accurate, is presented within a context that gives it meaning and relevance, and can lead to an increase in understanding and decrease in uncertainty. Agent of change in conflict resolution.

Interaction:
proactive, structured, and intended exchange of Information and Egoity in an attempt to resolve conflict.

Melfox Mindset:
seeing a partner as an ally, as opposed to someone to defend against. During Interaction: seeing resentment as the adversary to be battled with a partner through cooperation, empathy, and understanding.

Outcome:
conflict resolution results of Interaction (unresolved, irresolvable, or resolved) and the resulting impact on the relationship health with one's partner, self, family, and world.

partner:
other person in a relationship with whom you are working to resolve conflict, and restore trust and respect through understanding.

postulate:
inquisitive statement suggesting further discussion, contemplation, or exploration before confirmation.

resentment:
feeling of distain caused by the non-acceptance that an individual presumably is, did, or believes something that does not match one's belief about or expectation of that individual.

startlement:
initial, instantaneous reaction and feeling of surprise at the moment of perceived threat awareness.

Traditional Relationship Logic
seeing a partner as a threat to defend against, as opposed to an ally. During conflict resolution, seeing one's partner as the adversary, not resentment.

****

INDEX

INDEX

INDEX